Training for Results

SECOND EDITION

A Systems Approach to the Development
of Human Resources in Industry

MALCOLM W. WARREN

President, Performance Technologies, Inc.

ADDISON-WESLEY PUBLISHING COMPANY

Reading, Massachusetts

Menlo Park, California · London · Amsterdam · Don Mills, Ontario · Sydney

Library of Congress Cataloging in Publication Data

Warren, Malcolm W.
  Training for results.

  Bibliography: p.
  Includes index.
  1. Employees, Training of. I. Title.
HF5549.5.T7W37 1979   658.31'24   78-73373
ISBN 0-201-08504-6

Second Printing, March 1984

ISBN 0-201-08504-6
BCDEFGHIJK-AL-8987654

Preface to Second Edition

There ought to be a compelling reason for revising any piece of writing, once it has been published. Either the facts have changed substantially, or the author has found that his or her assumptions, premises, or theory structure have changed significantly. The latter is my compelling reason. Surely, the facts have changed but minimally since 1969: Cost parameters have enlarged; some new and impacting teaching and training models have been developed; and the field itself has gained stature and sophistication. These elements, though, tend to be a constant growth and by themselves did not justify a revision.

However, there have been three significant changes in my own thinking over the past ten years which I believe constitute a change in direction. First has been the development of a performance-centered model for obtaining and maintaining desired performance. The development of this model has changed the way we look at training and the training function. Since it includes training as one of five possible change elements, it has forced consideration of a broader set of tasks for the training function; indeed, it has suggested a new function entirely, that of performance management, of which training is but one part.

Second has been the realization that concentration on building a more effective training technology has led us into a trap. We have bent our efforts toward refining the ways we develop and manage instruction without examining how that instruction is delivered. Yet experience demonstrates that effective management of the processes used to ensure quality and consistency of training actions by the users are at least equal in importance to instructional excellence.

Third, my perception of the roles and relationships between instructor and learner has changed. More and more, training appears most effective when it is learner-centered rather than instructor-centered. It follows, then, that instructional technologies must become more learner-controlled and that training design and delivery need to be shaped to this end.

Given these significant changes in thinking as compelling reasons to revise this book, we have also been able to bring it up to date in technical areas and to clarify some of the applications. Several tools in the form of work guides and checklists have been incorporated in this edition, many of which have been suggested from time to time by the readers.

As ever, I am indebted to many, trainers and trainees alike, with whom I have worked over the years and who have helped to shape my conception of behavior management and who have contributed to my own growth.

Edina, Minnesota   M. W. W.
February 1979

Preface to First Edition

During the past ten years a fundamental change has been taking place in the role of training in business and government. Training is no longer, like the house organ, nice to have if you can afford it. It is becoming a basic tool for increasing the effectiveness of the organization. In the past, alternatives to training were easily available. Needed skills could be obtained in the labor market. Processes and procedures could be simplified to reduce skill needs. Managers could be nurtured within the organization or found outside.

Today we are seeing the alternatives disappear. The rapid growth of new technologies, the automation of repetitive tasks, and the introduction of entirely new business concepts are changing the functions of people in organizations. Needed skills are less available in the labor market, and the age and experience levels of job seekers are lower. Nonrepetitive tasks are increasing, as is the breadth of skills needed to function in the new technologies. The entire focus on skills is changing from the direct production situation to system control situations. The organization no longer has time to grow managers in an environment which rapidly changes the function and accountability of its management.

The organization's problem becomes not whether to train, but how. It is no longer a question of whether the cost of training and development programs can be borne, but one of building a training function to meet desired goals. In 1964 at a meeting of training people, Dr. George S. Odiorne said,

> Training in the modern corporation can't be economically conducted on a basis of casual, chaotic, or sporadic activity. The basic purposes of training must meet these requirements:
>
> 1. It is based on a unified concept of economic contribution to the objectives of the company.
> 2. It is rooted in the management process, and isn't an additional or peripheral function, but a way of getting a job done.

3. It makes a measurable contribution to the organization's goals.

Ten years ago when training became a major part of my job, I tried to find some help in the basic concepts of training. I found no written material which dealt with the kind of work I was doing and few practitioners who were able to help me deal with these basics. I began a trial and error search for ways of dealing with need identification, instructional design, cost estimating, and evaluation of programs and methods. The problems I faced were the result of my not having a general set of principles or approaches which could be consistently applied to the work at hand.

During these years I have read a number of books and articles in the fields of training and education. From them I have learned how to use audiovisual equipment effectively; but I have learned little there that would help me choose instructional media best suited to specific training situations. I learned how to use a blackboard, but not how to decide when it was appropriate in bringing about behavior change. I learned to write a lesson plan that would ensure accurate and complete content, but not how to design instruction that would ensure the participants' learning the content.

I found much that would help me develop some general approaches that do work. The work of B. F. Skinner and the developments in programed learning that grew from it gave me one major thread. A second came from the work in individual and group behavior by Roethlesberger, Tannenbaum, Schein, and others. I found another thread in the work in human communications, both in the psychological and physical fields of study. Most important to me was the discipline gained from systems theory, which provided an approach to the analysis of human behavior in relation to the organization in which it existed.

This book, then, is an attempt to put on paper the fabric I have woven into a general approach to training. Its subject is the use of training systems to meet organizational needs. Three objectives are proposed:

1. To assist the experienced manager of training and development to develop, revise, and maintain training systems which will meet organization objectives and which can be measured in terms of organization values.

2. To provide general management with information they can use to establish an effective training and development function, evaluate the results of that function, and obtain the services or programs needed.

3. To provide the individual given responsibility for a training function information which can be used to establish an effective, up-to-date, and cost-effective training system.

A number of individuals and organizations have contributed to this book and to the synthesis of ideas presented here. My special appreciation goes to these contributors:

To Geary Rummler, Carl Semmelroth, and Dale and Karen Brethower, of the Center for Programmed Learning for Business of the University of Michigan, for their help in formulating the analytical approach to the identification of training needs and the specification of behavioral objectives. I am particularly indebted to Geary for my first introduction to the concept of training as a system.

To Richard R. Keeffe and the management of Sylvania Electronics Systems Division, Eastern Operation, for support in implementing professional and technical training actions using specified behavioral objectives. Their willingness to invest time and money in the analysis of organizational requirements and to experiment made it possible to test training in terms of organizational economics.

To C. W. Kitzinger, President of Oldberg Manufacturing Co., and Ralph Lingg, Manager of the Youngstown Division of Oldberg, for their help in developing the supervisory training system described in Chapter 14.

To E. L. Muckensturm, Director of Employee Relations, Oldberg Manufacturing Co., for his contributions in the areas of labor and union relations as they affect training and performance standards.

To Paul Putman, Chairman of the Board, and P. M. Grieve, President, of Questor Corporation, for their support and particularly for their interest in the use of training as a management tool to develop an effective organization out of many parts.

And to my wife, Beverly, for her critical assistance in developing both the form and content of this book as well as for her patient editing of the copy.

M. W. W.

Toledo, Ohio
May 1969

Contents

11 Administrative Skills Training   169

12 Sales Training   183

13 New-Hire Orientation   201

Introduction

By Geary Rummler

Nearly everyone would agree that what the training function in every organization needs in order to be more effective is more money and authority. But I seriously question that supposition. What would be the effects of appointing a vice-president of training and of providing unlimited training funds and companywide support? What would be different from the results we see now? Would there be training film products to rival Hollywood? Training "charm schools" second only to exclusive Swiss girls' schools? Job-instruction courses conducted by supervisors in tuxedos? What would you do? What would any of us do without our present constraints? How would the results be one bit better?

The point is, we can't get there from here. If training is going to meet the challenge of the effective utilization of human resources, it is going to have to change what it is and what it does—its goals and its procedures.

Today, the trainer is a *technician*. If training is ever going to develop into a useful force in the organization, the trainer is going to have to become a *technologist*. A technician applies a technique. A technologist applies a science. A technologist engineers.

To be effective, training departments are going to have to change their present conceptualization (whatever that is) of their role to one of solving human performance problems to assist the organization in meeting its goals. And subsequently they will have to change the skills they have from those of a technician to those of a technologist—applying the science of human performance.

What is the need? At a time when jobs are becoming more complex, there is an increasing shortage in qualified personnel. In addition, there are extensive social pressures for organizations to assist in developing currently unqualified personnel. Human resource is now emerging as the most important natural resource to nearly every organization. And yet people are still the most exploited, wasted, and misapplied of all the natural resources. The training function is probably the single most critical function in the effective use of human resources to meet today's pressing personnel needs. Training must transform the raw natural resources into an effective and productive final product. It will be done no other way.

But can the training function in most of today's organizations meet such a challenge? It certainly seems doubtful. As a rule, the training department enjoys little support in its own organization. It is often poorly budgeted, and that budget is particularly susceptible to cutbacks when the organization tightens its belt. The department appears to enjoy little respect from the rest of management. In most instances it is told when to train and what to train by someone else. It is very often perceived by the rest of the organization as a group of meeting-runners—just one step short of being in show business.

This is hardly a viable situation for a function which must close the human performance gaps in our organizations. Few training people would argue with this description of the status of training. Some corporate training heads might take exception and point to their plush offices, large budgets, and sizable staffs. But chances are, at some level in their organization, division or plant or branch, their training person is being asked to set up the projector for plant manager meetings and is continually being requested to use training to solve nontraining problems in quality ("It's going to hell—do something!") or supervisory attitudes ("They don't identify with management") or a dozen other areas. I will readily agree there are a number of outstanding exceptions to my dismal-sounding generalization. But most training people would agree and would even offer a number of reasons for the predicament. The common statements of rationale are: "We are located in the wrong place in the organization . . ."; "If we could just get out from underneath personnel . . ."; "We need to be more professional . . ."; "Management in this organization just is not training-oriented—we can't get a budget to do anything." All these observations are true.

Yet this problem seems to exist only when we are dealing with management of human resources. I don't hear the same complaints from those who deal with the physical, technical, or financial resources of an organization. Controllers have no problem obtaining the personnel or budget they need to carry out their functions. The staff people who acquire, design, and install new processes or equipment have high credibility in the eyes of the organization. And these people often have no more "vested" authority than the trainer.

It may be that the financial specialist, the industrial engineer, and the market researcher have demonstrated that they have technologies which can serve to make the organization more effective. It may be that they have shown they can contribute to growth and profitability. I suggest that the problem is not so much that management doesn't understand training, but rather that trainers have given management little to understand. Perhaps the trainer has not been able to show how training results would be different if there were money and authority.

As long as trainers think of themselves as technicians and talk about the "many tools in their bag," there will be no change. And no organization is going to budget much money for a Vice-President of Training Technicians!

There is an alternative—the trainer as a technologist, as a human performance problem solver. Actually, the alternative requires two things—a technology and an approach. In this case the technology is behavioral technology (the application of the science of human behavior), and the approach is the systems approach.

The technology of human performance is here. It is the outgrowth of the work of behavioral technologists who were originally concerned with the design of self-instructional systems. It has built on the work of the Air Force Human Factors Engineers and studies of the NTL. It is manifest today in such places as the Behavioral Technology Curriculum for Business, of the Center for Programmed Learning for Business at the University of Michigan, the Center for Educational Technology, Catholic University of America, and Westinghouse Learning Corporation.

The systems approach as applied to training and human performance problems is not so well developed and, appropriately, is the subject of this book. Unfortunately, "systems" has become a fad word in training. Mal Warren treats the *concept* of systems here as it should be—not in the context of a systematic checklist for training logistics, but as the conceptual framework which will make it possible for training to realize its full potential. We all know that the quality of a solution to a problem depends on how we initially perceived or defined the problem. Likewise, looking at human performance problems in an organization from a systems viewpoint makes possible solutions to "training problems" heretofore impossible, and with these solutions comes a new and more productive role for training.

Mal Warren is the person to write this book. As a trainer himself some years ago, he first began to apply some of the basic principles of systems engineering to the training function. Since then he has designed and implemented a number of original and effective training systems. This book is a unique combination of theory and "what to, how to." The theory involving the systems concept is balanced with operational discussions at each point. And the theory is not put forth as an academic abstraction, but rather is a sound generalization from years of experience.

Chapter 1 states the need for the systems approach to training and draws the subtle and important distinction between the training function and the training operation. Chapter 2 presents the general systems theme for the book. The key elements in a training system and an eight-step approach to solving training problems are presented in Chapter 3. The eight steps include steps such as "estimating return on investment" which are generally not found in most training checklists, but which are now made possible through this approach.

Chapter 4 is typical of the next five chapters in its mix of theory and operations. The argument for thorough analysis as part of the systems approach is made and followed by specific recommendations as to whom to interrogate and what questions to ask as part of the analysis. Chapters 5 through 10 discuss the important problems of method, estimating costs, instructional design, management of training, and evaluation in the systems context.

Most authors would have stopped here after assuring the reader that these concepts would work equally well with skill training and management development.

But Mal Warren has taken six diverse and important training needs (among them, skill training, technical and professional training, sales training) and devoted a chapter each to discussing how the training-systems concepts apply. The final chapter discusses the implications of the systems approach to the administration of training in today's organization.

This book is important. It should serve as an additional impetus to those of us who have already started down this road, and it should serve as a blueprint for others of us who have felt things aren't quite right in training, but haven't been sure where to turn. Guided by the concepts in this book and armed with a technology, we can bring about a great deal of change with an adequate budget and proper organizational placement.

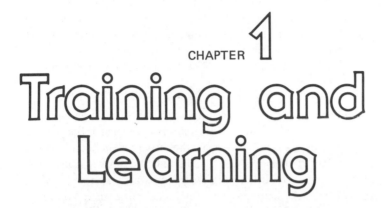

CHAPTER 1

Training and Learning

TRAINING FOR RESULTS

Training is inevitable. Like old age, it attacks each of us whether we like it or not. At birth, or before, we begin training to operate within our environments. When the training is satisfactory, we speak of adjustment or adaptation to life. When the training is unsatisfactory, the result is failure, neurosis, or perhaps psychosis. This generalization provides a fairly valid basis for further discussion of training or development, since any action taken to train an individual must be considered in the light of his or her prior experience and the behavior which must be developed in the current environment.

But if training is inevitable, why all the fuss about training program development, development planning, need identification, etc., in an organization? It would seem that since "Experience is the best teacher," training in an organization is also inevitable. All that is really needed is a hire and a job; in time the hire will be trained.

An intelligent management looks at this inevitable process and asks some questions. Is experience actually the best teacher? What is the cost of training a qualified person? How do we know when the person has been trained? How long do we mean when we say, "In time, the hire will be trained"? Most important, management asks, "How do we know that the person has been trained to meet the goals we have set?"

These questions and the implications they raise require that training or personnel development be clearly defined in terms of management's goals, the fulfillment of which is the organization's first concern. From this viewpoint, training must be evaluated in terms of its contribution to these goals. The first question is not how, or even who, but rather why. If experience is the "trainer" who can best help the organization meet its goals, then experience will be chosen to run the training function.

To define training goals, it must be assumed that the organization under analysis is able to determine what it wants to accomplish. The term "organization" is not restrictive; any group of human beings or combination of humans and things falls

1

into this conceptual definition. Organizations tend to formulate goals, and as the organization grows more complex, the goal-setting process becomes more formal. The complex organization defines its goals in terms of specific objectives or milestones. The business firm or governmental department establishes profit plans, five-year plans, product or task missions, system objectives, etc. Voluntary groups set study goals or program objectives.

One common characteristic of this goal-setting process is attainability; management believes that the goals it sets can be accomplished. Three seven-year-olds setting up their lemonade stand believe that they can earn five dollars for the purchase of a ball and two bats. If they are astute managers, they have researched the market by talking to mom and dad. If their analysis is valid, and the market really exists, they have satisfied one of the conditions or constraints which affect the attainability of their goal. They must then consider other constraints, such as: (1) cost and availability of raw materials—lemons, sugar, water, and ice; (2) facilities—a stand, sign, glassware, and location; (3) human resources—skills to make lemonade and sell it; and (4) cost of operation and price to the customer. If the constraints remain constant and the children operate within them, they can attain their goals: a ball and two bats.

Just as in larger, more complex organizations, this small group of entrepreneurs must establish goals and then make use of the best data available to determine the constraints within which the goals can be attained. Once the goals are set, these three budding managers can make the decisions for action needed to meet them. If the constraints change, either the goals must be altered, or actions must be taken to satisfy the new constraints. For example, if none of the children has the skill to make lemonade, they will have to buy it ready-made (thus increasing costs), hire someone to make it, or get one of their number trained to make it.

Within the framework of organizational goals, the goals of training or development become quite specific. Training is one management tool used to develop the full effectiveness of an essential organizational resource: its people. The function of training, then, is to bring about the behavior changes required to meet management's goals. When considered from the point of view of a system's overall mission, a training function is no longer an extra operation within the organization; it is an essential subsystem used to fulfill the larger system's specific mission. Thus management asks, "Is training the most effective method to develop the human resources needed to meet our current and future goals?"

TRAINING AND ITS ALTERNATIVES

When training is considered as a method for achieving organizational goals, its importance is determined by management in terms of increased profits or reduced costs. Management does not decide to train so much as it determines what human resources are required to fulfill its goals. The decision to train is based on the need for certain skills, knowledge, and attitudes. Training, however, is not the only way to maximize the contribution of human resources to organizational goals. It is one alternative among several. Consider the following example: An organization establishes a goal of a 10% increase in sales. Responsibility for accomplishing this objective might be assigned to a sales function, which, after analysis, might decide that the goal can be met by increasing the number of qualified prospects obtained by each salesperson. This constraint could be met by improving the performance of existing sales staff in cold-canvass selling techniques. The choice of this alternative implies a training program designed to increase each individual's effectiveness in cold-canvass selling. However, an increase in qualified prospects could be achieved by other means as well. The organization could hire people already skilled in cold-canvass selling, new markets could be opened to acquire additional prospects, point-of-sale advertising could be increased, territories could be changed or automobiles furnished so more calls could be made. Possibly the entire sales force could be eliminated and a wholesale distribution system established.

This simplified example can serve to show the process through which a results-oriented organization must go before it decides to use training or some other form of personnel development in meeting its goals. This is nothing new. The option of a business firm to hire skills rather than to develop its own has been a basis for human resource planning for many years; in fact, it often governs the very shape an organization will take. Business concerns that consciously choose to promote from within, or grow their own management, tend to develop an organizational identity quite different from that of companies that go into the hiring market to meet each new set of personnel needs. There are sound reasons for either approach. The latter brings in new ideas and varied approaches to goal accomplishment. The former builds consistency and loyalty to the organization.

Other alternatives to training must also be considered. Work simplification can eliminate the need for skills; automation can be used to replace human resources entirely; and changes in work flow or work processes may make better use of skills within the organization. Any of these alternatives to training may not only result in more advantageous utilization of existing skills or a reduction in total staffing needs, but also actually effect a total behavioral change within the organization leading to higher productivity. The most common example of such an alternative is the change from functional management to task or program management in the defense industry. This alternative, however, is extremely complex, requiring formidable management skills and a high level of sophistication to deal with the special inter-relationships involved.

COST EFFECTIVENESS IN THE TRAINING DECISION

The maximum utility of training as a method for meeting constraints or achieving goals is fully realized only in comparison to other alternatives. Then the choice of training as the best of the available alternatives is based on its cost effectiveness in achieving the desired result. The full utilization of any personnel development system depends on this orientation; training becomes not just a way of providing a series of educational programs, but rather one more means for accomplishing organizational goals.

Using cost effectiveness as the basis for a decision requires an analytical approach to not only training actions themselves, but also the results anticipated from such actions. If there is a need for skilled machinists, a choice between hiring and training should logically be based on cost effectiveness. Management can take the position that if it costs $750.00 to hire a machinist in the local market and $700.00 to train, the decision would be to train. The real problem in determining which alternative to use is deciding just what is meant by the word "machinist." Is our $700.00 worth of in-house training equal to the $750.00 worth of outside training we are buying? Perhaps in the case of a machinist the answer can be based on factual observation. We can establish a skills test and have our outside hire and our inside trainee take the test before being qualified as machinists. If both score the same on the test, then obviously training would save us $50.00. However, a look at the apprentice or trade training programs in existence today shows a complete lack of significant standards for measurement. Considering the difficulty of developing standards to measure qualification in skilled or semiskilled occupations, development of such standards for a first-line supervisor or operations researcher may seem nearly impossible.

Management demands for cost effectiveness from all subsystems making up the organization create problems to which the training subsystem must find solutions. The individuals responsible for the training subsystem are, of course, accountable for the quality of their training and the efficiency of their programs. However, they must also ensure that the training done meets the requirements of the organization in the most cost-effective manner. It should be part of the training subsystem's job to recommend alternatives to training actions when those alternatives can more economically supply the organization with usable human resources.

TRAINING AND DEVELOPMENT

In presenting this approach to training, three terms have been used without definition: personnel development, training, and management development. Attempting to explain these terms is like trying to define "supervisor." Of any seven definitions, four will disagree. However, in this book these three terms are defined as follows:

Personnel development is any direct action taken by an organization to change the behavior of any of its members. Any training action is a system for personnel development, as are most internal communications systems, motivational campaigns, and even management policy letters. The primary concern of personnel development is to achieve behavior which will help the organization meet its goals.

Training and *management development* are operating terms falling within the general classification of personnel development. Perhaps the easiest way to define these words is to make a comparison between them on several points (see Table 1).

TABLE 1

	Training	Management Development
Purpose	Supplies specific knowledge skills, or attitudes needed to meet organizational goals (usually the performance of specific tasks within specific standards of productivity).	Supplies individuals prepared to meet company goals in specific positions or functions (i.e., people who have the ability to perform whole groups of tasks).
Scope	Deals with specific tasks or subject areas.	Deals with a complex of tasks, training individual for an area of responsibility (a group of responsibilities or functions).
Problem approach	Problems arise from sub-standard conditions or the absence of desired conditions, caused by lack of knowledge or skills or by unacceptable attitudes shown by individuals or groups.	Problems concern the improvement of existing conditions by reinforcing or adding to present knowledge, skills, or attitudes.
Point of view	Supplies qualified people to meet specific job requirements.	Supplies qualified people to meet organizational goals.
Selection	Participants are chosen because they lack skills, knowledge, or attitudes required by job requirements (i.e., because of what they don't have).	Participants are chosen because past performance has demonstrated their potential for new responsibilities (i.e., because of what they do have).
Evaluation	Compares participant's performance to training criteria or job standards after completion of the program.	Evaluates the participant's performance continuously in terms of organizational goals.
Identification of need	Needs are based on present or anticipated performance of tasks.	Needs are based on organizational needs and planned human resource requirements.

In system terms training and management development have totally different missions. Training supplies specific knowledge, skills, or attitudes needed by the organization to meet its goals. It is oriented to the completion of specific tasks within standards of productivity. Management development supplies individuals prepared to meet company goals in specific positions or functions. In other words, it prepares individuals to perform whole groups of tasks. *Training* industrial engineers in the technical skills and applications of Master Standard Data provides a manufacturing organization with the performance required for this method of work measurement. Individuals are trained to complete the task of work measurement consistently and competently. *Developing* a manager of an industrial engineering function would include training in MSD technology along with other systems of work measurement. Stress is placed on the evaluation and administration of work-sampling techniques so that the manager can more effectively design and administer a work-measurement program.

Training further differs from management development in that its problems result from substandard or nonexistent conditions caused by lack of knowledge or skills or by unacceptable attitudes within individuals or groups of individuals in the organization; management development deals with the problem of improving existing conditions by reinforcing or adding to the present knowledge, skills, or attitudes of individuals within the organization. Here, then, is the critical difference in their system mission: the problem solving of training versus the individual growth programing of development. The selection and evaluation of participants vary accordingly. Participants are chosen for training because they lack skills, knowledge, or attitudes needed to satisfy job requirements; for management development they are chosen because their performance demonstrates a potential for further responsibilities. Training participants are evaluated only for that area of their job performance within the scope of the training program, whereas management development participants are judged in terms of their total job performance and contribution to organizational goals. Finally, training needs are based on present and anticipated task requirements, whereas management development needs are based on planned human resource requirements to meet organizational goals.

In summary, we can differentiate between training and management development in three ways:

1. Training deals with current needs; management development with predicted needs.
2. Training is job-oriented; management development, person-oriented:
3. Training usually deals with specific task requirements; management development with organizational requirements or task complexes.

The effect of both training and management development is to change human behavior. They have a common objective: the development of human resources. It has been said that a business organization is distinct from its competitors in only one respect: its people. An organization's plant, processes, equipment, even its new technical breakthroughs, can be duplicated by its competitors. But its human resources cannot; they can only be pirated. In today's business environment human resources are the most expensive and valuable asset of an organization. The development of this resource, the change of individual behavior, is crucial to the success of any organization, whether it be three seven-year-olds in the lemonade business or General Motors.

RESPONSIBILITY FOR THE TRAINING FUNCTION

Responsibility for effective deployment of an organization's resources lies with the organization's management. The successful utilization and development of human resources are no different from those of physical materials. In either case responsibility must rest with general management.

Accountability for human resource development may be placed anywhere within the organization. Most often it rests with industrial relations or personnel operations. Less frequently, but often more effectively, accountability is placed with line supervision. Where line supervision functions effectively in training and development, in the establishment of standards and the evaluation of performance, the system can be quite efficient. Usually, however, personnel development comes rather low on a line manager's priority list. The day-by-day pressures on a production supervisor to improve quality, reduce scrap, etc., seldom permit the kind of performance analysis needed to develop effective training actions. The demands of the job require the solution of "right-now" problems, not the development of programs to achieve "next-week" performance. A sales manager taking a sales trainee out on calls is often too involved in sales quotas to permit the trainee to "muff" a call. Instead, the manager does the talking, hoping that the trainee will learn by observing. When this kind of thing happens, general management calls in a staff trainer. The staff trainer usually realizes the importance of the function, but often lacks the knowledge and skill to carry out the analysis necessary to identify specific task requirements or performance standards.

Regardless of where accountability for training is placed, the training function is a necessity. It must serve to not only produce the means for changing behavior, but also analyze and recommend alternatives to training whenever these alternatives are more cost effective. On the other hand, a training operation need not exist as such. Many organizations requiring behavior change cannot afford the luxury of a training operation, nor need they. Training must be considered as a subsystem within the organization, not as a physical entity with names on doors and several thousand dollars worth of audio-visual equipment. What makes a training subsystem valuable is its ability to bring about required behavior change in terms of skills, knowledge, and attitudes, not the number of programs it runs or its ability to utilize the newest technological advances in the field of education. An organization may be able to forego the luxury of a training operation, but it cannot afford to ignore the necessity of the training function.

It is important that the concept of the training *function* be distinguished from that of the training *operation*. The training function is the subsystem or group of subsystems which bring about controlled behavior change within an organization. The training operation is a mechanical means for carrying out the training function. Confusion between the formal means of training and the functional action for bringing about behavior change is one of the chief reasons why management so often fails to use training to its maximum effectiveness as an agent for meeting an organization's goals. Too often an organization acquires the machinery for training in the form of a training department without developing the function which this department is to perform. No profit-oriented business would ever purchase machinery before it had decided on a product, yet many businesses establish a training operation without defining its function.

THE OBJECTIVE OF TRAINING: BEHAVIOR CHANGE

The mission of a training function is to bring about behavior change. As a result of its action individuals will do something differently. The behavior change brought about by the training function must be measurable in terms of the organization's requirements. This is a crucial point. To provide an employee with knowledge which cannot be applied or the results of which cannot be observed would appear pointless in terms of the organization's requirements. There is, for example, no point in training a machinist in the use of precision gauges if they are never used in the production of the company's product. Similarly, there is little value in teaching a supervisor the skills of delegating unless the organization has some means to measure ability to delegate after training. Without measurement, management cannot determine the utility of the action.

Before we can attempt to change behavior, the required behavior must be known, and the means to measure the change in behavior must be found. Until these two constraints are satisfied, the effectiveness of training actions cannot be known, and their functional utility becomes guesswork. Furthermore, behavior change must be measured in terms of not only training, but also what the person does after training in the actual job environment. It is performance on the job that is important, not performance in a training program. There is little point in training a person to become a skillful painter of pictures if he or she is to paint houses. A real test of behavior change is how well the trainee performs in terms of task accomplishment. The only valid result of training or management development actions is a measurable increase or improvement in an individual's contribution to organizational goals. If any general rule for a training function were to be stated, it would be: "If you can't measure it, don't train for it."

KINDS OF BEHAVIOR CHANGE

Behavior changes brought about by the training function can be divided into:

> Change of skills
> Change of knowledge
> Change of attitude

Changes in skills may be measured by a change in production. For example, as a result of skill training, a sheet-metal worker can operate a brake and produce a precise 90-degree bend in a sheet of steel. Or an operations researcher, given sufficient data about an organization, can produce a mathematical model of that organization which, when programmed into a computer, will provide valid predictors of the future of that organization based on specific variables. In essence, skills can be measured by output. The objectives of skill training can be quite explicit. They define what an individual does, and the results can be objectively evaluated in terms of what he or she produces.

Behavior changes involving knowledge are quite different. Here the trainer deals with "concept" or "principle." The sheet-metal worker's knowledge can be measured in terms of ability to explain how a brake works, to tell what the requirements for a 90-degree bend are, or to discuss the requirements for a satisfactory sheet-metal bend. The operations researcher might be called on to define the business simulation, to explain the mathematical theory behind linear programming, or possibly to describe how to apply simplexing as a technique. It is behavior changes in terms of knowledge that can often be measured by pencil-and-paper testing or some similar device. Providing the supervisor with knowledge about delegation is not too difficult. The trainer can very quickly bring a supervisor to the point of defining delegation, explaining how it works, and discussing its effects. It is far more difficult, however, to improve the skill of delegation without knowing what it is and without being able to observe the supervisor on the job to evaluate delegation of responsibility to subordinates.

Attitude change is, of course, the most difficult of behavior changes. In dealing with attitude we are dealing with an entire internal system which is summarized as an individual's feelings about something. It is generally held that an individual's attitudes control the way he or she acts. Any actions or tendencies toward action that result from an individual's attitude system strongly affect his or her productivity and that of others within the organizational environment. Therefore, attitude is a training problem. In changing behavior involving attitude change, the training function affects a great deal more than the individual being trained. Yet how can attitude change be measured? There are three ways: first, by the individual's verbalization of his or her feelings; second, by the subjective evaluations of others about the person; third, by the individual's total productivity within the organization. The first two measurements, however, will hardly satisfy a results-oriented management, for it is only in terms of the individual's productivity that attitude can be measured in terms valid to the organization. Therefore, the third measurement, change in productivity, is the most valid of the three. It is not high morale that has dollar value, but rather the results of high morale.

Attitude change becomes critical when we are talking about management development. When an accountant is being prepared for the responsibilities of a controller, the real objective of behavior change is not a matter of improving accounting skills or knowledge of financial analysis, but rather of changing his or her view of the organization. The accountant must, in effect, be trained to think like a controller and not like an accountant. Unfortunately, in most cases no evaluation can be made until the person is actually in the position of controller, and then success or failure as a manager can be measured. Also, unfortunately, this is a little late to evaluate the person's competence to hold that position. The usual method for measuring attitude change—attitude scales, disguised techniques, or semantic-differential rating systems—are difficult to validate. Other means must be sought. On the most rudimentary level, frequencies of absenteeism or tardiness can be measured. Beyond this, quality and quantity of overall productivity can certainly provide an objective measure of attitude. Admittedly, there are many intervening variables affecting productivity, such as skill level, tool efficiency, environmental influences, quality of supervision, etc. If productivity is used as a measure of attitude, these variables must also be measured.

From the foregoing, it is obvious that attitude change and its measurement requires the highest level of competence in the training function.

TRAINING AND PERFORMANCE STANDARDS

Two things are necessary if the behavior change brought about by the training function is to be measured: a standard of performance against which to measure, and the means to make the measurement. If the training function is to provide a qualified machinist, the organization must establish standards for that individual; it must know what a qualified machinist is and does. If performance is to be measured, the standards of performance must be quite specific. For example, if a machinist is required to change spindles on a milling machine, he or she must know how to do it, must take only a certain amount of time to do it, and must know when to do it. And the organization must be able to measure those capabilities; it must be able to point to an individual and say, "He is qualified because he can identify a dull spindle before rejects occur, but he changes no more than two spindles per shift." Or, "It takes her no more than eight minutes to make the change, and she knows which tool room to go to for the tool and how to complete a requisition for the change item." With knowledge of this kind, the trainer can design a program that will develop sufficient skill to meet the requirements for a qualified machinist. Having established performance standards, the trainer can prepare the criteria by which to measure the trainee's progress through training, step by step. The "final exam" is developed in terms of the performance required from the trainee machinist on the job. Of course, this example includes only one small part of a qualified machinist's job. It has not covered such steps as which tools are used, what movements are made in changing the spindle, how placement of the spindle is checked, or the other machine tasks that are part of the job. The analysis of those requirements is part of the trainer's job. However, before this analysis can be carried out, the trainer must know in specific terms what results are to be obtained. Where performance standards are not readily available, the training function must develop the information for setting them.

Once the difficult job of defining performance standards has been completed, the trainer can undertake the simpler task of developing measurement criteria. These criteria *must* measure what they are intended to measure, for it would do no good to test, say, a house painter's skill in painting a picture. The trainee's behavior change must be measured not just by the standards of the training program, but also by performance on the job.

If the standard requires demonstrable skills, the means of measurement is clear: observation. The real problem of measurement is the selection of key or typical tasks which will measure the trainee's ability to meet the performance standard established. If a person is being trained for a soldering operation, it would not be necessary to test performance in every soldering situation, but only for the seven or eight typical connections which can demonstrate skill. An important measure of the effectiveness of the training function is its ability to measure behavior change accurately without spending too much time or money on the process.

The development of measurement criteria requires that the training function carry out the task analysis and system interrogation which will provide it with adequate knowledge of both the standards of performance and the processes required to obtain that level of performance. It is in this area of criteria development that the practice of purchasing commercially developed, generalized programs or the implementation of traditional company training programs becomes inadequate for effective behavior change. Effective utilization of any training program, new or old, in-house or outside, must be based on the specific needs of the organization in terms of the performance desired. Further, a training program must incorporate measurement criteria which are valid in terms of the organization's needs. A program to develop supervisory skills may fill the needs of several kinds of organizations, but whether it will be adequate for the needs of a specific organization can be known only after the preformance standards of that organization have been defined and the measurement criteria for the program validated against those standards.

The responsibility of the training function goes beyond the development of training programs; it must achieve the desired behavior change in individuals or groups. The training function must also search out alternatives to training and assist management in selecting the best course for meeting organization goals. The training function is responsible for the development of the organization's human resources. When a training action is required, the training function is expected to present the best available means to bring about the desired behavior change and to measure the change once it has been brought about.

TECHNOLOGY OF BEHAVIOR CHANGE

The training function's areas of technical competence must include not only the skillful analysis of human resource needs and performance standards, but also the theory and methodology for bringing about controlled behavior change.

From the point of view of the training function, only in recent years has the technology needed to bring about controlled behavior change become developed enough for application. Fundamental research into human learning processes has been carried on for many years. Unfortunately, the results of most educational research have had little applicability in the world of adult organizations. The fundamental need in the training system is a technology which can, when intelligently used, bring about a very specific kind of measurable behavior change. Research in the field of education has never sought techniques for bringing about specific behaviors, since its objective has maintained a more generalized outlook for individual learning. The industrial situation, however, requires something quite different; it requires that the behavior change be both measurable and of utility to the organization.

Over the past 30 years, considerable experimental attention has been given to the specific problem of controlled behavior change. The remarkable progress made in the use of training simulators is an excellent example of the application of research by behavioral scientists into the learning process. The "revolution in education" brought about with the introduction of programed instruction has also demonstrated the applicability of this kind of research. Our concern here, however, is with the technology of behavior change and not with the theoretical implications of the research.

The body of experimentation that provided us with this technology had centered on the stimulus-response system. Although this research orientation can be said to have had its beginnings in Pavlov's classical research in conditioned responses, it is B.F. Skinner's development of a model of operant behavior that provides us with the basis of a usable technology. The technology resulting from research into the stimulus/response system focuses on observable responses made to a controlled stimulus. The learning process consists of modifying the learner's responses to a given set of stimuli by reinforcing desired responses and permitting unwanted responses to be extinguished. The learner's entry behavior, the measurable portion of prior learning experiences, furnishes the responses to be modified.

Suppose that we were training a buyer trainee to read blueprints. One criterion for training might be that when shown an orthographic projection, the trainee will identify the object represented. We might begin by presenting a block with the word "top" appropriately placed and ask the trainee to identify the top of the block. This response is clearly called up from the individual's prior learning experiences. We might next ask the trainee to identify a picture of the top of the block; then, to pick out the pictured block from a group of similar blocks. This might be followed with a new block having the top notched but not labeled. The process would continue with objects of increasing complexity until the trainee could identify one object in a group of similar objects when shown an orthographic projection.

The trainer's initial attention is on the response. The goal is to develop a training action that will bring about a response in the trainee indicating that the desired behavior change has taken place. In almost all training situations this behavior at the end of training is rather complex. It is made up of a number of different kinds of responses. Unlike the psychologist's laboratory, where each individual kind of response can be differentiated, or at least narrowed, the real-life training situation must deal with combinations of responses grouped together and summarized as trained behavior. Trained behavior is that which can be observed and to some degree measured. Breaking this desired behavior into its component responses makes the training job easier. The trainer's job becomes in reality the development of a series or group of stimuli which will bring about the desired set of responses. In psychological terms the training program is a learning environment in which the stimulus/response sequences are carefully controlled. This chapter began with the statement that training is inevitable; it would be more accurate to say that learning is inevitable. The trainer's job is to bring about a learning process which is controllable and which can be repeated. A training program then becomes a group or series of stimuli which the trainer knows will lead to desired responses. This concept presents the trainer with a heavy burden. It is no longer sufficient to develop subject matter or even exercises which present the content of the subject; it now becomes necessary to structure this content in such a way that observable responses are obtained which demonstrate that the trainee has acquired the skill, knowledge, or attitude being taught.

The trained behavior must be observable or measurable; a second constraint on the training system is that the trained behavior must be transferable to the job. The problem of transfer has been a fundamental concern in research on learning. With this problem in mind, the skilled trainer tries to make the training environment approximate the job environment as closely as possible. Perhaps the best example of this has been in the use of simulators in military training. In an industrial organization the problem is somewhat more complex, since the trainer must face the problem not only of what behavior can be transferred to the job, but also of what behavior can survive on the job. Training a supervisor in the techniques of supportive management may bring about little change in on-the-job behavior if superiors and peers bring pressures to bear which prevent the maintenance of this kind of behavior. A behavioral scientist would say that environmental conditions bring about the extinction of the trained behavior. The trainer would probably say that the organization really doesn't want this kind of behavior to take place and will not permit it to survive. A particularly cynical trainer might add that continued attempts to bring about this kind of behavior would cause him or her not to survive.

In structuring the stimuli of the training environment, the skilled trainer will make use of *reinforcements* to ensure that the desired responses stick. The training design will include stimuli which give some positive pay-off to the trainee for learning the desired responses. Early programed instruction provided this positive payoff by letting the trainee know when he or she was responding correctly and by praising the accomplishment. Today, we see reinforcement technology as more complex and more varied in application: we speak about managing the *consequences of performance* both in the training environment and on the job after training. The ways in which desired performance is rewarded and undesired behaviors are extinguished are the subjects of consequence management.

Another aspect of the training environment stemming from behavioral research is the design and control of *feedback*. How the trainee gets information about how he or she is doing has a direct impact on performance. Lack of usable and timely feedback tends to inhibit trainee progress. On the job, the lack of objective performance feedback frequently leads to undesired behaviors.

These elements drawn from research in behavior coupled with a wide range of what really happens in training and posttraining situations provide us with the working models from which to build successful behavior-change systems.

The first is a model of individual behavior (Fig.1). In this model a situation of stimulus (S) is presented to the performer (P), who responds in some way (R). The response has a consequence (C) to the performer, which will affect the way he or she responds to the same or a similar situation the next time it is presented.

Let us suppose that a sales representative is the "P" in our model. The rep is presented with an objection from a prospect (S). The rep answers the objection (R). If the response is a good one, the rep is rewarded by the opportunity to make a trial close (C), which will tend to cause the rep to answer similar objections in the same way in the future. The more often the response is successful, the more often it will be used.

Suppose that during sales training, the rep is placed in the usual "role play" situation. The objection is presented, and the trainee's answer, though basically a good one, is subjected to detailed criticism. The effect of this kind of consequence may cause the trainee to avoid that answer in the future rather than to help her or him to polish the response!

Again, suppose the trainee goes into the field for the first time, tries out the answer, and fails to get anywhere with it. The new rep may search for different ways to answer the objection or may try to avoid similar situations entirely by not calling on that type of prospect. The rep may also learn to avoid training programs as a waste of time and effort.

This leads us to the second model: a model for performance management. If we accept this model of performer behavior, we will find it helpful to construct a framework for managing the subsystems which affect that performer's behavior on the job. Our model consists of five subsystems plus the organization environment within which they function (Fig. 2). This model describes the subsystems we will design, change, or maintain in order to bring about desired performance. Changing

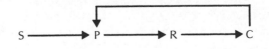

Figure 1

what goes on inside the performer is left to practicing clinicians and others who believe that they can change psyches.

The *expectations* subsystem defines the processes for specifying what a performer is expected to do. This includes task results and outputs. It also includes the organization's rules of behavior, required procedures, as well as those unwritten but expected behaviors found in every work group. Expectations set for a supervisor may specify the quantity, quality, and cash standards for his or her unit's production. Rules of behavior may specify the management style expected by the organization. Specific procedures for hiring or firing may be expected. Informal expectations might require the supervisor to be on the job early for coffee with his or her peers. The expectations and the ways they are communicated strongly impact on individual performance.

Feedback defines the processes by which the performer gets information about his or her performance in relation to expectations. Managing the form, objectivity, timeliness, and usefulness of feedback becomes critical in obtaining desired performance. Performers need to know how they are doing in order to adjust their performance. Incomplete feedback can lead to performance problems usually attributed to poor attitude or lack of skill.

The processes that reinforce behaviors are defined by the *consequence management* subsystem. Both financial and nonfinancial elements are included. The way

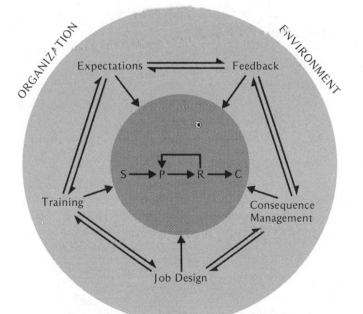

Figure 2

reward is linked to performance, the frequency of reward, and the type of consequence administered are all factors to be considered in bringing about desired performance.

Job design defines how the work situation will be managed. Methods, subtask sequencing, equipment, tools, materials, and job information are the elements to be considered. Task interferences need to be reduced and task supports created and maintained.

Finally, the performer must acquire and maintain the skills required to perform to expectations. Knowledge and skill acquisition processes are defined by the training *subsystem*.

Underlying these subsystems is the organization environment. The organization's values, interpersonal processes, and climate affect individual performance. To the organization development practitioner, the primary focus should be the organization environment if desired performance is to be obtained. To the strict behaviorist, the organization environment is of little concern. The critical question is not whether the organization environment affects performance, but rather whether anything can be done about it. Where relevant action can be taken, action must be considered.

This book focuses on the training subsystem. No performance change action exists in isolation, however. Training cannot be successful without acting on the other critical subsystems which impact on the performer. We must deal with the whole performance system.

The broader subject of human resource management will be left for another occasion. Just as this book is not about human resource management, it does not deal with learning theory. The technologies of both provide the training function with specific and effective tools for bringing about and maintaining desired performance. Therefore, in discussing the practical day-to-day operation of a training system, these technologies become important resources.

SYSTEMS FOR BEHAVIOR CHANGE

The purpose of this book is to provide a working synthesis of research in the behavioral sciences and the management of systems which will enable the individual responsible for the training function to develop and administer cost-effective training and management development actions. Chapters 2 through 9 develop a step-by-step process for establishing a training system and preparing an effective training program. Various roles of the training operation are discussed to show how effective organizational interactions can be created to provide an effective framework for training actions. Next, the development of specific training programs is analyzed, beginning with the identification of organizational problems and needs and the establishment of performance standards. The heart of this analysis is the utilization of techniques for organizational investigation and task analysis. The development of training criteria will be detailed together with a program for obtaining management support of the training system. This section will conclude with a system for program evaluation which can measure trained behavior against the criteria established for the program, on-the-job performance, and, it is hoped, return on investment.

Chapters 10 through 16 apply this approach for the solution of common training problems. The primary objective of this section is to demonstrate a consistent process of analysis, development, action, and evaluation which can be applied to achieve measurable behavior change, whether the change involves an industrial skill, sales techniques, supervisory skill, or technical state of the art.

Chapter 17 covers the administration of an effective training function. It deals with the problems of creating and maintaining a successful training operation, including selecting and training people, establishing and maintaining record systems, and building an inventory of training aids and facilities.

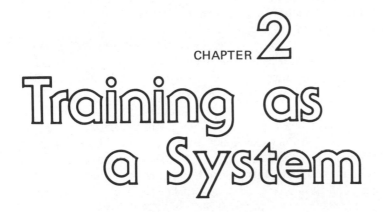

CHAPTER 2

Training as a System

THE SYSTEMS APPROACH TO TRAINING

From a systems point of view, the design of an operation to successfully carry out the training function becomes a problem of creating a system to accomplish a given end result as mission. In the case of training, this mission is to effect a group of planned and predefined behavior changes in the organization. At a generalized level, a system may be defined as an organization of pieces which interface or operate together to accomplish the purpose for which they were designed. The pieces in a system may be smaller systems, or they may be single components or elements which cannot be further broken down.

DEFINING THE SYSTEM MISSION

A basic rule of system design is that the system itself is defined by its mission. For example, one cannot design and build a chair without first defining the mission of that familiar, but too frequently uncomfortable, system. In examining the mission of the system known as "chair," we discover that defining the system mission is not as simple as it might first appear. Let us say that the chair's mission is to support a human being in a sitting position. Now it becomes necessary to define "human being" and "sitting position." The height, depth, and width of the seat, the angle of the back, whether or not there should be arms, the weight and structure of the human being to use it—all become part of the mission definition for this simple system. It might even be advisable to get rid of preconceived notions about chairs by not using the word at all.

The design of the system begins with a desired end result: maintaining a human being in a predetermined position for a given length of time in order to carry out a defined set of functions. These might be anything from a restful snooze after dinner to tying dry flies for the next fishing trip. This approach to the design of chairs has resulted in some unusual assemblies, but has also resulted in some fairly effective systems to meet this kind of mission. But the design of a seating system for a human being is not merely a matter for entertainment. It can be crucial, as, for example, when designing a person-carrying space vehicle.

Most chair (seating) systems are organizations of pieces. These pieces may be termed components (a term usually applied to electronic systems) or elements. These elements are the basic building blocks of a system. By themselves, the various elements have little utility; i.e., they cannot themselves fulfill any defined mission until they are organized into a system. In the case of the chair, we have legs, seat, back, possibly arms, perhaps fabric covering, springs, foam rubber, etc. Bring them together and organize them into a system, and there is a chair. But the chair by itself cannot achieve its mission to provide support for a human being in a given position. Before that can take place, there must be a human being. The total chair system, then, consists of the floor on which the chair rests, the chair itself, and the human being sitting in it. In effect, the total seating system is composed of three subsystems: floor, chair, person. The points at which these three subsystems come together are commonly known as *interfaces*.

INTERFACE IDENTIFICATION AND CONTROL

As a system becomes more complex, the identification and control of interfaces become extremely important, since interfaces form junctions which permit communication between subsystems. If the interfaces are clear and well controlled, communication is effective. If not, communication can become badly garbled or filtered. In the latter case, two efficient subsystems may make up a very inefficient total system. Consider the problem that arises if a football quarterback cannot communicate clearly with the rest of the team. No matter how good each player is, the team is unlikely to meet its mission, victory on the playing field. Or, in the case of the seating system, a situation could be visualized in which the floor system is an inclined plane. Unless this peculiar interface problem were dealt with, most chair subsystems would be ill-suited for meeting the entire system's objectives. It might also be worthwhile to examine certain peculiarities in the human being subsystem, such as weight, dimensions, or posture. Unless these aspects are taken into consideration, the entire system could turn out to be at least inefficient, possibly even disastrous.

PROCESSING SYSTEMS

Moving beyond the chair system in complexity and into an area more applicable to the design of training systems, we come to the organization of pieces which process or change things. In this type of system, a raw material of some sort, be it sheet metal or information, is fed into the system. Within the system, this *input* is processed or changed to produce an *output* consisting of a finished product or specified data. The greatest body of literature in the field of systems theory or systems engineering deals with this type of system. It relates three things to the system: the input, the processing system itself, and the output. The input is the raw material or data entering the system, and the output is defined by the system mission. (See Fig. 1.) Inputs to a computer system may consist of punched cards—actually the signals caused by the holes in the cards. The output may consist of the printed forms produced by the printer or perhaps more punched cards. (See Fig. 2.) In a computer the card reader, the processor or processing unit, and the printer all form parts of the system. The complexity of the computer system increases when one deals with the subsystems making up the overall information-processing system. At this level of system definition, one must deal with a software system which provides processing instructions (or program), or the information needed to produce the output required to fulfill the total system mission. Another subsystem is designed for the storage and retrieval of information. Still others are designed for processing input data into the system and output data into usable form. Each of these subsystems has a well-defined mission which contributes to the overall mission of the system. (See Fig. 3.)

As the computer grows in complexity, so do its various subsystems. These subsystems must be organized through carefully controlled and defined interfaces to accomplish a specified objective or mission. The large computer has often been described as a kind of general-purpose system, with its mission defined by the program, or instruction subsystem, which in turn controls the processing operations. Even this subsystem can be divided into further subsystems: Consider that programs are first written in a programming language, itself a subsystem, and that this programming language must be translated through an interface into an object language, another subsystem, which can be used by the computer to process the input data.

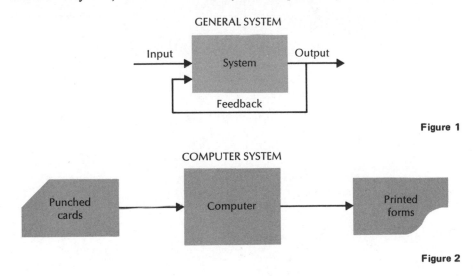

GENERAL SYSTEM

Input → System → Output

Feedback

Figure 1

COMPUTER SYSTEM

Punched cards → Computer → Printed forms

Figure 2

COMPUTER SUBSYSTEMS

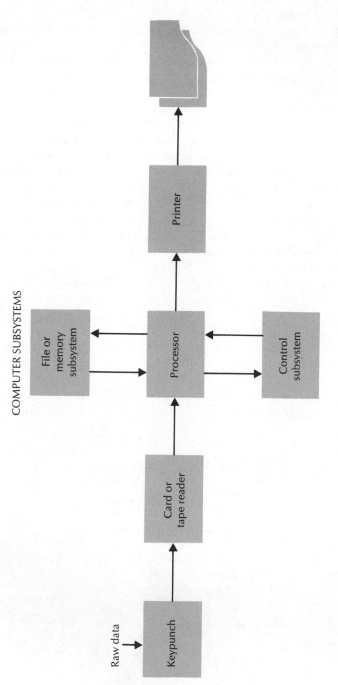

Figure 3

THE ASSEMBLY LINE AS A PROCESSING SYSTEM

The computer is an ideal model of a complex processing system. Unfortunately, when discussing an electronic data-processing system, we have a tendency to ignore one kind of subsystem with which we are concerned: the human operator. A better model might be an automobile assembly line. As a system, the assembly line uses as its inputs partially completed assemblies or sheet-metal formings which have been produced by various subsystems within the manufacturing system. Engines and power trains, chassis, bodies, seats, wheels, etc., are all end products of other subsystems. In terms of the product mission, i.e., the completed automobile, the assembly line itself forms only one major subsystem of an automobile manufacturing system.

Differentiating between subsystem and system is really a matter of viewpoint. We can regard the assembly line as either a total system or a subsystem in relation to the manufacturing system of an automobile company. Even here, the manufacturing operations form only a subsystem of the total corporation, which may include such other systems as marketing, distribution, cost control, reporting, purchasing, etc. To an economist, the automobile company itself is a subsystem within the economy; to a government planner, the industrial economic system may be only one subsystem to be included in long-range national planning. In our view, the merits of calling any system a subsystem is rather like arguing how many angels can stand on a pinhead! It makes for interesting table talk, but to anyone other than a systems theorist, it serves little purpose.

The mission of the auto assembly subsystem is to produce a given number of vehicles of a certain type on a certain schedule and, it is hoped, within a given cost limit. The assembly line itself is divided into a number of smaller subsystems, all of which perform parts of the assembly operation. At given stations in the assembly line, there are interfaces where subassemblies, the *output* of various subsystems, feed as *inputs* into the assembly-line system itself. The control of these interfaces is extremely important, since it would be rather awkward if red doors were supplied when and where a blue automobile body appears. The control of these interfaces is usually the responsibility of a traffic subsystem whose mission is to furnish the right subassembly at the right time and place to ensure that the finished product meets the purchaser's specifications. Anyone who has ever completed an order blank for a new car has participated in furnishing inputs into this control system.

The assembly line itself contains a large number of subsystems. Some consist of one or more human beings trained to perform a specific operation with certain tools; the tools too are parts of the subsystem. Each of these person/machine subsystems has well-defined missions and well-controlled and specified interfaces with one or more other subsystems in the assembly operation. One of these subsystems might consist of a group of human operators whose only mission is to carry out temporarily the subsystem process of other human operators, providing relief time for them. Thus the total system is able to maintain continuous operation for the specified time periods needed to produce the required number of finished vehicles.

FEEDBACK

One extremely important aspect of this or any other system is feedback. The designers of any complex system incorporate within it a method for obtaining information about system efficiency. With this information they develop methods for correcting variances or improving the effectiveness of the system itself. The information is furnished through a feedback loop, which obtains information at key points and feeds it back to points where corrective controls can be applied. In terms of the product mission of an assembly line, the various inspection points are examples of feedback sources. The inspectors themselves furnish the feedback information to the control aspects of the system. (See Fig. 4.) In the automotive model this may be a quality-control subsystem, or it may be a manager who can take action to correct a deviation from the standards required to produce the finished vehicle. In some systems the subsystem providing the feedback includes an automatic means for control and correction. The thermostatic devices on a heating system or the governor on a steam engine are examples of this type of feedback and control system.

PERSON IN THE SYSTEM

This discussion of the auto assembly line as a system is useful in that it relates the human operator to the system. An individual is not considered as a unique, separate entity who works at a job in a manufacturing operation, but rather as a critical subsystem without which the remaining subsystems could not be organized or made to function. The relationship of the human operator to the machine and product elements of the system permits the system designer to develop a total organization. This is not to dehumanize people by placing them in relation to the system in which they operate. Instead, it becomes necessary to look at people in a new way, perhaps as we looked at the chair in a new way. In the case of the chair, we have found new ways of using the existing materials to more effectively carry out the desired functions. When people are related to the systems within which they operate, we find new and more effective ways for them to accomplish their own ends and the organization's goals. It then becomes possible for individuals to know what their employers really require, how their performance will be measured, and how they contribute to the accomplishment of the organization's objectives.

Someone once said that you should never treat a person like a machine. But consider how a machine is treated: We never expect it to perform a function for which it was not designed; we always supply it with sufficient energy to do its job; we carefully maintain it; we never overload it; and we certainly never expect it to perform its function before it has been properly set up to do so. On the other hand, we often expect people to do things beyond their capabilities; we frequently fail to provide them with the motivation to do a good job; we often let them work in an environment which, at least psychologically, fails to maintain them, and we seldom let them know specifically what they are to do or really train them to carry out

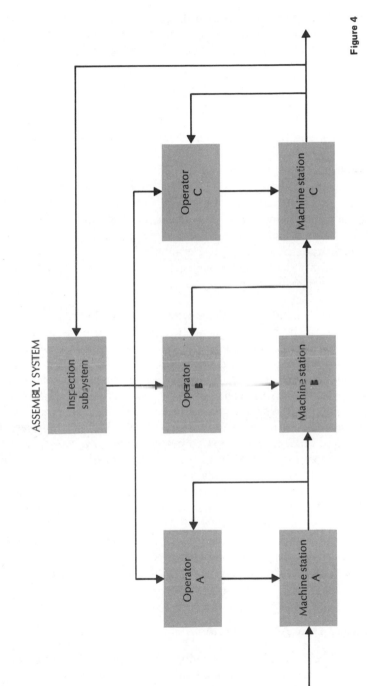

ASSEMBLY SYSTEM

Figure 4

their functions. By relating the worker to the total system, one might say that we can begin to treat a person as well as a very expensive machine. We can also begin to help an individual realize full potential as a human being who can make decisions and initiate actions.

MAINTENANCE SYSTEMS

Both the computer and the automobile assembly line have been used as models of complex processing systems. However, we must also consider systems that do not change things to produce a product or energy, but have as their mission the maintenance or servicing of existing systems. A good example might be a local telephone company. Its mission is to maintain the existing flow of information. This system contains within it processing subsystems such as the electronic switching systems which connect calls. A look at the continual service functions of the telephone company demonstrates how an effective maintenance system operates. Inputs are received in the form of signals indicating equipment failure and specifically designated subsystems consisting of people and machines repair or replace the faulty components.

Another example is the maintenance system in an Air Force strategic bomber group. Here each of the aircraft subsystems is maintained on a continuous and well-controlled schedule. In addition, signals can be received which indicate faults within the aircraft subsystem, and designated subsystems can then take action to repair the faulty unit. Feedback systems are critical in these maintenance systems.

Even in a maintenance or service system, however, the operation closely follows that of a processing system. The distinction is between change systems and maintenance systems and is one of mission definition. In a processing system the *change* of an input produces a required output; in a maintenance system an input (information in most cases) that allows modifications to ensure the output—the operation of the system at a given standard of performance—is continued. If it were not for the importance of maintenance systems in our daily lives, it might be possible to consider them only as subsystems within larger processing systems, since they really serve the long-range objective of processing systems. In the case of the Air Force strategic bomber group, maintenance is performed so that the mission of the group can always be carried out. In other words, it contributes to the long-range mission of the squadron, the delivery of bombs to a specified target on a predetermined signal.

THE ORGANIZATION AS A SYSTEM

Let us now consider the business organization as a system. We will not at this point concern ourselves with the organization's subsystem role in the community or in the national economy, but will quite arbitrarily call the business organization "the system." The first chapter of this book described the organization in terms of its objectives or missions. As with any processing system, a clear definition of a business organization's objectives will define the organization itself. Likewise, once the mission is defined, it will become possible to design and organize the subsystems and subsystem interfaces necessary to fulfill the mission.

A small manufacturing company can serve as a simplified model of the business organization system. Let us suppose that a small manufacturer intends to produce fiberglass sailboats. At first thought, the mission of this system might be stated as the production of 1200 fourteen-foot fiberglass-hulled centerboard sailboats per year. It takes no analysis to see the weakness of this mission definition. With a little imagination we can visualize 1200 well-built craft piled up at the back door of the factory, gathering dust until the firm's creditors sell them at auction. This definition of mission has left out an important segment of the business organization's system; it had failed to consider either the distribution and sale of the product or the required profit return. A restatement of the mission that includes these aspects might be the production and delivery of 1200 fourteen-foot fiberglass centerboard sailboats at $1800.00 each, with a net return of $100.00 per boat.

Without refining this statement of mission further, we can attempt to design a manufacturing system to fulfill this mission. First, the organization will require a subsystem for procuring the raw materials necessary to produce its product. The mission of this subsystem must include not only the procurement of the right materials at the right time, with delivery as required by other subsystems, but also the purchase of these materials at a cost that will permit the unit profit specified in the mission statement. Actually, this purchasing subsystem itself could be divided into other smaller subsystems: one for fiberglass for the hulls, another for wood parts, another for fittings, still another for fabric for the sails, and finally one for purchase of materials for masts and booms. Considering the number of boats, however, the entire procurement subsystem would probably be rather small and self-contained.

Once the materials have been obtained, they will provide the input for the production subsystem, which will perform the various processing functions to produce the finished boat. Before manufacturing can take place, of course, a design subsystem will have to produce designs for the hull, sail, mast, and related items along with prints and instruction information. Then machines and machine operators can produce the boat.

A marketing subsystem will be required to obtain purchasers for the finished product, and once the marketing subsystem has fulfilled its mission, a packing and shipping subsystem and a distribution subsystem will be required to get the finished boats to buyers. A billing subsystem will be needed to collect payments and bank profits. Good system design requires that there be a control subsystem to obtain the feedback information needed to ensure efficiency of the system in both product quality and cost effectiveness. This control subsystem will be part of the management subsystem and will probably also furnish data for a planning subsystem which will determine the tactics and strategies necessary for the organization to grow into new markets and new products.

Since this business organization is a human/machine/product system, it will need a personnel subsystem to obtain, train, and maintain the human resources required to carry out subsystem operations. Designing a model of the major subsystems in this business organization presents little problem. The mission of each of the major subsystems can be made clear and the interfaces and inputs well defined. Difficulties begin to arise when the smaller subsystems and components are organized to carry out the mission of each major subsystem. These problems result from the fact that very few systems are purely processors of information or material or people. For example, the purchasing subsystem in our boat company, although essentially an information-processing system, also has as part of its mission the actual placement of the material in inventory for use by the manufacturing subsystem. Most people who hold purchasing or procurement responsibilities agree that they are primarily processors of data in that they must obtain information from their design and production subsystems detailing the requirement of the materials to be purchased. They then process this information, comparing it with vendors' catalogs and information obtained directly from vendor representatives. On the basis of this information, they make a decision to purchase samples for examination. These samples are examined by the design and production subsystems, and if the samples are acceptable, these subsystems inform purchasing to go ahead and buy. The purchasing subsystem then executes the purchase orders and processes the information necessary to make payments to vendors. When orders are received, information about their receipt is again processed by purchasing for use by an accounting subsystem. Many purchasing agents who have the mission of acquiring raw materials never themselves see or handle those materials.

If we were to ask the personnel manager of our boat company what, from a systems point of view, he or she processes, the answer would probably be "people." An analysis of the personnel system would very quickly indicate that this manager processes not only people, but also information about people. If one were to look at one of the largest personnel subsystems in existence, the federal Civil Service, one would find that most of the system has no direct involvement with people. It deals instead with the information supplied by and about people through the medium of application forms, test results, performance evaluation reports, payroll records, etc. Considering these two aspects of the personnel subsystem, a useful operating model can be designed which will form the basis for analysis of the training and management development subsystems in an organization.

THE PERSONNEL SYSTEM

To maintain our sanity and avoid constraints of grammatical logic which will lead us from subsystems to subsubsystems to subsubsubsystems, we will label the personnel subsystem as the personnel system. The objective or mission of the personnel system is to provide the other systems of the organization with human beings who can and will perform the tasks needed to accomplish the organization's overall mission. To meet its objective, a number of subsystems are required.

First, human resources must be acquired. This acquisition subsystem is usually labeled "employment," but as a system, it actually carries out functions not usually considered as employment tasks. Essentially, the employment subsystem recruits and selects people and places them in other subsystems. Recruitment implies going outside the existing organization to obtain the necessary skills, but from the system's point of view, recruitment within the existing organization would be just as important as outside recruitment. Therefore the acquisition or employment subsystem would continually search the existing organization for individuals ready for transfer or promotion. In order to carry out the recruitment function, the employment subsystem would continually interface with the other subsystems to assist them in clarifying their human resource needs, not only to learn their requirements, but also to acquaint them with market availability. The selection and placement functions of the employment subsystem are equally complex in their interfaces with the other systems.

The second system of our personnel model could be generalized as a maintenance subsystem. Its mission is to maintain an environment in which all human operators continue to perform as required. This subsystem carries out a number of functions: employee and labor relations, wage and salary administration, payroll, employee benefits and services, health services, perhaps design and development of tools and equipment, plus the acquisition of facilities that will enable the human operators to carry out their tasks efficiently. It would appear that some of the subsystem functions mentioned don't belong to a personnel department, and indeed they may not. However, if maintenance of the work force is the defined mission of the subsystem, the functions must be carried out somewhere within the organization, and more important, all of the elements contributing to the mission must be considered in terms of interface and feedback.

The problem is not allocation of accountability to a specific department, but rather design of a system that can carry out the mission efficiently. If an industrial engineering department carries out job analysis and job evaluation and never interfaces with a wage and salary system, the development of wage scales that will maintain a work force is likely to be rather ineffective. Similarly, a production supervisor who has no interface with the subsystem handling employee relations might get into real trouble because of inability to comply with company policies on a matter such as leaves of absence (which in some organizations can be rather complex).

If a maintenance subsystem is included, one would suppose that the personnel system would also include a change or development subsystem. The functions of this subsystem would include human resources planning, organization planning, training, management development, and perhaps system design. The primary mission of this development subsystem would be to provide the organization with the kind and quantity of people needed for growth and improved performance.

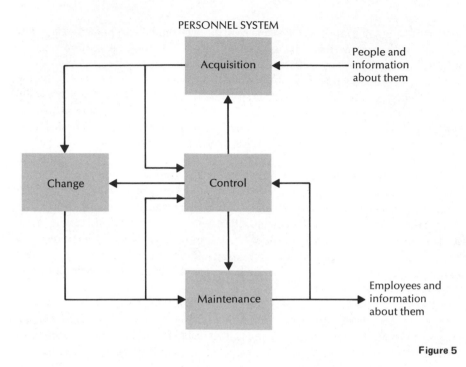

Figure 5

Finally, the design of an effective personnel system requires a control subsystem to collect and maintain data the personnel system requires for continued efficient operation and for a data bank to be used by other subsystems. (See Fig. 5.)

THE TRAINING SYSTEM

Increasing magnification one step, the term "system" can be used to refer to development. We can now focus on a *development system* and one of its most important subsystems, training. Earlier in this chapter, the mission of the training subsystem was broadly defined as the attainment of a group of planned and predefined behavior changes required by the other systems in the organization to carry out their missions. The development and presentation of specific programs is only part of this subsystem's objective. Its functions also include the interrogation of all systems within the organization to identify their requirements in terms of human skill, knowledge, and attitude, and the performance standards used in their feedback and control systems. It must also provide the other systems with information on the performance of individuals undergoing training and recommend methods other than training which can obtain the behaviors they require.

ELEMENTS OF THE TRAINING SYSTEM

A general model for a training subsystem which could operate in any organization consists of six elements. These elements, which are themselves subsystems, are: research, analysis, development, operations, delivery, and evaluation.* (See Fig.6.) The mission of the research subsystem is to provide the training subsystem with data to improve the effectiveness of the entire organization. It also has the mission of training the rest of the training subsystem. Some research functions are investigation of outside training sources; examination of training techniques, programs, and operations of other organizations; research into the technology of training and education; and investigation and evaluation of aids and materials that could be applied by the training subsystem. In other words, the research element is accountable for maintenance of the training subsystem at the state of the art. It is essentially an information-processing system. Most of its input data are obtained outside of the organization in which the training subsystem operates, and its outputs are furnished to the training subsystem itself. This element has interfaces throughout the organization as well as within the training subsystem. In areas of task analysis it might interface with the organization's production subsystems or possibly with its industrial engineering subsystem, if one exists. If computer techniques are needed for such actions as management games and business simulations and if a department for central data processing or operations research exists within the organization, an important interface for the research subsystem will be found there.

The research element would also be made accountable for the investigation and validation of testing techniques, both as measurements of entry behaviors and as a tool for evaluating the effectiveness of training programs. This would require interfaces with the acquisition or employment system, since entry-behavior tests would probably be assigned to a selection process unless the organization could afford the luxury of two testing operations. The research element might also investigate techniques for obtaining and utilizing skill inventories, furnishing this information to

GENERAL MODEL OF A TRAINING SUBSYSTEM

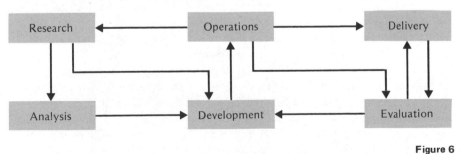

Figure 6

---

*These are subsystems by definition, since their missions can be defined. They are, however, elements of the training subsystem. The term "element" will be maintained for clarity.

the training subsystem and to the personnel system's control subsystem. These subsystems would include the information in a personnel master file as a data source for selection of new hires and promotional or management development potentials.

Finally, the research element has the added accountability for researching and evaluating alternative technologies for bringing about performance change in the organization. Part of its mission is to ensure that the organization has the capability of solving performance problems and enhancing its overall effectiveness using technologies outside of the training and development disciplines. Through this element the training function can become the organization's major resource for technologies affecting standard setting, performance appraisal, reward systems, feedback processes, organization development interventions, etc.

The element having the function of training analysis has three critical missions. First, it must identify the organization's training needs and evaluate them in terms of cost. Second, it must identify and specify the behavior or performance that must be obtained to satisfy the needs. Third, it must analyze the tasks for which training is provided so that training actions can be developed to obtain the required performance. Implicit in these three missions is the responsibility to advise the organization on training alternatives and to recommend whatever training and/or alternatives are best suited to the organization's needs. Inputs to this element would come directly through investigation of the other systems in the organization or indirectly through subsystems responsible for organization and personnel analysis, for establishment of performance standards, for product or process planning, etc. Results of the analysis would be provided to the other elements of the training subsystem for use in research, operations, or program development. Recommendations for alternatives to training would be provided directly to the system under analysis or to the training system's operations element for implementation.

The development element would design and produce specific training actions[*] required by the organization. Its functions include selection and utilization of subject-matter experts both within and outside the organization; selection of training methods; instructional design; development of lesson plans for leaders' guides; selection or development of audiovisual aids, texts, workbooks, cases, etc.; utilization of inside and outside sources for production of necessary aids and materials; and selection and purchase of necessary equipment.

From the research element, the development element would receive recommendations for training methods or techniques; from the analysis element, specifications of trained behaviors to be obtained and recommendations for the choice of subject-matter specialists who would help develop training programs. The finished programs would be supplied to both the operations elements for implementation and, when possible, the evaluation element for validation.

---

[*]The term "training *action*" is used to underscore the concept that the training system does considerably more than create and present classroom training *programs*. Training actions go far beyond the concepts of training programs, including, for example, individual coaching, self-development, on-the-job training, job simplification, job aids, etc.

The mission of the delivery element is the effective interface between instruction and the trainee. Its activities center on the place or places at which the trainees have contact with the instruction and the instructors. In an institutional setting it deals with the teachers and the classroom setting itself. Where training actions are diverse and decentralized, it may handle a number of activities ranging from laboratory learning management to criteria testing in self-instruction. Its role in the decentralized situation becomes quite critical because it is the quality control agency which ensures that the training being delivered is implemented as planned by the development element and supported in the job environment. Using inputs from the evaluation element, it makes on-site revisions of training materials and instructional approaches.

The operations element has two mission areas. First, it must effectively administer training actions, including such functions as scheduling, training, selecting instructors and trainees, and arranging for facilities and other logistic aspects of an ongoing training operation. Second, it is accountable for the day-to-day maintenance of the training subsystem itself: internal record keeping, maintenance of a library of materials, internal assignments and communications, communications with management (particularly the reporting of results and costs), and other maintenance functions which might be lumped into care and feeding of training troops.

The operations element is accountable for the management of both on-line training and the training operation itself, if one exists.

The last element in this general model has as its mission the evaluation of training performance, training program effectiveness, and training system efficiency. This system could be part of the analysis element or of the delivery element and could, in fact, be part of some system outside of personnel, in which case it might serve an auditing function as well as one of feedback and control. If the organization does not require an internal audit of training operation performance, it is possible for an evaluation element to operate as part of the training subsystem. Most of its inputs come through the other elements of the training subsystem, and its outputs furnish the training subsystem with its major source of feedback for improvement of system performance. If the information supplied by the evaluation element is valid, no other audit of performance should be necessary. It may be useful, however, to have the organization's control system make audits of cost effectiveness in relation to budget constraints.

This generalized model describes the elements required in a training subsystem. It does not, however, necessarily imply six departments, sections, or even six people. Rather, it sets forth the missions and functions that must be carried out somewhere in the organization.

ASSIGNMENT OF THE TRAINING SYSTEM

The specific use of this model within an organization is dependent on the assignment of responsibility for the functions described. Most often the training subsystem is made part of the organization's personnel system. Historically, there have been a number of reasons for this assignment. Where the personnel system is responsible for the acquisition, maintenance, and servicing of human resources, it seems logical that this system also be accountable for the internal development of those human resources.

If the personnel system is to be responsible for training actions, it must be capable of carrying out not only operations, development, and delivery elements of the training subsystem, but also the analysis required for effective training. In most organizations this becomes quite difficult, since the personnel system does not usually have the interfaces necessary to identify needs or establish standards. As a result, many training subsystems may exist within an organization. For example, the marketing and sales systems may have their own training subsystems, accountable to a sales manager for the training of salespeople. A production subsystem may assign skill training to individual supervisors or to job trainers. During the Second World War, the fantastic requirements for semiskilled personnel brought about a program for developing job trainers through the "job instruction training" program. Large numbers of supervisory personnel were trained as trainers, and new employees were assigned to them for skill training on the job. This assignment of the training function is still used as an effective way to develop basic skills in manufacturing. It is also essentially the technique used in on-the-job training in many white-collar jobs. Here, a training subsystem exists in each department, with a supervisor or department head accountable for the training actions.

The weaknesses implicit in an organization's use of many training subsystems are fairly obvious. First, individuals accountable for the training subsystems may not themselves be able to carry out the analysis and development necessary for effective training. Second, evaluation of performance by these many training subsystems is seldom tied to the training itself, so that no use is made of feedback information to improve the efficiency of the training action. Third, when each department or function is responsible for training its own members, there is little opportunity for training to include requirements other than those of the specific function or department. Overall organizational goals set by top management may be ignored in the training actions that take place. Further, training totally within a department or function may bring about not only duplication of effort, but also the loss of overall organizational goals in the competition for growth between departments and functions.

But as a model system, training within each department, with the department's manager accountable for the results of training, should be the most effective approach to training actions. The department manager is equipped to establish specific performance standards for the operation as well as to identify nonstandard performance or determine what skills are lacking within the department. The manager should have the expertise necessary to carry out required departmental tasks or at least have within the department resources to supply the expertise. Even in an ideal model, however, the department head may not have the resources to develop a training action that will obtain the needed performance, but may instead have to call on an outside source for program development.

Few real systems approach the ideal. Work-load demands seldom permit allocation of time for analysis of performance in training terms. Standards are frequently subjective and inconsistent within an organization, and there is seldom enough time allowed to specify these standards in terms of the specific kinds of performance desired. Further, the time needed to analyze substandard performance or missing skills and knowledge is not available within an operating department. Those most able to supply expertise are usually those who are best at their jobs, and as a result of their own proficiency, they are called on to carry out many tasks to "get the job done." There is little motivation for individuals in a line-responsibility situation to train new people or to increase the proficiency of those whose performance is substandard.

An organization's training needs are not filled by assigning responsibility for training to a personnel department or to various line systems. Something more is required than a statement of training responsibility on a job description. This is particularly true when a supervisor bears the responsibility for training individuals in a section or department without receiving either the tools for carrying out this responsibility or the motivation for ensuring its completion. After all, a production supervisor is paid to maintain production standards. Specific instructions for the accomplishment of this task are seldom if ever outlined; the supervisor must find a way! If somehow an individual supervisor could do all the jobs alone, management might well be satisfied—at least for the moment. The continual demands made on a supervisor's time make it impossible for that person to train people effectively. Nor can a centralized personnel operation fill training needs if there are no interfaces with line systems through which training needs, performance standards, and evaluation methods may be identified. Also, the personnel department is not likely to have within it the subject-matter competence to develop effective training actions for a line system.

The solution to the problem of filling training needs lies not simply in the assignment of responsibility for training, but rather in the assignment of responsibilities *for the elements in the training subsystem*. Not only must these elements be specifically assigned, but also feedback must be provided so that management may evaluate each element's performance in terms of the total training mission. It is not likely that two training systems will be identical any more than two organizations are identical. Design of an effective training subsystem must be based on the organization as it is, not as it might be or according to a paper model organization chart.

REQUIREMENTS FOR EFFECTIVE ASSIGNMENT OF TRAINING

Four constraints must be considered in designing, developing, and maintaining the training system in the real organization. These constraints will have to be defined for each element of the training system. They are:

> accountability
> interface
> competence
> capability

The identification and definition of these limiting requirements determine the kind of training operation the organization can use.

Accountability determines the assignment of responsibility for results of each element in the training subsystem. Defining the mission or objective for the element determines the results to be measured. Accountability answers the questions "Who? How? What?" and it can be assigned to a number of places within an organization. Accountability for the analysis of needs and standards for skill training, for example, could be placed with an industrial engineering or "control" organization, such as quality control. It could just as easily be assigned to a specific individual reporting to a production manager. It is simply a question of where in the organization the mission of the analysis element can be most effectively accomplished. Assignment of accountability is also governed by the method for measuring accomplishment of the element's objective. This means that the results to be obtained by the element must be specifically defined in terms of (1) what is to be done and (2) when it is to be accomplished. The assignment of accountability for analysis is crucial, since it establishes the objectives for the remaining elements of the training subsystem. It is only after needs have been identified and performance standards have been established that development, operations, and evaluation can take place. Results obtained by an analysis function must ensure that the needs identified do in fact reflect the requirements of the systems involved and that the standards established will produce overall organizational results. As an organization's size and complexity increase, the need for more analysis elements (i.e., assignments of responsibility for the analysis element) also increases.

The second constraint in the design is the definition of interface requirements of the various elements of the training subsystem. The interfaces determine the manner in which elements of the training subsystem obtain information and resources, as well as the means for getting trained behaviors into the system and reporting results of training actions to organizational management. The initial problem is to provide the kinds of interfaces needed to bring information into the training subsystems. The analysis element of the subsystem must interface with line organizations in such a way as to obtain accurate, complete, and timely performance data. An interface must be provided with the system that sets performance standards for the tasks under investigation. A typical example would be training for basic skills of new hires in a production facility. Data on performance standards come from job descriptions used in the hiring process; the training operation assumes that these are accurate, complete, and timely descriptions of the performance to be obtained through training. Far better sources for these data would be the supervisor to whom the new hire will report after initial training and the quality control system, which determines the standards for the finished task. In this example the training needed would be identified through interviewing, testing, and a demonstration of performance by the new hire. Here the interface requirements are twofold: (1) the analysis element of the training subsystem must be part of the hiring process; and (2) the training subsystem must be in a position to interrogate line supervision and quality control (the production system) for information on continuing and/or changing standards.

The third constraint on training-subsystem design is competence. Each element described in the model system requires its own particular knowledge and skill. The analysis element requires sufficient knowledge of organizational functions and missions to identify areas where analysis is needed. In addition, it must have the skills to investigate needs and standards in terms of human behavior so that the results of the analysis are meaningful. The special competence required by the development element falls into two areas. This element must have the skills necessary to a program for changing behavior, that is, the specialized technology of training. It must also have available to it special information about the tasks for which training is required. In a large organization these two areas of competence are seldom compatible. Competence in the fields of both training and cold-canvass selling, for example, are rarely found in the same place. Effective sales training, therefore, requires one of three things: a subsystem with competence in the techniques of both training and sales, an effective sales subsystem which has available to it a consulting subsystem to provide training technology, or a training subsystem that can obtain subject-matter expertise from the selling organization. The constraint competence places on the design of a training system must then be combined with the constraints of accountability and interface. If competence is not contained within the training subsystem, interface must be provided for obtaining it within the organization, and the systems must share accountability for training with the training subsystem itself. As the training subsystem takes shape, the interrelationships of these constraints become more and more a part of the system design.

The fourth constraint, capability, deals with the limitations on workload and budget. Assignment of the training-analysis element to a department manager, for example, is dependent on the time that person has available to analyze accurately and completely department needs and standards. However, budgetary limitations might well preclude the personnel from properly carrying out the required analysis. Handling this constraint to obtain an optimum system can critically affect the size and scope of the training mission. Within these four constraints of a training system, the training operation can be structured to meet the needs of the organization in the context of its existing systems.

The structuring of a training operation can be approached in three ways: (1) by establishing a fully functional operation accountable for all elements of a training subsystem; (2) by establishing a staff operation accountable for one or more of the training subsystem elements; or (3) by having a consulting operation furnish specialized services to the systems accountable for training actions.

THE FUNCTIONAL TRAINING SYSTEM

Let us use a manufacturing company as one example of an organization with a fully functional training system. In this example the manufacturing system, under the direction of a plant manager, is fully accountable for meeting cost and delivery objectives of the organization. The plant manager is accountable for the utilization of both physical and human resources, but is assigned production quotas and quality standards by corporate management, which also directs distribution, marketing, research and development, and other organizational systems used to meet the corporation's overall missions.

The primary mission of the training system is the development and maintenance of skills of hourly production machine operators. Accountability for the accomplishment of this mission is assigned to a training "department." Being fully accountable for training actions, the training department must, therefore, have interfaces which will permit it to be cost effective in its analysis and development elements. It must also have both the training technology and the plant technology to develop effective training programs. Since training efforts are directed at the machine operation, the training department is best placed in the subsystem where it can have continual interaction with both line supervision and the machine operators themselves. The question, then, is "Where in the organization can the training constraints be met and the mission carried out?"

One system having these qualifications is industrial engineering. We will, therefore, place the training department there. Industrial engineering has within its scope of responsibility job and task analysis and can provide essential inputs on standards and needs. Performance evaluation of trained operators is also part of the industrial engineering function and gives the training department both the competence and capability to carry out analysis and evaluation. The analysis element must also have an interface with the personnel system so that data about experience, abilities, aptitudes, etc., on new hires and existing workers can be used in the development of training actions. A training manager who reports to the industrial engineering manager directs the development and operations elements of the training system. The training manager operates the facility in which actual job training for new hires takes place and provides specific "up-date" training in the production facility as job methods change. The program is developed from the analysis of needs and standards, by means of the training technologies most applicable. As the manufacturing system grows and requires the training of more operators than can be handled in existing facilities, the development element employs other training technologies as indicated to meet the goals of the training operation. The training manager is, of course, accountable for researching new training technologies which can bring about the behavior required by new technologies in work methods and machine operation of the industrial engineering system.

In this example the limitation of the total mission of the training system permits a fully functional operation, and the nature of the mission assigned makes the industrial engineering system the most appropriate place for the training operation.

The functional training operation described would be radically changed, however, if the manufacturing manager were no longer accountable for training actions in his or her organization.

THE STAFF TRAINING OPERATION

If a training function were to be operative at the corporate level, with a mission including the development and maintenance of all skills needed in the corporation, the change in constraints would require an entirely different kind of structure. Accountability for the training function might then be assigned to the personnel system, so that the central personnel records might be used for necessary information and to track individual development in the organization. With the training operation moved from the tasks for which training must be provided, the need for clear interfaces becomes a major problem. The analysis element of this training system must be provided with means of communication which permit investigation of needs and testing of performance standards at the operator level.

Similar problems exist in the development and evaluation elements of the training system. The corporate training operation would have a difficult time supporting subject-matter experts in all of the various special fields required for training. Performance evaluation would also require investigation at the operator level. One solution to these problems is to place elements of the training system within the systems serviced by the training operation. Training specialists in each system could carry out the analysis and evaluation of training actions and act as subject-matter experts for the development of new training actions. The individuals assigned as training specialists could also carry out the training delivery and be given direct accountability for the results of training in their systems. This kind of operation could be successful only if the individual training specialists were assigned their training functions as an integral part of their overall responsibility. In other words, if budgetary constraints did not permit full-time assignment to the job, it would be necessary to structure the individual job-evaluation system to ensure that the actions necessary for successful accomplishment of the training mission would be taken and that individual training specialist reward would be merited proportionately on success of training and not only on the unrelated functions of the job. The competence and capabilities of these training specialists are crucial to the success of a functional training operation of this type, no matter how effective the other elements of the training system might be. There is no possibility for accomplishing the mission without effectiveness in the analysis, evaluation, and delivery elements of the system.

The problem of satisfying the constraint of capability in a functional training operation in a complex organization makes a staff concept more attractive. Accountability for training in a staff-training operation is assigned to the individual systems in which the training takes place. The research element is the only one not operated within the individual systems. The staff-training operation is accountable only for the specialized technologies required to develop and carry out training programs. The identification of needs, analysis of tasks and jobs, and establishment of performance standards, as well as evaluation of performance after training, are carried out by formal or informal subsystems within each organizational system. In addition to supplying technical assistance to the line systems, a staff-training operation is accountable for the cost effectiveness of training actions and for the evaluation of overall organizational training effectiveness. Thus the training operation becomes a feedback and control system for the organization.

The staff approach to the structuring of the training operation is quite the opposite of the functional approach. As in any effective staff system, the training operation provides information, control, and coordination and is only indirectly accountable for attaining the training missions. Effective utilization of such a training system is dependent on the effectiveness of the training subsystems in the line organizations. Since each line organization determines its own needs and standards, provides the subject-matter expertise to the staff operation for the development of training programs, and probably also carries out the training actions, the contribution of the staff-training operation to the success of the overall training mission is responsive rather than creative. A clear definition of interface between the staff operation and the individual training subsystem is primary. If these clearly defined interfaces cannot be provided, the staff approach to training is not likely to be effective. It might then be useful to use a consultive approach to training.

THE CONSULTIVE TRAINING OPERATION

In the consultive training operation, accountability for one element of the training system is assigned to the training consultant. In most cases it is the development element. It is here that the specialized technology of behavior change is employed. With needs and performance standards specified by the system requiring consultation, the consultant and the subject-matter experts from the originating system together develop a training program to meet specific criteria. Once development is complete, the program is returned to the system for delivery. Recommendations might be made for evaluation or clarification of trained behaviors so that accountability for the results of training is wholly with the system requiring the training action.

Regardless of the approach used in structuring a training operation or training department, the primary consideration for success is the clear definition of the system's objective and a full understanding of the constraints to be applied. Unless the training system is designed with clear constraints, there can be little expectation that the training operation, whether functional, staff, or consultive, can operate effectively.

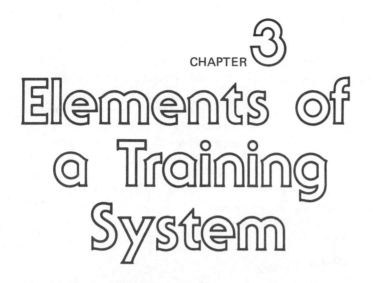

CHAPTER 3

Elements of a Training System

THE TRAINING SYSTEM

The training-system design provides a model for a training operation that can fulfill its functions under any organizational circumstances. It provides a structure for identifying training needs and for creating, developing, presenting, and evaluating specific training actions. The system design also defines the operating entities that will assume the functions of the training-subsystem elements. The training actions themselves are processing systems requiring interaction of the same six elements: research, analysis, development, delivery, operations, and evaluation.

THE RESEARCH ELEMENT

The research element of the training operation has continual interface with the other subsystems of the organization. Its techniques and methodology, however, can best be discussed in relation to the other elements of the training system. In applying the generalized training-subsystem model to specific areas of behavior change, the role of research can be seen to be both implicit and explicit. The tasks of the research element may be grouped into two categories: search and application. Search tasks comprise activities such as collecting and examining published materials, seeking out and contacting organizations that might be applying effective new training approaches, and participating in professional and/or academic courses and conferences. These search activities are not limited to training alone; they also go into fields that might add to the organization's state of the art: industrial engineering, marketing, systems, production, etc. Management games as a training method, for example, originated in the creation of probabilistic models for market forecasting and military war strategies. In the category of application are the tasks of analyzing search data for potential uses in the organization and of modifying new concepts and approaches, where appropriate, to fit with existing or planned training actions.

41

The best reason for separating the research element from others in a training subsystem is the need for freedom to examine and evaluate a wide range of data. If well managed, the other elements will be required to produce predictable results; they will not have the luxury of trial-and-error experimentation. But the research element requires the opportunity to experiment if it is to produce new ways of doing the job. Further, the research element must have the opportunity to examine nontraining technologies and to develop ways of introducing them to the organization in a sensible fashion. Frequently, specialists in the training field tend to automatically reject actions that are not instructional in nature. We know from experience, however, that a significant proportion of performance problems can be solved more cost effectively by nontraining actions.

THE ANALYSIS ELEMENT

Although each element of the training subsystem must function effectively for the system to work, the analysis element is the key to the success of specific training actions. This element defines the scope of the action: objectives, criteria, and constraints for the design and implementation of the specific training action. Definition of the mission of the specific training action, the *training plan,* is the primary task of the analysis element once it has made the decision that a training action is required. If its decision is otherwise, its task is to make alternative recommendations.

The training plan consists of eight parts:

> Problem definition

> Need identification

> Establishment of performance standards

> Trainee identification

> Establishment of training criteria

> Cost estimation

> Estimation of return on investment

> Scheduling

Problem definition

Inputs to any training system are of two types. In the first type the problem (which is seldom well defined) is introduced to the training operation as an observation that someone or some group isn't doing something properly. This is usually followed with a statement by management that training had better get going and do something about it. This input can come from any place in the organization: quality control when rejects are too high, industrial engineering when methods are poor, the general manager when organizational results are below projection. The other type of input is obtained at the initiation of the training system. In this case the analysis element in the subsystem itself goes into the organization to seek out areas where improved performance can be obtained through training. Whether this action is initiated by the training system or by other systems, the first job of the analysis element is to find the problem and define the scope and limits of the investigation which will develop the data necessary for design and implementation of the training action. The problem must be defined in terms of the value of the results (output) of present performance. A problem exists if this output does not meet organizational requirements. Usually it can be defined in terms of the additional cost of or the reduction of profit due to ineffectiveness or lack of the required level of standards in the present performance. The problem, then, can be stated in terms of results and cost of results. The definition, of course, identifies the system(s) in which the problem(s) exists and which will be investigated. It also provides the organizational limits of the investigation.

Need identification

After defining the problem in terms of cost to the organization, it is necessary to identify the specific behaviors or performance responsible for the problem. In identifying training need, the training analyst is identifying the performance which is at present judged to be substandard or nonexistent. When one uses the training plan to design and develop a specific training action, the identification of need describes the entry behavior the trainee will bring to the training action. The training plan will then define training needs in terms of the individual or subsystem behavior which needs to be improved. The identification of training need, if made before the definition of the problem, may turn out to be a long and expensive process without value to the organization. By first defining the problem in terms of its cost to the organization, the training analyst can decide on the value of further investigation. It may be that the substandard behavior itself, though extremely poor, is not costing the organization enough to make further investigation or training action cost effective. In defining the training problem we are discussing the value of given results to the organization; in identifying training need we are discussing the behaviors that bring about those results.

Establishment of performance standards

The standards established by the training analyst in the preparation of the training plan will tell what the organization may expect when training is done. Like training needs, performance standards are studied as specific behaviors: the former define substandard or nonexistent behavior, the latter the standard behaviors—what the individuals or groups of individuals will do in observable, measurable terms to achieve given results. The standards can be stated generally as typical performance or specifically as the performance of an individual or group currently achieving the required performance level. In the first case standards are stipulated which have been judged as valid and obtainable; in the second case, standards are based on existing, sucessful behavior.

Since we are discussing the development of a program plan, the establishment of specific performance standards for all aspects of the task involved may be overly complex and overly expensive. If the training analyst is dealing with a complex of tasks requiring many skills and diverse knowledge, particularly in a nonrepetitive situation, it may be more useful to discuss training objectives; that is, the results to be obtained at the desired level of performance. Thus the objectives can be stated in terms of specific contributions. This is, of course, the other half of problem definition, since by stating objectives and the value of achieving these objectives, the training analyst is in essence stating potential solutions to the problem defined in the analysis.

These approaches to training standards are each valid in their own way. In the first case the assumption is made that a model or ideal performance can be created. The analyst reasons that for a given result to be obtained, certain identifiable tasks, each with a measurement point, must be performed. These measurement points are parts of the task which can be tested to determine the results obtained. They provide standards for determining the acceptability of the performance. In this instance the analyst may use presently performed tasks to structure the model, or, if a model cannot be built on the basis of presently performed tasks, tasks must be designed which can be structured into the model to obtain performance standards. In the second instance the analyst identifies individuals or groups whose performance is "standard," and their performance then becomes the standard for the individuals to be trained. The analyst here assumes that if the results are acceptable, the tasks performed are acceptable also.

Trainee identification

The identification of trainees for planning will not only provide management with the raw numbers of individuals to be trained, but will also provide the other elements of the training subsystem data they will require for the development and operation of the training task. In the identification of trainees, the analyst will have to develop the numbers of the initial training group and will also project the numbers of trainees who will take part in the training action in the future. Both of these pieces of data are necessary for program development and estimation of costs. It will also be necessary to identify the present organizational levels of the trainees, the subsystems in which they work, and their physical location so that the operations element can ensure the facilities needed for the training task. Most important, the current performance levels of the trainees and their prior training must be known in order to establish entry behaviors into the training task. Thus the identification of trainees in task planning goes somewhat beyond the picking of names out of a hat or of asking line managers to recommend individuals to fill their quotas for training.

Establishment of training criteria

Whether the training analyst has established the standards as specific performance or as objectives to be reached in the training action, the criteria that will be used to measure the desired performance or behavior change must be defined. Training criteria provide the test situation or test questions to be used in evaluating training performance at the end of training and in the job environment. In effect, these criteria are the outputs of the training task system, or at least the output measurements. The criteria developed will delineate the specific tasks that are typical and necessary to achieve the desired standard of performance and the measurement points in those tasks. The criteria selected will be inclusive; that is, they will complete the scope of the training task and be all that is required to achieve the specified performance. They will describe not only the behavior expected, but also the method by which measurements will be taken. As in other aspects of the systematic development of cost-effective training actions, these criteria must be stated in terms of what can be observed and what can be measured.

Cost estimation

The presentation of estimated costs included in the training plan must provide management with a reliable basis for making a training decision. Management will be called on to invest organizational resources in the training action, and the training analyst must be able to provide cost estimates that will give a true picture of the total investment to be made. A number of elements of costs have been developed for the training plan, starting with what might be called "general and administrative expenses" for the operation of the training system. In addition to this continuing expense, the cost estimate will include labor-hours in the form of expenses for carrying out the training analysis and for developing program materials. If outside sources are utilized for program development, the contract amounts will substitute for the labor-hour estimates. The cost of production and reproduction of the aids and materials must be included, as well as the actual cost of production or purchase of any text materials. Instructors' salaries or fees must be considered, plus specific cost for outside tuitions, fees, facilities, travel, food, and lodging. Finally, to give a true picture of the training task cost, one element of cost usually left out should be included: the trainees' salaries. In organizations that have a labor charge system, this is a simple matter of estimating the labor cost that will be applied to the charge number assigned to the training task. But in organizations that pay no salary, as in the case of volunteer organizations, some estimate must be made of the actual salaries or a value applied to the time spent in the training effort. This matter of trainee salaries or wages, so often a hidden cost in the development of training actions, can contribute as much as 70% to the total cost of the training action. An interesting cost problem arises when considering the case of sales personnel who could be out in the field adding sales volume. Estimate of sales loss for the period of training should also be added to complete the picture of actual cost for the training effort.

Estimation of return on investment

Return on investment, as used here, really means a description of cost benefits; that is, the relationship of the investment in the training action to the amount of dollar value or other measurable value achieved if the behaviors or performance specified in the training program are met. If management is expected to make a decision to take the actions proposed in a training plan, it must be able to predict the value of this action to the organization. Specificity in this estimate is the key to an intelligent decision. It is at this point that the importance of establishing measurable standards for the performance becomes clear. The investment that will be made in the training action will be in terms of dollars; therefore, to be completely valid, the return ought to be established in terms of dollars. Consider the problem raised by an intensive new-hire orientation program: Investment in such a program can be extensive in terms of instructor time and dollar investment in materials. Yet the establishment of dollar measures for the performance that will be obtained as the result of an orientation program is extremely difficult. Knowledge added to the trainees' repertoire in an orientation program seldom has direct application to their first job assignments. It could be said that the purpose of an orientation program is an attitude change which, during the training program, provides a transition from the school environment to the business environment; yet the specification of measurable values for this attitude change is difficult. This is not to say that such measurable standards cannot be established—only that they are difficult.

Scheduling

In presenting a training task plan to management, it is necessary to develop the when, where, and how long, so that if management makes the decision to effect the training action, logistical planning can be completed and the trainees identified can be released from their present assignments for the training action. In establishing a starting date for the training task, the training analyst must fully consider the time it will take to develop the program itself and also the production requirements of the system in which the training action will take place. The optimal scheduling of training actions is most likely when system productivity is least affected. Heavy workload periods in the year and even in the day or month can seriously affect the ability of a training action to bring about desired performance.

The choice of facility for the training is also important in that it will affect both cost and convenience. The facilities required for the training action will, of course, be dictated by the methods chosen as well as the geographic location of the trainees. The scheduling of specific facilities must also take into consideration other uses of those facilities. Priority must be set according to the contribution of the various training actions to organization effectiveness. In this way specific training plans must fit into an overall training operation plan to make the best use of time and facilities. The training analyst must also specify to management the duration of the training itself so that the loss of trainees' productive time can be weighed against the cost benefits of the training action. Here, both the methods chosen and the criteria developed will determine the length of time that the trainees actually spend in the training action. This is part of the time constraint to be considered.

The training analyst must also look into the possibility that the planned action will put the trainees into a work-overload position. On-the-job requirements may make severe demands on the trainee during the period of training. These workload requirements might dictate that training be given in three-hour sessions once a week in one case and in another case that a 40-hour week be applied to the training task. Scheduling must also take into consideration the capability of the training system. This includes availability of instructor time, whether in-house or drawn from outside sources, as well as the workload of the development element in the training subsystem itself. This scheduling will seriously affect the make-or-buy decision in any given training action, for if time is not available in-house, the greatest competence in the world will not be sufficient to meet an overall training schedule that places available training personnel in a severe overload situation.

Development of a training plan and proposal requires considerable data gathering and analysis. It may be that in the development of this plan the training function will recommend actions other than training, but without the necessary investigation and analysis, it is impossible for management to make profitable decisions of any kind in relation to behavior change. Development of data and analysis for each of the eight parts of this training-task plan discussed above will be covered in later chapters. Considering the labor-hours that will be invested in developing this kind of a task plan, its uses and applications must have measurable value. The primary value of this kind of intensive investigation and analysis would be obvious if all performance problems brought to the attention of a typical training operation were in themselves significant. Unfortunately, this is not always true. Requests for rapid-reading programs, personality-improvement programs, and the like, plus the wide range of attitude-change and orientation programs, can make this initial analysis a very expensive part of the overall training operation. To spend two or three hundred dollars worth of time investigating a large number of potential problems, the solution of which may or may not be useful, can be a significant investment resulting in the inclusion of some extremely profitable behavior-change actions and the elimination of others which would be of little value. Such an investigation, then, might reduce the number of potential training problems accepted by the training subsystem for analysis.

In those cases in which the training-task plan is developed and the analysis completed, the finished plan will serve several functions. First, it will provide management with the necessary data to make a decision regarding investment in a training action. This becomes more than a budgetary decision, since the training operation will use this decision as a tool to obtain organization or system-management support for the training action once it is implemented. Simply, the training-task plan will be the means to sell management on the training action. It is therefore extremely important that the benefits brought about by a recommended training action are given in terms that management can find useful.

The training plan will also be used by the other elements in the training system in filling those parts of their missions that relate to the proposed training task. The development element will use criteria and recommendations about methods to develop instructional design materials; the operations element will use the estimates of cost and schedules to set an overall operating plan. Within the organization, the criteria will also be used for evaluation, as will the standards established. And, as we will see, development of performance standards and task models and the task analysis that is done may be useful to the management of the system in which training is taking place.

The training plan, then, will be the central input document from which all further efforts in the training task will be taken. Therefore, the investment made in the development of an accurate and complete training task plan will be measurable at several points within the organization.

THE DEVELOPMENT ELEMENT

The development element deals with specific training actions. It begins to function after the analysis element has completed the training plan for a specific action and has had this plan accepted by either the organization's management or the system or subsystem in which the training will take place. Considering this element as a processing system, its mission can be defined as the production of an instructional design and materials to carry out the actions required to fulfill the training plan. The instructional design is the "how to" for meeting the objectives of a training plan. It includes the step-by-step strategy and activities into which participants in the training action will be placed. From this design, materials are developed which will be used by the instructors and participants in the training action: conference leader's guide, audiovisual aids, workbooks, job aids, programed instruction, or whatever else may be needed to carry out the design's process. The basic input to this element is, of course, the training plan, which was the output of the analysis element. The items of this plan most important to development are the criteria and the budget and scheduling constraints the analysis element has stipulated for the plan.

The development element makes a further analysis of the criteria in order to determine how the required behaviors can be obtained, in what order they should be learned, and how they might best be grouped to obtain greatest efficiency from the training action. Included in this development analysis is the selection of the proper methods for getting the highest possible level of efficiency in terms of time and cost. For example, the plan for training first-line supervisors in the area of human relations might include behavioral criteria in which the supervisor is required to select a subordinate for promotion, ensuring that the best available person is chosen and that other subordinates will continue to maintain their present levels of activity. The development element would have to seek out alternative methods for getting this kind of behavior. It might be determined that a supervisor will have to learn enough about basic concepts of human motivation and self-image to be able to explain them in talking about the selection process. Or, it may be decided to employ a series of role-plays in which the trainee-supervisor must "live" through a number of situations, making and communicating judgments about people. Through this kind of process, the development element determines strategies and techniques to use in bringing about behavioral changes to meet the criteria of the training plan.

Along with the training plan, two additional inputs to this element are important. The first is subject-matter knowledge when the content of the planned behavior change is not part of the training subsystem's area of competence. This input most commonly comes from within the system in which the training is to take place, but it may also come from outside that system or outside the organization. Subject-matter experts, i.e., the people who will be called on as resources, might be selected by the development element or by the analysis element, or they might be imposed on the training subsystem by the organization in which the training is to take place. The other input to the development element is the technology of behavior change. This may be part of the repertoire of those accountable for the development element, or it may be brought into that element from the research element, or, possibly, from outside the organization.

Often the development element itself will be entirely outside of the organization in which the training action is to take place. It is in this case that outside training consultants are most usually called into the organization. These outside sources will normally be chosen not only for their expertise in the technology of training, but also for their subject-matter expertise. Some cases in point include specialized training in time-and-motion study, marketing, sales, and operations research. One of the most frequently used sources for this element of the training subsystem is the American Management Association, through its seminars, workshops, and courses. Also gaining acceptance and popularity are the highly specialized and highly technical advanced courses in the state of the art offered by a few universities.

Where the development element operates within the organization, its outputs take the form of an instructional design describing the steps to be taken and the materials to be used to carry out the training action. If the training action is to be a "one shot" affair, the development element will probably produce all of the necessary materials for it, but if materials will be needed in quantity, the development element may produce only dummies, roughs, or models which will be duplicated elsewhere. In the cases in which the development element is drawn from an outside resource such as a training consultant, it can be expected that all of the materials needed to carry out the entire set of training actions will come from the consultant.

In situations in which production is necessary, it will be the operations element that will coordinate the necessary duplication or production processes. This will be one of the missions of the operations element in filling its part of the training subsystem's performance of specific training actions.

THE DELIVERY ELEMENT

Essentially, the role of the delivery element is to implement the training action and to ensure maintenance of the training action's quality. The delivery element becomes accountable for all of the logistic details for getting the trainees, instructors, instructional design, and materials together at the right place at the right time. It will also arrange for the right place, since one of its missions is the acquisition and maintenance of facilities for training. In an institutionalized setting this could as well be handled by the operations or managing element of the system, but where facilities are decentralized or temporary, it becomes part of the delivery process and an essential piece of quality control. It is the delivery element that is responsible for providing instructors or for training individuals within the organization to act as instructors for a specific action at a specific location.

The delivery element has the additional responsibility of building support processes which will maintain the trainees' skill and knowledge levels on the job after the training action itself has been completed.

THE OPERATIONS ELEMENT

The operations element is essentially the administrative system accountable for control, coordination, and reporting as the training action goes on the line. The training operation's own support processes are the responsibility of the operations element, including the care and feeding of its troops, their selection, and overall quality control of the training operation's products.

Since this chapter is intended only as a discussion of the interrelationships of the various training elements as they apply to a specific training action, the responsibilities and missions of the operations element for general planning and maintenance of the training subsystem are not considered here. Some of these responsibilities will be discussed in later chapters as they apply to training facilities and the acquisition and maintenance of personnel for the training system.

THE EVALUATION ELEMENT

The evaluation element works in parallel with the development element to produce the strategies and materials for judging both the training action and the trainees' performance. This element's mission as it applies to the specific training action is the production of three feedback processes. It evaluates the trainee's performance at entry into the training action, at the close of the training action, and on the job.

In addition, the development element may request that those responsible for the evaluation element provide feedback processes for application during the action, so that revisions and modifications can be made within the action itself. Further, the evaluation element may possibly be called on to produce testing strategies for use in the analysis of training needs. The most common of these are attitude or opinion surveys administered to large segments of organization personnel as a means of identifying specific needs for training or other forms of management action.

This discussion of the step-by-step procedure through which elements of the training system interrelate to produce training actions describes a processing system. It is not intended to furnish a table of organization for a training department. All of these elements may be performed by one person (a training manager), or each element may be carried out in a different department of the line organization or even farmed out to consultants. But whether a functional, staff, or consultive approach is used, effective implementation of a training action requires that these elements be present and that the functions described here be carried out.

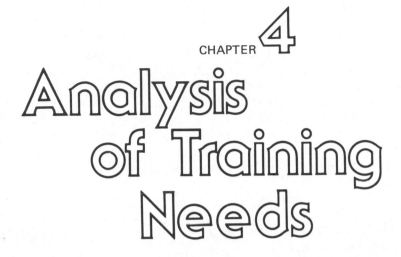

CHAPTER 4

Analysis of Training Needs

DEFINITION OF TRAINING NEEDS

The success of a training-system design is measured by its ability to fulfill its mission. This mission has generally been defined as the development and maintenance of the human behaviors or performances required by an organization to meet its objectives. The training action, then, is evaluated in terms of the performance of those who have been trained. Thus effectiveness of a training system is not measured by the number of programs it produces or by the quality of its handbooks and training aids, but by the contribution of those trained to the organization's goals.

The first three steps of the analysis element's training plan deal with need: problem definition, need identification, and establishment of performance standards. To produce improved human performance, the training system must analyze both existing and required performance. Individual training actions are then designed to satisfy the performance needs of the organization. The statement "Training meets needs" is heard often enough to raise the question "Exactly what is a 'need'?" The president of a corporation "needs" better middle managers. The sales manager "needs" more effective salespeople. The program chairperson of a club "needs" more and better conference leaders. These are all statements of need, but none provides a common definition of "need" that can be used in the design, development, or presentation of a training action.

For a definition of need to be useful, it must define the behavior or performance to be changed. One approach is from the end results of the performance under examination. When a manager evaluates the performance of a subordinate, a number of aspects of that individual's behavior can be measured. One may be talking about busyness or ability to get along with people (an O.K. person) or even the results the person obtains. If the third aspect is the basis of evaluation, there must be an end product to examine. From this point of view, need is defined in terms of performance standards. Instead of saying, "I need better salespeople," the sales

53

manager says, "I need salespeople who bring in no less than 30 orders per week with an average billing per order of $3000.00." The sales manager can fairly easily define the desired standard of performance, but what does the club's program chairperson use as a performance standard? Is there a standard for a successful conference leader in a club? What results must a conference leader in this situation obtain when a satisfactory job is done? Well, our program chairperson might say that a conference leader must hold the interest of the group for an hour and a half, using as measures of this interest the 30-minute question-and-answer period that the conference group will have and the discussion of the conference subject that will continue without structuring or direction for the duration of the coffee period. These might be pretty high standards for many clubs, and the training action required to obtain this kind of performance on the part of conference leaders might be costly in both time and program development.

But even if standards of performance can be expressed, definition of need in terms of training has not been completed. If the training action contemplated is to produce performance to a standard, the need must also be defined in terms of the present performance or behavior; that is, the definition of need must also include what the potential trainee is doing now. The definition of present performance is given in terms of results *not* obtained or behavior *not* taking place—the actions or lack of action causing the deficiency. A corporate president observes that middle managers are not planning their workloads or are not fully utilizing people in their systems; the production control supervisor observes that clerks are not completing inventory control forms properly; or the club's program chairperson observes that conference leaders are not holding the interest of the group, or, even further, that there is no one to lead discussions.

Most training managers often hear "These people can't do. . . ," or "These people won't . . . ." When present performance is defined in terms of something *not* taking place, it is not the present performance that is being identified. Rather, it is a statement that performance is not meeting the expected standard. The manager identifying the need is really saying, "Jones is not performing according to my expectations." In the case of the production control supervisor, "standard" implies that the scheduling forms be completed correctly, and it is assumed that they are to be completed correctly 100% of the time. The inclusion of present performance in the definition of need goes beyond this statement. In the analysis that must take place for the design and implementation of effective training, it is necessary to know the results now being obtained. In the case of the inventory control form, it is necessary to know which parts of the form are filled out correctly and which incorrectly. It is also necessary to identify the other results obtained by the individuals completing the inventory control forms. These individuals will also be involved in other tasks, and these tasks and the system into which they are organized may be contributing to failure to meet the supervisor's expectations or standards for the inventory control forms. Thus the analysis of need must include an analysis of the total system for which training is proposed.

DEFINING PRESENT PERFORMANCE

There are three reasons for including present performance in the definition of need. First, it provides the basis for analyzing the trainees' entry behavior. If a training action is taken, the designer of the action can then use these entry behaviors as the starting point of the training action. Without this knowledge, a training action would have to begin with the assumption that no skill or knowledge is presently available in the trainee's repertory. This is seldom true. In the case of the inventory control clerk, it would be a rare occurrence, unless the clerk were a new hire, that none of the form was completed correctly. It will usually be discovered that certain parts of the form are filled out correctly by the group. Based on knowledge of entry behavior, the training action can eliminate unnecessary training for behaviors already existent.

Second, the difference between entry behavior and required performances will be the basis for determining the value of the training to the organization. If there is a need for a training action or any other action for behavior change, it must have value to the organization. Therefore, the present performance must be costing the organization in terms of lost production, profit, or some other measurable unit. In the same way, obtaining the desired performance must in some way add measurably to the organization. It is this difference between present contribution and required contribution that puts a value on the training action. It also dictates the maximum amount that can be invested in the training action, since it would be expected that training, like any other effort within an organization, provide a positive return on investment, whether in terms of dollars or some other unit of value.

Third, the difference between present performance and required performance will provide the first step in determining whether training is the most effective action for obtaining the required behavior change. The analysis arising from the identification and definition of present and required performances may show that the tasks being performed and the processes by which these tasks are accomplished are those required to meet standards of performance, but that there are intervening factors extraneous to the operator which do not permit the required results to be obtained. It might be shown that a change in the system or in equipment is required. As frequently happens, the problem may lie with the system supervision which fails to provide the environment for actually obtaining the results they as managers require.

BEHAVIOR-CHANGE SYSTEMS

If the phrase *training to meet needs* is to be meaningful, the specific behaviors needed must be identified. The purpose of need identification is to provide an organization or system with a clearly defined end product as the objective of developing an action for behavior change. Each training action is in itself a processing system, and the organization need becomes the mission for that system. Since any training action is designed to bring about change, the description of the need must include all information necessary for accurate definition of the behavior change to take place.

Thus far, the term "training subsystem" has been used to describe the operations responsible for providing the organization with training actions. Now we introduce a new use of the term "system." Each training action is in itself a processing system that brings about behavior change in individuals or groups carrying out human operator roles. The difference between these two uses of the word "system" is similar to that between the description of an electronic data-processing system consisting of pieces of equipment and the program or instruction system that operates within the computer. Each training program or training action, then, is itself a processing system. In effect, we are discussing specific training actions as systems. The mission for each training system must be clearly and accurately defined, as are the missions for any operational or functional system. This mission is a definition of training need. Therefore, before an effective action can be taken, the identification of need must be as specific and complete as the definition of mission for a production system.

The identification of training need, i.e., performance required to meet objectives or standards, can be made at three levels: the system level, the subsystem level, and the individual level. Any training-task system or individual training action will affect change at all three of these levels. Most training actions will require interfaces between individuals and subsystems, and many require interfaces among the major systems of the organization. When managerial skills are considered for training action, identification of needs may be required at the organizational level. The effects of managerial behavior are felt in several systems. At this level, needs can be identified or expressed in such terms as the organization's product, markets, or methods of operation. The decision of an organization to change its product line might bring about training tasks throughout all the systems in the organization. In the same way, a decision on the part of top management to impose a new system of management on the total organization might require training actions reaching every individual in every subsystem. For example, general management might decide to operate on a cost-benefit system or a cost-effectiveness system. Once the alternative is chosen, it is likely that every manager in the organization would have to be trained in the techniques of cost and operating analysis. The identification of need at this level is, fortunately for trainers, rarely assigned to a training operation. In most organizations the training operation is seldom in a position to carry out the interrogation, investigation, and analysis required to define needs on such a wide scope. Usually the highest level of need analysis made by the training subsystem is at the system level.

At the system level the identification of needs is really part of the definition of system mission. For it is this definition of mission that defines the performance standards for the human operators of the system. Required performance is essentially that performance needed to obtain the objectives of the system. This is the end result. It must be present if the system is to be successful. At the system level we will be working with many possible kinds of performance: operating methods, quality of product, cost effectiveness, utilization of personnel, utilization of facilities and equipment, etc.

IDENTIFYING TRAINING NEEDS IN THE OPERATING SUBSYSTEM

The analysis of training needs in a production system can serve as an example of the ways in which the analysis element works in the interrelations within a system. The definition of mission for a production system includes statements of the cost constraints within which the product must be processed. As this constraint changes, the manager of the production system may find it necessary to reduce costs in order to meet mission requirements. Rather than take the obvious first step of a 10% layoff of production-line employees, he or she may make a performance analysis of the various subsystems which make up the system. As a result of this analysis, the manager may find that a number of subsystems are performing below the standard required by the cost constraints established in the definition of the system's mission. The inventory control subsystem may be setting up inventory requirements which do not make most effective use of investment dollars. In comparing present performance against required performance, the manager may discover that the subsystem accountable for inventory control does not have the skills necessary for cost-effective inventory turnover. Further investigation may show that inputs received by the inventory control subsystem from the production control subsystems or from the manufacturing subsystems are themselves inadequate to bring about effective inventory turnover even if the inventory control subsystem had the skills to apply sound investment principles. Thus at a system level, training needs can be identified that affect several subsystems within the system. In this case four or five training-task assignments may go into operation in the several subsystems interfacing with the inventory control process; one training action to bring about a performance change in the inventory control subsystem itself, and other actions to ensure the proper data inputs so that this subsystem can do its job once it has been trained.

The approach to need identification at both the subsystem level and the individual level is similar to that for the system. Again, the question is one of what outputs or results are to be obtained to meet subsystem or individual performance standards. The results of the analysis at each level point downward to the next level, as, for example, the analysis of need at the system level for the production system pointed to an unmet performance requirement in the inventory control subsystem. A definition of needs in terms of the various skills, knowledge, or attitudes required in that subsystem will again point downward to the next level, that of the individual. At each level, specific missions, objectives, or performance standards must be established before the need for behavior change can be identified. In situations in which this multilevel analysis does not take place, even the best training actions seldom produce the required behavior change. When this happens, management says, "Well, why did we bother? Training didn't do any good," and the fault is usually laid at the feet of the manager of the training operation. It is rather like training an insurance salesperson to sell more volume and having this new business turned down as unacceptable by the underwriters. Failure to analyze the requirements of underwriting or the interface relationships between underwriting and the sales force results in a behavior which, though it may meet performance standards of a sales organization in terms of signed applications, fails to meet the requirements of the total organization in terms of acceptable, profitable business. The training action itself may have been quite successful, with measurable improvement in sales performance in terms of increased number of signed applications, but the failure to identify the training need at the system level in this case, particularly the underwriting-sales interface, makes it impossible for this performance to have value in the system.

TRAINING-NEEDS DEFINITION

Training needs are defined by comparing present performance with a standard of performance. If a performance or behavior change is necessary, either present performance is substandard, or a required performance is nonexistent; substandard in the case of a sales force that is not producing a required volume of profit and nonexistent for the same sales force when a new product is introduced about which they know little or nothing. In either case the determinant is the performance standard established for the individual, subsystem, or system. Broadly, there is no such thing as nonexistent performance or nonexistent condition, since any group of trainees brings entry behaviors to the training task. The analysis of these entry behaviors, however, is likely to be simpler in the case of the nonexistent conditions where no wrong behavior is being reinforced in the present environment. In other words, when substandard performance is being considered in the training situation, the individuals being trained have been doing something that has been accepted by management and for which they have received some sort of "payoff"; this behavior, which was rewarded and supported, may have to be unlearned or eliminated from their performance. When this kind of condition is present in an operating system, need analysis at higher levels becomes crucial, for it is in this kind of situation that changes affect supervision or interfaces. Often the entire process in which the performance takes place must be changed in order to change behavior in the individuals being trained. For the inventory control subsystem this may mean changing the kinds of inputs it receives and training related subsystems in the preparation and transmittal of the inputs. In the insurance situation the changes might be more complex. Perhaps training will be required to obtain commitment from the underwriting system to the mission of the sales system or vice versa. Possibly new missions or a new interface relationship may be required. The interface relationship might include a change in incentive plans so that the underwriter shares in sales commissions or salespersons are given an additional bonus for acquiring "profitable" business.

In the case of the nonexistent performance or condition, there has been no reinforcement of wrong behavior within the organizational environment. In dealing with a substandard performance, it is not the training action itself that becomes more difficult, but rather the identification of the individuals or subsystems to be trained. A substandard condition seldom exists in a vacuum; if it does exist in the subsystem, it is being supported somewhere in the organization. Without this support it could not survive. As a result, the analysis of need must go beyond what appears to be the problem area.

IDENTIFICATION OF PERFORMANCE STANDARDS

The first data requirement for the analysis of needs is the identification of performance standards throughout the organization. Again, these performance standards must identify the specific results to be obtained and must be measurable. Without some means of measurement, there is no way to determine whether this standard of performance is being obtained. Whether the system of measurement is subjective or objective, a matter of qualification or quantification, the ground rules have to be set before any training task can be designed.

Considerable stress has been placed on the measurement of behavior change and on the purpose of that measurement, namely, to tell all those involved—trainer, trainee, and manager—what has been changed. When the measurement is objective, the standard of measure will have the same significance to anyone concerned any time it is applied. But subjective standards are also valid so long as everyone concerned accepts and understands them. Someone makes the statement, "My judgment will be used as the standard of measurement." Well, why not? This is, after all, the form of measurement most frequently applied in human activities. However, if the measurement must be subjective, then the training analyst must be able to identify the judge and secure agreement that the judge is competent and qualified to provide the standard. Similarly, where quantitative measures cannot be developed, qualitative ones should certainly be applied. Even if unable to determine how much of a behavior is required, the analyst must at least be able to identify it when it is there.

PRESENT PERFORMANCE VERSUS REQUIRED PERFORMANCE

The second kind of data required for the analysis of training needs is data on present performance, and, as before, these data must refer to specific measurable performance.

The third type of data required for analysis of training needs relates to the processes or tasks required to meet established standards so that those processes or tasks which are not part of the present performance can be identified. Detailed descriptions of the specific tasks and their sequential relationships will be used to establish the performance criteria by which both the training tasks and the trainees' behavior change will be measured. If the problem were simply the design of a job or job family, the data required would relate only to those performances required to obtain the standard. However, since a training action is to be designed, the same task or job analysis must be done on the existing performance in order to determine the specific behavior changes to be brought about. Thus from the training point of view, crucial data relate to the processes or tasks not now being performed but which are required to achieve the standards. These process or task data also include the identification of the individuals or subsystems to be trained; that is, they pinpoint those who are not doing what is needed.

IDENTIFICATION OF SYSTEM PROBLEMS

In addition to data relating to the tasks or processes performed by the individuals or subsystem under analysis, information about the system itself and its interfaces is also needed. This description of the system and system interface must include identification of all tasks required to meet the standards, both those performed within the subsystem under study and those from other subsystems which furnish inputs to the subsystem and utilize its outputs. The identification of specific inputs and outputs is particularly important, since the inputs determine the limitations on the task performance of the subsystem and the outputs provide definition and measurement for the performance under analysis. These data must include not only the physical inputs and outputs, such as raw material and partially finished products, or raw information and processed data, but also the interfaces with the subsystems providing the inputs and using the outputs. Data relating to subsystem or individual outputs must include the requirements of the receiving system or individual. For example, if the subsystem under analysis is a series of machine operations and each machining operation is considered an element of the subsystem, the input requirements of one machining operation will determine the outputs of the preceding one. This could be crucial if performance standards for, say, a surface grinding operation requires that steel blanks be ground into rectangular blocks plus or minus 0.005 in. and the next machining operation requires the input blocks to be rectangular to within 0.0003 in. The outputs of the first element will never meet the input requirements of the second. Therefore, the identification of inputs and outputs must be both descriptive and measured, since it must define the material or other item being processed, the individual or subsystem receiving the output, and the flow between elements.

Finally, data will be required for analyzing the causes of the substandard performance or behavior. These data will include the process description, input and output identification, description of controls and measurements within the system, identification of interface, and statement of standards. Thus data requirements for analyzing the causes of the potential training need summarize all other data requirements.

DIRECT INVESTIGATION OF PERFORMANCE

Three sources are available for obtaining the training analysis data: direct investigation, management interrogation, and system design and projection. The quality and utility of the data obtained will differ in each case. Direct investigation, of course, requires that data collection and analysis be carried out at the level of the subsystem or human operator. This is the process of observation and interview with the people who make up the subsystem under analysis. It is most useful in identifying present performance, processes, and interfaces and is partially useful in establishing required performance standards of the subsystem. Direct investigation, whether through some form of oral or written interview or by direct observation, can be extremely accurate and complete when carried out by a competent training analyst. It can also be extremely time consuming, since many of the behaviors or processes observed do not directly relate to the performance under investigation.

MANAGEMENT INTERROGATION FOR PERFORMANCE DATA

Since the training analyst is concerned with performance rather than with designing the method for obtaining the performance, ability to identify the key contributing factors to the performance is likely to be the most important problem. Interrogation of management can overcome this problem. If we assume that the management questioned is competent to evaluate and describe the tasks and behaviors in its area of responsibility, data obtained from this source are particularly important in identifying required performance and established standards for the subsystem. Whether this information is obtained through direct interview of management personnel or from management reports to one of the control subsystems, the training analyst is still dealing with forms of management interrogation. The use of existing control data is particularly important, since the information in these reports is the same data used to evaluate performance of the system as a whole. The reports may also be the system for evaluating performance after training, and it is therefore useful to obtain data which are commonly understood throughout the system. Usable control reports will detail performance against plan or budget, cost reports, inventory turnover reports, sales against projection or quota, etc.

SYSTEM DESIGN FOR ACCEPTABLE PERFORMANCE

The third data source, system design and projection, is necessary when a training need arises out of a major change in the subsystem under analysis. In this case a design is developed for meeting a level of performance, and the performance or behaviors required of subsystems or individuals are projected from this design. For example, the introduction of an electronic data-processing system for production control will require totally new kinds of documentation throughout the production process. As these documents are designed, changes in performance will be required in various subsystems to complete the software items for computer usage. The various required tasks and the standards of performance for them would then be projected from the design itself. This approach to training analysis can also be useful in existing systems to develop a model against which the existing system processes can be compared. These comparisons would then be used to identify possible process or interface changes which would enable the trainee to more easily achieve the required performance.

APPROACHES TO TRAINING-NEEDS ANALYSIS

Two approaches are available for the identification of training needs and the analysis of tasks and the processes involved. The most common approach is from the tentative identification of substandard existing performance or behaviors; an individual or group of individuals in the subsystem is identified as doing something wrong or as not doing something that the manager of the subsystem thinks ought to be done. For example, a sales group may not be producing sufficient volume, marketing may not be bringing in enough new business, there may be too many rejects in the punch press department, there may be too much overtime in the accounting department, and so on. This is the approach taken when the general manager sends out the plaintive cry, "My managers simply cannot manage!"

The second approach is from the establishment of performance standards; management states what is required and demands that the training operation obtain that level of performance. No matter which approach is used, or whether both are used, the same process of analysis is required to identify training needs and to define processes or tasks required to meet the performance standards.

ESTABLISHING THE SCOPE OF THE INVESTIGATION

The first step in the analysis is to develop an orientation toward the problem; that is, the training analyst must set the limits within which the particular training task or group of training task systems will operate. This limitation of scope will determine the subsystems or parts of a single subsystem to be investigated, the kind of performance or process to be analyzed, and the data sources to be used. Such a limitation of scope appears to contradict the stated necessity of system analysis for identifying all tasks, inputs, outputs, and interfaces involved in any process. Ideally, complete analysis of the processes, documents, machines, and human operators within any system and group of subsystems which interface with it would be necessary to develop an effective training action. In fact, development of a total training system will be the objective of the analysis element of the subsystem. However, in developing specific training-action plans, it becomes necessary to limit the breadth of investigation in order to focus on the problem causing the need. The training analyst will be dealing with a live, ongoing system and will be expected to obtain practical results in a reasonable time for any given training task. It becomes important, therefore, for the analyst to be able to provide management with a reasonable target date for completion of the assignment and a reasonable idea of the kind of results expected. By limiting the scope of the investigation, the analyst can provide management with this data. Results of the analysis may show that substandard or nonexistent performance is not a training problem, or it may provide the criteria from which a training task system will be developed. But in order to come up with an acceptable answer in a reasonable time and at a reasonable cost, the scope of the investigation must be limited to a predetermined part of the organization and a predetermined set of processes, performances, or tasks.

The scope of investigation defines the start and end of the process or task sequence in which a problem has been identified. It also tentatively identifies the subsystem or individuals doing the processing or completing the task sequences. Let us assume that management has identified a substandard performance in a finance department as the inability of the financial analysts to produce a clear, concise, and usable monthly report of performance against plan. If a potential training problem has been expressed in such terms, the limitation on the scope of investigation can become quite important. For example, if the training analyst limits the investigation to that point in the process at which all data for the reports have been gathered, only the performance task sequence that involves only the organization and writing of the report will be investigated. If, however, the scope is expanded to include the gathering of pertinent financial data on the condition of the organization, the task analysis will include the financial analysis itself. This will become, then, not a report-writing program, but rather a program for the training of financial analysts in all aspects of their job relating to developing data on budget and performance against budget and plan.

DEFINING THE PROBLEM

Once a reasonable attempt has been made to limit the scope of the investigation, a specific definition of the problem can be made. The problem, again, is one of a substandard or nonexisting performance or condition. Therefore, in defining the potential training problem, the analyst must consider the processes being performed or the results being obtained through the performance. The definition must include the effect of this substandard or nonexistent condition on the organization in measurable terms. Thus the problem is defined in qualitative terms and its negative value measured. Both of these steps must be taken.

The discovery of substandard performance within an organization is nothing more than an interesting exercise unless that substandard condition affects the organization's ability to meet its missions. It must be assumed that obtaining the desired performance will result in a measurable reduction of cost or increase in profit to the organization. Even when this contribution is indirect, as in the attempt to bring about an attitude change, it must be specific enough to be described in measurable terms, and its effect must have some kind of value to the organization.

The questions to be answered in defining the problem are quite simple: What is being done wrong? Or what is not being done that should be done? What is it costing the organization? Since dealing with people means dealing with a fairly complex set of behaviors, it will usually be found that a group of tasks or performances is being done wrong and that the costs to the organization are additive. Thus the definition of problem must cover the entire process within the limits of the scope established at the beginning of the investigation.

In seeking a definition of the problem, the training analyst must follow the problem step by step from the input to the output stage. In gathering this information, the groundwork is prepared for comparing present performance to the standard against which trained behavior will be measured. Each task within the sequence must be examined in terms of the total process and results it produces and in relation to the tasks which precede and follow it. If the training analyst defines the problem, it will probably be presented in an additive form. Referring back to the financial analysis department, the problem might be stated as one of additional time required by management to read poorly prepared reports or additional cost to the organization due to insufficient financial reporting.

Upon analysis of the substandard condition, however, the training analyst might find a number of discrete substandard performances within the subsystem. The reports may be poorly organized, necessitating additional time spent in revision. The data may be poorly summarized or collated, resulting in additional hours spent in correcting or repeating the analysis, etc. It may even be that at the output stage, the manager of the department is required to spend expensive time personally revising the reports. All these quantitative measures of laborhours spent become additive in stating the entire problem.

ESTABLISHING PERFORMANCE STANDARDS

Once the problem has been stated in terms of performance and cost of performance, the next step in the analysis can be made. Ideally, this should be the establishment of performance standards. It has already been determined that correction of the substandard or nonexistent condition will make a measurable contribution to the organization. The problem now is to determine specifically what performance will be required to accomplish this end. As in the definition of the problem, the qualitative description of the standard must be made and a system of measurement created to ensure that the standard is indeed obtained. What will be done when the job is done right, and how will we know it is being done? The prime consideration now is the results obtained at the output end of the process under investigation.

EVALUATING PERFORMANCE CHANGE

When the training action itself is designed, it will be necessary to identify performance standards for each significant task within a task sequence so that standards can be developed for each step of any job. From the standards set for each task within the sequence will come the criteria by which the training action and the trained behavior will be measured. At this level of the investigation, the objective is to develop sufficient information about the acceptable standard of performance to make a decision about the value of bringing about this behavior. At some point the decision will be made as to whether the investment in training is worth the result that will be obtained through training. It is the standard of performance established at *this* point in the analysis on which this decision will be based. Continuing our example of the financial analysis department, the performance standard to be established would be developed from a description of the monthly report management wants. This definition would describe an acceptable report in terms of data, format, schedule, etc. The value of such a report would also have to be established. Just what is it worth to the organization's management to have the report they have just described? How much time will it save? What additional information will it provide that can increase profit or cut costs for the company? What is the advantage of the fact that this report can highlight certain kinds of information about the performance of the various subsystems within the organization?

One of the pitfalls of evaluation of standard performance can be seen in this particular example. The usual reply to the question "What is it worth to the organization?" is "The boss wants it!" For most of us in the business environment, this answer is sufficient, but from the point of view of training effectiveness, a contribution to the boss's sense of well-being is seldom sufficient to warrant increased investment in a training action. Perhaps we might say here that unless the boss's sense of well-being is reflected directly in the organization's profitability and directly contributes to the fulfillment of the organization's mission or objectives, the successful accomplishment of the standard of performance has no utility to the organization.

After performance standards have been established for the potential training action, they can be used to define present performance and the cost of the present substandard or nonexistent condition. At this point we ask what the present performance is. How does it compare to the performance required to meet the established standard? What is it costing? What will standard performance cost? What is the difference between the two costs?

During that part of the analysis in which performance standards are established, the training analyst identifies the performance which the system or organization management requires, i.e., the desired state of affairs. Standards are given in terms of the results which management wants to obtain. In analyzing present performance, it is necessary to examine what is actually happening in the organization, not what system or organization management *thinks* is happening. Furthermore, it entails the analysis of what individual operators are actually doing, not what they think they are doing. Thus interrogating a system requires not only that members of that system, particularly the management members, describe what is going on—what actions and what processes are being taken and what results obtained—but also at least some direct observation or direct evaluation of the processes, actions, and performances.

Since the results of any training action will be measured by the standards of the organization in which the action takes place, the analysis of present performance must be in terms of the measurements that the organization now uses to evaluate subsystem performance. Thus existing reporting and control documents provide a substantial proportion of the data used in the analysis of present performance. Often the organization's own internal reporting and control system will identify, or at least highlight, the problem under analysis. The attention of the training analyst is on those performance areas that have measurable outputs and that are key measurement areas according to the established standards. Therefore, the analysis of present performance is likely to be most effective when limited to those areas that contribute most directly to the subsystem's outputs.

DEVELOPING A SUBSYSTEM MODEL

After standards have been established, measurements have been set for the key performances required to meet standard output, and the present performance has been compared to the required standard, the training analyst's next step is to develop a model of the subsystem under investigation. This model will outline the specific tasks in the sequence that would be required to meet the standard of performance established for the subsystem. In establishing those standards, the analyst has specified outputs. In identifying the specific tasks and task sequences, the individual operations that will lead to those outputs are identified. A number of discrete operations are put together in a sequence to lead to the required outputs. The project involves developing a system flow model describing each key task, its input, output, and interface with other tasks. At a later point in the analysis, each of these key tasks or processes will have an individual operator identified with it, and the performance of each task will be associated with certain skills and knowledge required to complete it. This process expands the job-analysis process undertaken by the industrial engineer in a time-and-motion study or by the industrial engineer in developing a production-processing system or designing a production line. From the training analyst's point of view, the methodology is applicable to any processing system in which inputs and outputs can be identified and measured.

THE MODEL VERSUS THE EXISTING SUBSYSTEM

Once the task or process model has been completed, it can be matched to the process or task sequence that is producing the present performance. Each task in the present system can be compared to the task in the designed system, with differences in input and output levels noted and those tasks requiring training action identified together with the skills or knowledge required to carry them out. By this process, the training analyst is able to identify subject matter, the individual can be trained, and the outputs that provide the basis for establishing criteria can measure the behavior changed through training.

There are two points to consider in identifying the key tasks or processes: first, the importance of successful completion of the task to the total process; and second, the cost impact of those tasks requiring behavior change. The training analyst's objective will be to attain the greatest return on training investment. The tasks that can be most significantly improved in terms of dollar effectiveness will be those for which the greatest training dollar investment can be made. This process of analysis removes the possibility of training an individual in a task that can never contribute greatly to the total performance of the subsystem. For example, training a salesperson to correctly fill out an order form might be less important than training the same salesperson to maintain a prospect-call record. The decision would be based primarily on which specific task would contribute most to the overall sales performance, assuming that the objective of the sales system is to bring new business to the company. Of course, if sufficient training dollars were available and the return on investment for successful performance of both tasks were adequate, then training could be provided for both. In most cases, however, training dollars are limited, and the best investment must receive priority. It is essential to identify the contribution of each key task or process to the subsystem performance.

The final step in the analysis of the training need is to specify the key behaviors needed to carry out the tasks or processes at the required standard of performance. These key behaviors will become the trained behaviors described earlier. At this level, the training analyst is describing the specific observable actions of the individuals carrying out key tasks already identified. To sum up, the training analyst first describes the performance standards required by the subsystem; then identifies the key tasks that lead to this performance; and finally defines the specific behaviors involved in performing each task. Each of these three levels is described in terms of present substandard or nonexistent performance and required standard performance. The analysis of training need is now complete.

DATA FOR AN ACTION PLAN

The analysis of need must answer three sets of questions before an action plan can be developed.

Problem identification

1. What systems or subsystems are involved?
2. What system or subsystem missions are not being met?
3. What is the value of meeting the missions (or what is the cost of failure)?
4. What other systems or subsystems are affected and at what cost?

Need identification

1. What kinds of performance or behavior are required to fulfill the missions?
2. What are the required standards of performance or behavior?
3. How will performance be measured against the standards?
4. What is the present performance or behavior? What is to be retained, changed, eliminated, or added?
5. What inputs are required for standard performance? Can they be changed to improve performance?
6. What other missions are assigned to the system or subsystem? Do they impose performance requirements that interfere with the performance under analysis? Can they be changed to improve performance?
7. How is the system or subsystem organized? Does this organization make the required performance possible? Can the system be changed to improve performance?
8. What technology is required for standard performance? Does the technology exist within the system? Is it used?
9. What tools and materials are required? Are they available? Can they be changed to improve performance?

Trainee identification

1. From whom is the performance or behavior expected?
2. Do standards and requirements differ for the potential trainees? Do the differences interfere with performance? Can the differences be changed to improve performance?
3. Are the potential trainees in a position to meet requirements? Are other demands interfering?
4. Do the potential trainees know the performance or behavior expected?
5. Can the potential trainees meet the requirements? Do they have the ability?
6. What is their present level of performance?

DATA FOR A DECISION TO TRAIN OR NOT TO TRAIN

The next step of the analysis element is to develop data for a training decision. Now that the behaviors are known, it must be determined whether the required performance can best be brought about through a training-task assignment or through an alternative means. The analysis has described the individuals now carrying out tasks, and in most cases these will be the individuals who will undergo the training action. Through observation or direct interrogation, the training analyst will determine whether the individuals are now carrying out the tasks inadequately or incorrectly because they do not know how to do the job or for some other reason. The determination is a matter of "can do" versus "will do." Substandard performance often results not from lack of training or skill or knowledge (the can do), but rather because the individual for one reason or another will not carry out the tasks. If it is found that potential trainees already have all the skills and knowledge necessary to perform to the required standard, other causes for the problem must be sought.

Essentially there are three general causes of substandard performance: a system problem, a process problem, or a training problem. If the individuals presently performing the tasks do not have the skills or knowledge necessary to do their jobs, it is likely to be a training problem. If the potential trainees can carry out the task but do not do so because they are receiving improper, inadequate, or badly timed inputs (in other words, if someone else in the system is at fault), or because their interface with supervision is creating a situation in which they are not motivated to carry out the task, most likely the system itself needs revision rather than the individuals. It may be that the system does not create an environment in which the potential trainees are motivated to meet the required standard. Essentially, attitude-change training is a matter of system revision, including revision of the communication process which takes place between the individuals and their peers and superiors as well as of the reward structure of wage, salary, fringe benefits, etc. It may be that the performance problem can be solved by the establishment of a recognition system or other similar changes in reward structure.

If the training is good and the system is sound, perhaps the cause of substandard performance is the process itself. It may be that the task sequence was not designed to bring about the desired performance. This can easily be ascertained by comparing the existing process system to the model designed around the standards. It is here that particular attention must be given to any human-machine relationships within a task system in order to determine whether the equipment used by the potential trainee will obtain the desired results, given the individual operator has all the necessary skills and knowledge to carry out the task. The cause of substandard performance can, of course, be due to a combination of these factors as well as to any particular one.

With the cause of the substandard performance identified, a plan of action can be made. The training analyst can recommend that a system or process be revised, or that a training action be employed, and the next step in the training analysis can begin: developing training criteria. This becomes a process of translating the key tasks identified earlier into terms of observable behavior and designating specific means for measuring those behaviors. Three things are necessary for the development of training criteria. First, the behavior must be observable; that is, the potential trainee must do or say something. Second, these observable behaviors must be measurable; we must know when the trainee is acting or communicating correctly and be able to compare his or her performance to that of others or to a standard. And, finally, the "law of parsimony" must be applied; that is, the criteria developed must take the least effort, the least time, and the smallest dollar investment. The training analyst will identify those key tasks that contribute the most return for the time and money invested in bringing about behavior change.

The training analyst is now ready to list the criteria by which the performance of both the trainees and the training task itself will be measured during and/or on completion of training. These criteria must then be tested by the standards of the model design. Here the training analyst attempts to determine whether the performance standard required in each task will indeed be met if the criteria set for the training task assignment are fulfilled. This is the first feedback loop in the training action. If the training criteria met will not produce the required performance, the training analyst must make revisions to provide behavior to standard, before preparing the program proposal.

So far, no training has taken place, nor has a training program or training action been developed for implementation. Before development takes place, management must decide whether or not to train. It is at this point that the training subsystem will find it most helpful to obtain management support for any further action. It is also at this stage that a cost proposal can be prepared demonstrating the cost benefits or return on investment from training. All necessary data will be available; the training analyst will have already discovered what the substandard or nonexistent performance is costing and what the attainment of standard performance will contribute to the organization. The analyst will also know where and how present performance deviates from standard and, from knowledge of training technology, the kind of program necessary to correct the deviation. An analysis of the training criteria will provide an estimate of what the training task itself will involve. At this stage in the training system, the cost of not having trained behavior will be known, and management can then judge what kind of an investment in training is feasible.

PLANNING WORKSHEET

It is important that a proposed change action be tracked from start to finish. This kind of record keeping helps ensure that planning is consistent and complete. It also provides material needed to gain the "client's" agreement to the action. Finally, it can provide data for future use for both cost estimating and more efficient program planning. We often find ourselves reinventing training programs because we did not document similar programs in the past. With an effective planning document, we can index objectives, criteria, and actions for future use.

A typical planning worksheet includes the following items:

1. *Program initiation:* Who started the ball rolling? The client? From training? From a third party? Why was the action initiated? How will it benefit the "client"? The organization? The trainees? The training operation?

2. *Problem definition:* What is wrong? What will be true if the problem is solved? Who is affected? How did the problem surface? When? How will the "client"

know when it is solved? Who will be involved in the solution? Where are they? What can inhibit or prevent a solution?

3. *Problem impact:* What is the cost of the performance problem so far? If it continues? What can be gained by solving it? Who will gain?

4. *Objectives:* What are the objectives for the proposed actions? How will they be. measured? By whom? When?

5. *Criteria:* How will the desired performances be defined? What criteria will be used? Who will approve them? When? How?

6. *Performance standards:* What will the performance standards be? Who will approve them? When? How?

7. *Trainee specification:* Who will be trained? How will trainees be selected? How many? Where? What might interfere with trainee participation? What are potential costs of participation? What are the scheduling constraints?

8. *Resource specification:* What resources will be needed if a training strategy is selected? A nontraining strategy? Dollar resources? Technological? Subject matter?

9. *Probable causes:* What kind of problem is indicated by the analysis: expectations, feedback, consequence management, job design, training, organization environment? Describe the cause(s).

10. *Planned solution:* What strategies and tactics will be used to change performance? What methods? Why? What are potential limitations to the proposed solution? What potential negative consequences will there be to the organization?

11. *Estimated costs:* What is the solution likely to cost?

12. *Time and action:* What are the start, milestone, and finish points? How will milestones be identified? Who will audit? How? Who will approve schedule? How?

ALTERNATIVES FOR BEHAVIOR CHANGE

On the basis of this analysis, the training analyst recommends to management the best alternative for bringing about the performance or behavior required to obtain the results needed to fulfill the system mission under investigation. In order of complexity and cost, the alternatives examined in the analysis might be described as follows:

1. Eliminate the mission from the required outputs of the system. This can be done if the mission itself has little or no value to the organization. The mission may be partly eliminated if it can be altered by changing the standards of performance required to fulfill it.

2. Change the way standards are specified and communicated to the performers to ensure that the performers' understanding of the standards of performance is

the same as that of those who will evaluate performance. Also, make sure that the receivers of the performers' outputs understand the standards of performance in the same way as the performers do.

3. Change the inputs into the system so that more usable material or information is available to the individual performing the tasks required to meet performance standards.

4. Change the output requirements so that fewer or different outputs are required from individuals performing the task. In the system this might mean changing the reporting form or possibly eliminating certain outputs normally required to fill the system mission, as in the case of first-line supervisors counseling subordinates. The counseling task as an output might be moved to another system.

5. Change the organization of the tasks themselves by eliminating extraneous ones or changing the sequence of performance.

6. Change the conditions under which the tasks are performed by removing or reducing other demands on the individuals performing the tasks. (These demands may conflict with the task under analysis).

7. Change the internal feedback system by providing more control points within the task system through which individuals performing the tasks can evaluate and change their performance.

8. Change the consequences for performance by introducing directly related positive consequences for performance improvement and withdrawing positive consequences where performance does not improve. Both financial and nonfinancial rewards should be considered.

9. Replace individuals not presently performing the tasks to standard with people who do or can.

10. Change the control system by increasing the amount of control data from and to the system or by adding additional constraints limiting the freedom of action of individuals performing the tasks. For example, procedural control over the tasks being performed might be increased, cutting down the number of alternative judgments that can be made by individuals. This could be an acceptable alternative in redesigning a first-line supervisor's job. (It may not be a palatable alternative from the social scientist's point of view, but in some situations it can be quite effective!)

11. Redesign the entire task system so that the mission can be fulfilled through the performance of a wholly new set of tasks. This, in effect, is what is done when a process is automated or when new machinery is introduced into the production situation.

12. Improve the performance of the individuals presently performing the tasks through a training action.

DEVELOPING TRAINING CRITERIA

Only if the last alternative is recommended as the most cost-effective means for obtaining the desired results can the training analyst move on to the next step: preparation of a training action plan. In this step the first action will be to develop training criteria as the basis for instructional design for the training action.

Training criteria do three things: (1) describe the conditions that call for a response; (2) specify the response the trainee will make after the training; and (3) establish the standard to be met by the trainee. For example, the criteria for a program to train a sporting-goods salesperson to sell camping equipment might specify:

1. *The condition:* "Using an erected sample of a No. 10-13 deluxe tent . . . ."
2. *The response:* ". . . point out ten special features, including fabric weight, thread count, aluminum spring-loaded poles, chemical waterproofing, inside zippers, nylon screens, extra sun protector, reinforced corners, headroom, and pleasing appearance."
3. *The standard:* "The trainee will point out the features without reference to printed material and will specify one benefit to the user for each feature identified."

If the training action is also to train the store salesperson in sales techniques, this criterion might be specified otherwise, stressing user benefits rather than features, requiring a demonstration of the use of benefits to obtain buyer agreement and the use of buyer agreement to make trial closes on the sale. Thus the same condition can be used to structure three kinds of responses and three separate standards of performance. The different responses in this case will require different training designs to obtain the desired performance standard. There is a difference between teaching product knowledge and teaching the techniques of benefit selling or the skills of using leading questions and trial close approaches. Each has its own requirements, and all are necessary in the complete training of a successful salesperson. However, if the trainer is interested only in the introduction of a new product, the feature and benefit responses may be all that is required. In structuring training criteria, it is important to note that they are key behaviors; that is, they are the essential elements of individual performance in a given task or series of tasks which can be used as limiting measurements for the performance. If the criteria are met, it may be said that the trainee can perform all parts of the job at the required standard even though the criteria do not include every discrete behavior which may be observed in carrying out the specific tasks.

The training analyst is saying that the training action will bring about the particular kinds of performance specified by the criteria—no more, no less. If more is required, additional criteria will have to be specified. If less is required, some criteria of conditions, responses, or standards can be eliminated.

COSTING AND SCHEDULING

There remain two areas to be included in the training plan that will be offered to management for approval: an estimate of the costs of carrying out the proposed actions and a schedule for completing these actions. Cost will be estimated from data supplied by both the development and the operations elements of the training subsystem. The operations element will furnish data from past experience as well as estimated costs for both development and implementation of the action. These costs cannot be estimated until the development element of the subsystem has made a preliminary selection of method and has decided on the strategies which will be used in carrying out the action. Thus from this point forward, the training plan is a combined operation of the three elements: analysis, development, and operations. Scheduling data will be developed by the operations element from existing training actions and prior data on development time. Again, this is a coordinated effort of the three elements.

PERFORMANCE–ANALYSIS CHECKLIST

An effective needs analysis should specify the performance problem and identify probable causes. A complete performance analysis will investigate each element of the performance-management model. The checklist presented here is a guide to the kinds of information needed. The data collected should be sufficient to provide "yes" or "no" answers to the checklist questions. "No" answers indicate probable causes.

Expectations

1. Outputs specified: What? How many? How often?
2. Outputs produce desired outcomes?
3. Performer expectations match output requirements?
4. Boss expectations match output requirements?
5. Receiver expectations match output requirements?

Feedback

1. Actual outputs known to performer?
2. Feedback timing permits adjustment?
3. Feedback usable by performer?
4. Feedback neutral or positive in reinforcement effect?
5. Actual outputs known to boss?
6. Actual outputs known to receiver?

Consequences

1. Consequences for meeting requirements exist?
2. Consequences for meeting requirements known to performer?
3. Consequences perceived as performance-related by performer?

4. Consequences perceived as performance-related by boss?
5. Consequences perceived as performance-related by receiver?
6. Consequences for meeting requirements positive to performer?
7. Consequences for approximating requirements exist?
8. Consequences for approximating requirements positive to performer?
9. Consequences for not meeting requirements exist?
10. Consequences for not meeting requirements known to performer?
11. Consequences for not meeting requirements perceived as performance-related by performer?

Performance environment

1. Other outcomes specified?
2. Other outputs specified?
3. Other outputs produce outcomes?
4. Performer expectations match requirements?
5. Boss expectations match requirements?
6. Where same receiver is involved, receiver expectations match requirements?
7. Performance free of task interference?
8. Performance free of consequence interference?
9. Performance free of demand interference?
10. Activities relate to performance requirements?
11. Performance priorities known to performer?
12. Role norms relevant to performance?

Job design

1. Input requirements met?
2. Processing requirements met?
3. Subtasks efficiently sequenced?
4. Physical environment free of task interference?
5. Performer controls tasks and subtasks?
6. Intrinsic reinforcers present?

Interface requirements

1. Required interfaces known to performer and interface?
2. Interface expectations met?

3. Performer and interface goals congruent?
4. Goal competition not a factor?

Interaction requirements

1. Substantive issues not a factor?
2. Value issues not a factor?
3. Competitive issues not a factor?
4. Power issues not a factor?

Performer skills

1. Performance criteria known to performer?
2. Performance compares to criteria?
3. Training feasible?

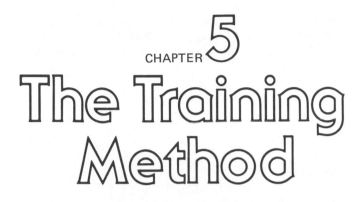

CHAPTER 5

The Training Method

STRATEGIES FOR TRAINING

The training-action plan prepared for management approval provides the development element with its primary input. At this point the plan still lacks the cost estimate and schedule, which are to be drawn out of feedback from the development and operations elements. Both cost and schedule are dependent on the strategy proposed by the development element for meeting the training criteria established by analysis. The proposed strategy is the "what, where, who, when, and how?" of the training action from which an instructional design and the materials required to implement it are developed.

The key to the strategy of a training action is the selection of a method or methods to be applied in the instructional design. The media and technique that make up the educational or training method determine the structure, scope, and limitations of the instructional design. Several considerations must be examined in choosing a training method, but the primary one will be the training criteria, selected to ensure that the desired behaviors will result from training. If training criteria are to be the primary consideration in the selection of method, it becomes impossible to select an approach for the sake of the method itself. Selection of method on the basis of novelty, common usage, past success in other programs, or intellectual curiosity is dangerous to the achievement of effective training results. Yet arbitrary selection of method for any of these reasons is all too frequent. A particular problem arises when those in the development element of the training system are comfortable with one or two approaches they have used in the past. The appeal of prior success is seductive beyond reason to the trainer with intensive workload demands. The same danger exists in selecting outside specialists for program development; they often receive a greater payoff for their technical proficiency than for the results they obtain. It is far easier to measure the quality of the artifacts that characterize a training method—aids, materials, texts, etc.—than it is to evaluate behavior change. But the purpose of training is to bring about behavior change, and the training design in all its parts must be directed toward this end if training is to be cost effective.

SELECTING A METHOD

The next step, then, is to select the method or methods to be employed. From this selection a cost estimate will be made, scheduling recommended, and, on approval of the training plan, an instructional design prepared. The selection will be based on several considerations:

> training criteria

> trainee response and feedback

> instructor skill level and feedback

> approximation to the job

> adaptability to trainee differences

> cost

Each of these considerations needs to be examined so that necessary compromises or trade-offs can be made in selecting the most effective method. The final choice may not be the best from the point of view of learning theory, but it should be the most effective combination possible within the imposed constraints.

Training criteria

Training methods must be sought to bring about the required behavior, and the methods available must be checked against each of the three aspects of the criteria. Since criteria are plural, a combination of methods may be required to meet them all. It must be decided whether the method under examination will bring about the required responses, whether it allows the response to be measured against the standard, and whether it can be used in the prescribed conditions.

In the case of the sporting-goods salesperson and the new tent, lecturing might meet all the requirements of criteria stipulating a listing of features. The lecture could furnish the information needed to make the response, and visual aids could present the conditions. However, if the salesperson will be required to convert features to benefits in front of a customer, role-play may be more effective.

Trainee response and feedback

To what extent does the training method selected permit the trainer to observe and correct or reinforce the trainee's behavior? How well does it enable the trainee to measure his or her own progress through the training task? The ideal training method would permit the trainer to continually observe the behavior of the trainee throughout the training action and to correct or reinforce behavior as necessary. Correction of behavior errors which prevent successful performance and reinforcement of every desired response of the trainee are essential to training success.

At the same time, the ideal method would enable the trainee to self-evaluate performance at all times during the training task. Linear programed instruction

techniques now in use, for example, permit the program writer or instructor to reinforce proper behavior and keep the trainee alert to progress by comparing written
responses to the correct responses. Programed instruction does not give the trainer
a means for observing the behavior, only for recording results. This can be quite
adequate in getting the trainee to describe, explain, answer, or choose. Where more
sophisticated programing techniques are used, motor-skill training and complex
decision-judgment kinds of behavior can also be brought about.

On-the-job training provides an example of a direct trainer/trainee relationship.
There is a continuing opportunity for the trainer to observe, correct, and reinforce,
and for the trainee to measure his or her own performance at all points in the training program.

Instructor skill level and feedback

In order to know whether the desired behaviors are being effected, the instructor
will need the same kind of feedback as the trainee. The business training environment is unlike that of the university in that the teacher/trainer is being measured
as well as the student/trainee. The trainer is measured on ability to bring about
specified behaviors and therefore needs to be able to appraise the degree of success
in achieving these behaviors. For this reason, it is necessary to consider how much
training will be needed to qualify an instructor in the use of the method selected.
This is one of the problems in selecting the on-the-job training method, since the
trainer is usually a supervisor or task leader with other duties more directly related
to the job reward structure. The same problem arises in the development of
programed instruction, wherein a skilled program writer must be either hired or
trained. Thus the competence—the skills and knowledge available in the trainer—
and the capability or time and motivation of the trainer become important considerations in the selection of a training method. If a full-time training staff is
available with competence in all the potential training methods and with the capabilities to carry out the training task, this factor need not enter into the selection of
method. But where trainers must be selected from other systems in the organization, these are extremely important criteria in method selection.

Approximation to the job

Here the question is how nearly the selected method will approximate the environment in which the trainees will actually perform after training. Will the conditions
of the training environment be close enough to those of the job so that the trainee
will be able to transfer the new behavior to the work situation? Anyone who has
ever hired secretarial personnel has faced the problem. The poor applicant who has
learned to type on the latest model machine complains bitterly that adequate performance is impossible on the beatup old model typewriter to be used on the
job. Or consider the sales manager who has seen a new sales trainee demonstrate

effective sales techniques in the classroom over and over again and finds that in the field, the trainee demonstrates none of these skills with customers.

Adaptability to trainee differences

How well does the training method adapt to differences in learning rates, entry behaviors, availability of trainee time, and trainee attitudes? Here again, the ideal training method would adapt to each trainee in a training group, allowing the individual to proceed at his or her own pace, with motivation and payoff designed for particular attitudes and environmental background. Programed instruction comes close; on-the-job training comes even closer, but if the training group is homogeneous in terms of its entry behaviors and educational and other environmental background factors, other methods will meet the trainer's needs. The high school or college classroom environment is a good example of a case in which the student/trainee has been conditioned to respond to the lecture, discussion, and demonstration instructional systems. These systems work quite well, especially when the environment can be totally closed, as in a residential or boarding school. But even here the size of the training group seems to be an important factor in the development of materials. It would appear that the smaller the class size or the lower the teacher/pupil ratio, the more effectively typical educational methods adapt to the pupils' particular needs and attitudes.

Cost

Three items enter into cost consideration. The first item is preparation; how much will it cost to develop the program using this method, and how long will it take? Can the program using this method be repeated at other times with different instructors? What is the actual labor-hour investment in developing all the materials needed to bring about the desired performance using any given method? Preparation cost is the most forbidding aspect of programed instruction. It is also the major consideration in using complex aids such as motion pictures or closed-circuit television. The last two training aids require a high degree of technical proficiency for effective use, not counting the actual equipment, i.e., film, videotape, etc.

The second item of cost is the matter of aids and materials. What will be the cost of equipment for audiovisual aids, texts, workbooks, machines, simulators, machine systems for programed instruction, etc.? Further, can these materials be obtained? Are motion-picture production facilities available for not only shooting the actual films, but also editing and producing the prints projected during the training task? Can the training program rationalize the $1000.00 per minute average cost for 16mm sound movie production or the $5000 to $50,000 investment in closed-circuit television?

The third item of cost to be considered is presentation. What will be the cost of actual training facilities, instructor fees, trainee salaries, or tuitions if outside sources are used? Part of the consideration of facilities is the availability of classroom or laboratory space on the premises. If it is not available, can it be obtained at a convenient location, or will the cost of transporting the trainees also have to be included in budgeting for the training task?

In general, then, the choice of method is based on the requirements of a planned training action. It must meet the training criteria within constraints set by the trainees, instructors, available facilities, and time and cost parameters set by management. Therefore, the various methods cannot be ranked as best or worst, but rather in terms of specific criteria to be met. Further, training methods are not mutually incompatible or discrete; they can be combined, altered, or varied to meet specific needs.

INSTRUCTOR-CONTROLLED VERSUS
LEARNER-CONTROLLED INSTRUCTION

Before examining the most common instructional methods, it may be important to consider two fundamentally different approaches to the training process. Historically, instructional processes have been instructor-centered. The instructor determined the methods to be used, the manner in which the content would be broken down, the sequence in which knowledge and skills would be acquired, the time blocks, and the facilities to be used for instruction. One result of this instructor-centered approach has been that much of the training offered has been designed and presented for the convenience of the instructor or the instructional system. Trainees were expected to conform to the requirements of the instructional system, arranging their time and habits for the convenience of the instructor. Frequently this has resulted in instructional efficiency but learning inefficiency.

More recently, we have been examining instructional design from the point of view of the learner and are discovering that learner-controlled instruction is more effective, particularly with adult learners. In learner-controlled instruction, the trainee knows in advance the criteria he or she will have to meet in order to achieve a specified competency level. The learner then controls the method to be used for delivering the instruction, the sequence of learning, schedule of instruction, and the evaluation of his or her own progress. The trainee in this approach has the opportunity to select the method to be used, or at least to participate in method selection and, indeed, may participate in the design of the instruction itself.

Learner-controlled instruction requires a very different organization of teaching/learning units, usually in shorter intervals, and is much more dependent on technically based equipment such as videotapes, teaching machines, and computers. It appears that the learner-controlled approach is rapidly gaining prominence for use with adult learners. Although development costs are higher than for instructor-centered approaches, both delivery costs and learning efficiency are improved.

TRAINING METHODS AND THEIR EVALUATION

Let us look now at the most common training methods in current use in light of what has already been said. The 14 that we shall consider are as follows:

Lecture	Incident process
Structured discussion	Role-play
Unstructured discussion	Role modeling
Experiential learning	In-basket exercise
On-the-job training	Simulation
Vestibule training	Management games
Case study	Programed instruction

Lecture

Examination of several hundred training programs given in several types of organizations indicate that well over 70% of all training actions use some form of lecture as their method. Lecture method may be defined as the presentation of course content by a subject-matter expert or instructor to a group of trainees who, during the period of the lecture, remain passive. By passive we mean that the trainee does not actively respond during the training session, other than to take notes, until there is a question-and-answer period. The lecture itself may be presented through a number of media. The instructor may make a live presentation, show motion pictures, or use closed-circuit television, videotape, or filmstrip with audio. The lecture may even be presented by tape recording alone, relying totally on audio transmission. If method is to be considered only on the basis of training criteria, the lecture method would seldom be chosen, since trainee response systems are not structured into the training process itself. When responses are called for, they take place after the actual training, and become primarily a test of retention rather than of response within the limits of a training criterion. Nor are the response requirements framed by conditions. On this basis, lectures alone are ineffective; they must be combined with some other training method to obtain the response needed to meet the conditions of training criteria. This is not to say that behavior cannot be changed through a lecture system, only that such change is difficult if not impossible to measure in terms of condition requirements and behavioral standards. Because of the passive nature of the participant in a lecture situation, there is little observable trainee response or feedback. The participant must await testing to discover progress with any certainty, and only the test situation gives the necessary feedback. A trainer has no opportunity to observe the trainee's response, to alter materials or presentation, or to ensure that the desired behavior change is taking place. Many practiced lecturers are able to sense a change in their audience and can judge their effectiveness during the course of a lecture. To a large extent, however, these observations are somewhat subjective and at best are only loose measures of a trainer's effectiveness. Still worse, few lecturers achieve this degree of empathy.

Where only canned media such as motion pictures, filmstrips, or videotapes are used, there is no opportunity to observe trainee behavior or any means for the instructor to evaluate the effectiveness of the communication.

The use of a question-and-answer period within or directly after a lecture is not entirely satisfactory for either the development of the trainee response and feedback or instructor feedback. Under normal circumstances, only a small number of participants use the question-and-answer period for feedback on content. The questions are usually quite specific and are easily drawn into subject areas outside the behavior change being sought. Much of the question-and-answer period, unless skillfully structured, is given over to ego questions by which the trainee demonstrates personal knowledge to the group. If ego questions were not limited to a small part of the participating group, they would be a far better measure of behavior change than the more specific question directed at the subject matter, since they at least indicate that learning has taken place, either in the lecture or at some time in the participant's personal history.

The positive feature of the lecture method is that the instructor's skill level need not be high in comparison to that needed in other training approaches. Training an instructor to effectively present material in lecture is not difficult. Therefore, by choosing a subject-matter expert as an instructor and utilizing his or her self-confidence, an interesting and successful lecture format can be developed. The subject-matter expert can be trained as a relatively effective lecturer through instruction and practice in the use of visual aids and special techniques for public speaking, such as varying pace, using surprise, etc.

In developing a training action restricted to company resources only, the lecture is often the most cost-effective method for building the training task. Combining it with other methods can result in extremely effective training. Later in this book we will discuss in detail the selection and training of instructors for the various methods that may be employed in an organization to bring about behavior change.

The two areas in which the lecture method is weakest are failure to approximate the trainee's job and inability to allow for individual trainee differences. Except for the school environment, the lecture never approximates the participants' actual job environment. Transfer of learned behavior from the lecture to the job situation is most difficult. The more elaborate the lecture facilities and the more professional the lecturer, the further the training is removed from the job situation. In this respect careful construction of classroom facilities, comfortable chairs, soundproofing, and controlled lighting actually become negative factors. By using tests of entry behavior, a lecture can be effective in adapting to individual trainee differences, *providing* the participants can be grouped homogeneously and frequent opportunities are created to test the participants' acquired behavior during the training sessions. Unfortunately, however, the lecturer is seldom given an opportunity to premeasure participants in groups, and it is often difficult to structure test sessions within the lecture format itself. Differing rates of learning speed cannot be considered in the lecture method, since the instructor is geared to a personal speed and to the training group as a whole. Thus the lecturer must gear the presentation to the lowest common denominator in the group in order to bring about at least some behavior change in all participants. This becomes extremely wasteful of the time of the fast learners, and its effect on them can be to create boredom and a negative attitude toward the training experience. Furthermore, without the opportunity to obtain feedback from the trainees, the instructor in the lecture situation cannot tell when participants are tuning in or tuning out the materials. Any evaluation must wait until the test period to judge the speed and quality of learning.

The major advantage of lecture as a method is cost. The elements of cost—preparation, materials, and presentation—are likely to be lower for a lecture-based course than for any other medium. Once content has been established, preparation of materials can usually be left to the instructor, with the assistance of any appropriate research facilities. Preparation time will be two to eight hours per hour of instruction time. Within these limits of preparation sufficient detail can be developed in the lecture notes so that other subject-matter instructors can present the content in a consistent manner.

The cost of aids and materials will depend largely on the size and number of the groups to be trained. If the training action is to be a single effort—that is, if the program is unlikely to be repeated after the first presentation—and if there are no time constraints on getting the job done, it will usually be most effective to use live instructors. If 100 people are to be trained and if they can be divided into groups of 25 or less, inexpensive visual media can be used for lecture aids, e.g., charts, blackboard, mimeograph, newsprint pad. With small groups where there is no need for duplication of visual material, the actual production of the visuals will not involve more than two hours of artwork per hour of lecture. If participant groups are to be larger than 25, the visual problem becomes somewhat more severe. More attention must be paid to the context of the visuals and to their form and media. The overhead projector is still useful, but the other aids described above are not. Transparencies become necessary, either in the 35mm or the 4" X 5" format, and with these media come higher production costs, for now artwork and photographic transfer are involved. Although the preparation of aids and materials for a larger group is more expensive than for a smaller group, the tradeoff must be considered in terms of presentation cost. In a large group, the cost per participant of facilities and instructors' time decreases rather quickly. This assumes, of course, that facilities are available for the larger groups.

In considering the cost of presentation, there is one element that can be quite expensive for a lecture approach: trainee time. Payment of trainee time as a training cost is not usually estimated when either calculating training cost or evaluating a method. However, if training is to take place during work hours, the loss of productivity and the actual wage or salary payment for the trainees must be taken into consideration. Since the lecture approach is not very efficient in bringing about desired behavior, it can be expected that the changes actually occurring will be limited. In terms of trainee time, this means an investment of large amounts of time to bring about small changes in behavior. This can make lecture an extremely luxurious approach to the training action.

Structured discussion

Essentially, a structured discussion is a small group meeting at which the instructor or conference leader guides the participants step by step through a process of questions, answers, and open discussion to a desired response. In a structured discussion, the instructor has prepared in advance the generally directed (or overhead) questions and specifically directed questions which will be used to cause all members of the group to emit the proper responses to meet the training criteria. The instructor controls the group at all times by directing specific questions to individual participants and restricts the discussion within predetermined limits to keep the group on the track and prevent it from moving outside the area of the desired responses.

In terms of training criteria, the structured discussion is excellent, provided the responses to be elicited are essentially verbal or written. As a method of bringing about behavior changes in motor skills, discussion can accomplish no more than a lecture with a written test. However, if the responses can be observed as verbal or written, structured discussion provides an excellent means for attaining, observing, and measuring participant responses. Trainee response is high, since the instructor has a constant opportunity to observe, correct, and reinforce trainee behavior. The small-group environment also has the advantage of giving the instructor the opportunity to use other participants to reinforce desired responses by obtaining their agreement and elaboration of the individual trainee's response. In the same way, the trainee has a continuing opportunity to discover how well he or she is doing by the comments of both the instructor and others in the group. Since group responses can constantly be tested during the discussions, the instructor receives adequate feedback to carry out a self-evaluation.

Instructor skill level for a structured discussion must be high. The instructor/conference leader must be highly adept in the use of overhead and direct questions and must have the ability to respond quickly to the participants so that the content can be continuously restructured for the group. Unlike the lecturer, the discussion leader must be less of a subject-matter expert and more of a skilled discussion leader; that is, we can expect one to be technically competent in the instruction medium as well as in the content.

The structured-discussion approach to training loses its value if the presentation is not made by a well-trained instructor. If the training action is to use personnel available to the organization, then, they must be able to be adequately trained. Trainer training must be feasible. If not, the designer of the training action will have to look outside the organization or have available trained instructors on the training staff.

Although the structured discussion does not approximate the job in terms of setting or task, the learning experience itself can approach the way in which learning takes place in many job situations. The active give-and-take questioning and answering, the process of analysis which leads to the discovery of problem solutions, can be structured to parallel the learning process the participant will find in the job environment. Although it cannot be said that the structured discussion duplicates or even simulates the actual job environment, the way in which learning takes place is similar to many occupational situations. This is particularly true in an organization in which supportive management is practiced and in which verbalized analysis is expected on the job. Structured discussion might be appropriate as a method in supervisory training programs, where a concept such as management by objectives is developed and then applied or practiced by means of another instructional method. Those in the training group would be able to discover and develop for themselves the concepts to be used in the other instructional methods. It must be stressed, however, that the types of behavior elicited are primarily verbal, so there can be little expectation that other observable changes will take place using structured discussion as the instructional method.

Because of the quality and immediacy of the trainee/instructor feedback in the structured discussion, the method is very adaptable to individual trainee differences. By judicious use of direct questioning, the instructor can provide additional learning and reinforcement for the slow learner and can give the faster learner the opportunity to develop the program content rapidly. One drawback, however, is that the system is essentially verbally oriented, and where verbal aptitudes are lacking in a participant group or a particular person, the necessary responses may be difficult to elicit. This can be an important problem when the participant group has not been controlled and both high and low verbal aptitudes are present. The participant who lacks verbal facility will often be placed in a highly defensive position in which self-image is threatened. When this happens, the instructor may find one or more participants either clamming up and refusing to take part in the discussion or resorting to highly critical, perhaps even sarcastic, language. An instructor who is skilled in this medium can avoid these pitfalls with judicious use of supportive questioning; in other words, the slower learners can be recognized immediately for their answers and protected from the faster learners by the instructor's support of their answers and discussion points.

The structured discussion as an instructional medium becomes very attractive from the point of view of cost where small numbers of trainees are involved. Once the desired behaviors are known, a skilled instructor can prepare the discussion questions. The instructor or instructional designer can set forth the criteria questions to be used as performance measures and from these questions structure overhead and direct questions to lead the group step by step to their answers. The pattern of questioning need not be rigid, provided there are no severe time restraints on individual discussion sessions. The instructor can change the line of questioning in the session itself and in fact develop a mutual learning process. As experience of the instructional designer or the instructor grows with the subject, preparation time for each session will diminish. Excellent structured discussion programs can be developed in as little as two hours per hour of learning experience. Even better from the point of view of cost are the materials necessary for the discussions themselves. The instructor will need a writing surface visible to the whole group—a blackboard, newsprint pad, or viewgraph cell. The primary visual aid will be the notes taken for the group as the discussion progresses. This is necessary as a reinforcing tool, enabling participants to refer to the points brought up during the discussion to build the learning experience. The presentation is also inexpensive so long as the total number of participants is limited; all that is necessary is a room and a conference table, as much comfort as is normally available in the job environment, and a reasonable amount of isolation so that concentration can be maintained. Because structured discussion is unfeasible for groups much larger than 15, the greatest expense is instructor and participant time. The close ratio of instructors to participants, 1:10 to 1:15, can rapidly increase the cost of this medium if there are many repeat sessions. The answer may be investment in training line personnel as skilled discussion leaders.

Unstructured discussion

The term "unstructured discussion" is used here to describe an instructional method controlled almost totally by the participants. It consists of a participant conference wherein problems may be stated or an agenda established, but within which the participants themselves formulate the discussion structure. An instructor may or may not be present during the session, but if present serves only as a moderator or, at most, a catalyst. The unstructured-discussion approach places an interesting constraint on the criteria established for the training task. The instructional medium itself establishes the conditions in which the responses take place. The group and the subject of discussion together provide both the stimuli and the feedback for each participant. Within the limitations of written or verbal responses, unstructured discussion provides the greatest freedom for participants, providing they have been prepared for such an experience by either their job situation or other training tasks. Unstructured discussion is often used to train participants in conference or committee processes.

The learning experience in the unstructured discussion is shaped by the group. The participants provide the subject-matter expertise, if it may be so termed, and work together toward the behaviors for which they are being trained. Usually this technique is used to resolve interpersonal conflict or to solve problems within the group. It may also be used to train a task team or management team to work together as an organizational entity. The opportunity for the instructor/moderator to observe and evaluate training responses is excellent, but if the greatest advantage is to be obtained from this method, it is not usually helpful for the instructor to correct responses. The participants themselves should provide the reinforcement and correction required for obtaining the trained behaviors. In the same way, the trainee has an excellent opportunity for feedback from the remaining members of the group. Feedback is direct and immediate and, if the training environment permits, quite openly accepted by the individual participants.

The instructor must have a clear understanding of the purpose of this particular instructional method. Divergence from the planned content must be expected, as well as conflicts within the group. The group itself must be allowed to resolve conflicts and maintain direction. Any intervention from the instructor should be only to help the group maintain task orientation. The advantages of this instructional method are precisely in the area of free interchange within the participant group. The "bull session" nature of this method is, of course, an approximation to the actual job environment. Indeed, it duplicates the system within which real-world problems are solved and conflicts thrashed out.

Restricting the group to a training facility removes restraints that might be placed on the participants in the actual job environment and provides them with an opportunity to practice new behavior patterns without danger of disrupting their usual task assignments or expected job roles. Because of the lack of instructional control over the participants in the unstructured discussion, the method is not particularly adaptable to individual learning-speed differences or individual attitudes. Individuals within the participating group will strive for dominance and form in-group coalitions very rapidly. The instructor/moderator may often have to intervene to point out that such in-groups are disruptive to the learning process taking place.

The cost of unstructured discussion as a method is quite low, having the same elements of cost as structured discussion. Small groups are required, but the greatest expense in the method is the time needed to develop the training criteria. The use of unstructured discussion must be carefully planned to take advantage of its freedom and job approximation, realizing the limited application of the method.

Experiential learning

Experiential learning goes one step beyond unstructured discussion by placing the trainee into a real-time, here-and-now, task situation. In most cases no instructor is employed. Prior to entering the task situation, the trainee is made aware of his or her learning objectives, although the trainee may construct these independently using broad objectives as the only reference.

Laboratory training is a special application of experiential learning in which the laboratory group creates the tasks and learning objectives, usually in terms of individual awareness learning or gains in interpersonal competence. In this special case a "trainer" is employed, primarily to facilitate the interaction of the group and to maintain, whenever possible, the group's focus on its chosen tasks and objectives.

Most often experiential learning takes place on the job site. The subject matter is the job itself. For example, experiential learning has been applied in teaching managers planning processes by placing them into the normal annual planning cycle, having them determine what constitutes their achievement of competence in planning, and then permitting them to go ahead with normal administrative or system guidance to complete their operational plans. Essentially, experiential learning is a controlled application of the notion that "experience is the best teacher."

Good experiential learning usually provides the trainee with a number of resources to link into as the need is seen. Depending on the extent of resource availability, the costs of delivering instruction in this method vary greatly. It appears to be most cost effective in skill aquisitions relating to career or management development.

On-the-job training

In on-the-job training both the trainee and the instructor operate in the actual job environment. Traditionally, the process is explained to the trainee, who then observes the process, describes it, and carries it out under an instructor's guidance. The trainee continues to carry out the process, being corrected by the instructor, until proficient enough to perform assigned tasks alone. The materials, tools, machines, etc., are those the trainee will actually use on the job. Responses are to conditions identical to those encountered in the actual job situation. Standards established for the responses are also real and pertinent to the tasks. From the point of view of response, condition, and standard, on-the-job training appears to be an ideal system for bringing about desired behavior. With skillful instruction, OJT is extremely effective. Its three major weaknesses are:

1. The order of instruction may not be the most effective for the behavior desired; in other words, certain parts of the task may be more effectively learned out of their normal task sequence. Because OJT takes place under production conditions, it is difficult to rearrange the order in which individual tasks are performed.

2. A high degree of instructor skill is required for OJT, since undesired behaviors or unrelated behaviors may be reinforced by an inexperienced instructor or one with more pressing duties.

3. A great deal of time and space is consumed by OJT because of the one-to-one ratio between instructor and trainee and the large amounts of time the individual instructor must devote to each trainee, particularly during the first stages of instruction. Further, since the training takes place within a production subsystem, a trainee's slowness or errors may disrupt the productivity of the operators receiving the trainee's outputs. Reject rates can go up and scrap can increase. These are expense items that must be expected when on-the-job training is used.

Since the instructor is present and in direct contact with the trainee, OJT provides excellent conditions for observing, reinforcing, and correcting trainee responses. Also, since the trainee is working in a real-task situation, reinforcement of desired behaviors can come through actual productivity. This is a powerful reinforcing tool; the trainee receives continual feedback from the production situation—from seeing results as they are obtained—and immediately discovers whether or not the tasks are done correctly. In the same way and through the same media, the actual productivity of the trainee, the instructor receives immediate feedback on the effectiveness of the instruction.

In order to make fullest use of OJT situations, the instructor's skill level must be high. The OJT instructor must be skillful enough to reinforce only the required or desired behaviors and to avoid "overteaching." Overteaching often occurs when the instructor is a highly skilled operator or subject-matter expert, particularly if deeply involved in and highly satisfied with the work. A tendency to show the trainee every way to do the job is prevalent. This leads to a number of extraneous behaviors on the part of the trainee, and although the extra information or skills may be interesting, they do not produce the most effective training system. It is particularly important that the training itself be very carefully structured so that only key behaviors are taught and performance of subtasks is frequently evaluated. There is little need to comment on approximation to the job with this method, since it *is* the job. It would be difficult to find a better way to approximate a person's work situation than the job itself.

The OJT process is highly adaptable to individual learning differences because of the one-to-one instructor/student relationship. It may also be assumed that since the trainee has been selected for and assigned to the tasks being trained, he or she will be highly motivated toward the learning experience; that is, motivation will be high at the beginning of the learning experience and, provided that the learning experience is unstructured, will continue to be so.

Cost is the greatest problem. Preparation of material and structuring of the learning order can be quite time-consuming, requiring frequent tests of the effectiveness of the learning order. Further, instructors must be carefully trained in both the content and the instructional method. If OJT is assigned to a supervisor as one of many duties, its effectiveness is lost unless the person has received special training such as "job instruction training," originated during World War II. Preparation of materials is usually limited to job aids that can be used as "reinforcers" for the trainee. The most expensive element is perhaps the presentation itself, since machine time, if this is an industrial situation, will be necessary for the trainee on a regular shift basis. In any event, whether it be a manufacturing environment or any other job situation, the cost of lost production must be accepted as a cost of training and estimated in developing training expenses. The cost of the instructor must also be recognized and considered as a major expense, since OJT does require large expenditures of instructional time.

Vestibule training

Vestibule training is intended to gain all of the benefits of OJT with few of its shortcomings. In vestibule training the on-the-job situation, the production system itself, is duplicated off-line. A separate area is set up in which the actual production processes can be carried out. Its effectiveness in meeting criteria closely approximates that of OJT. What is lacking is the production requirement of the on-line situation; that is, the trainee is neither under great pressure to maintain a standard of production at the beginning nor held accountable for a high reject rate in the first stages of training. The greatest advantage of the vestibule training over OJT is that it is the primary task of the instructor assigned to it. This is not something in addition to other duties, as is true of a task leader or supervisor. Since instructors can be assigned and trained for this specific duty, the training skills required to bring about behavior change can be developed in them. Also, the order of instruction may be varied to achieve the most effective sequence without jeopardizing or interrupting normal production processes. Skills being developed can be carefully structured so that undesired or unnecessary skills or processes are eliminated from the instructional process. The facility itself can be so designed that the one-to-one relationship usually required in OJT is not required for all instruction in the vestibule. Other forms of instruction can be added to the OJT process, since the vestibule, being isolated from the regular production facility, permits utilization of other training techniques and methods.

From the point of view of training, vestibule training offers all the other characteristics of OJT. Its major disadvantage is cost. The facility itself is a major overhead expense and can be maintained effectively only if sufficient numbers of individuals are being trained. The order of skill, the types of behaviors being trained, must be sufficiently complex to warrant the establishment of a separate training facility of this type.

Another assumption is that the skills themselves will remain reasonably constant. Otherwise, continual revisions in the type of equipment or the processes taught in the vestibule must be made. This will, of course, result in increased cost for maintenance of the vestibule.

Case study

In the case method the learning experience is developed through a well-documented description of a real-life or simulated situation. The trainee learns through analysis and solution of the problems implicit in the case documents. Usually the results of this analysis are presented in written form and are critiqued or discussed by the instructor. Often the cases are worked in small groups so that part of the learning experience is derived from the interaction of participants. Criteria defining the changed behavior can be carefully described in the case approach. The conditions for the responses are structured in the case documentation itself, and standards can be observed in the presentation of solutions. The form of response is normally written, and in most case studies the participant is expected to generalize from the solutions to particular cases. Trainee responses can be easily evaluated by the instructor, and the trainees receive direct feedback by the instructor's comments on their analyses and case solutions. Further feedback may be received where small groups work as syndicates on a specific case. Both the instructor and the developer of the case material receive their feedback with the submission of the completed case reports and can to some extent measure their training effectiveness by the effectiveness of the trainees' solutions to the problems.

It must be noted here that trainee response and feedback and instructor feedback do not take place during the learning experience itself but only afterward. The presentation of the completed case report is in itself a form of a test, although it can also be said that preparation of the report is a part of the learning experience. Frequently, indeed, this report preparation is as important as the solution to the problem. Unless the cases are structured for each participant, there is little opportunity to adapt the training material to the learning speed or attitude of the individual trainee. As a method, the case study was originated for the academic environment and presupposes a high degree of verbal ability on the part of participants. The materials themselves are in written form, and the response structure is written. Because of its form, a case study does not come very close to approximating a normal work environment, since all of the documentation and materials are prepared outside the working environment.

The major cost involved in the use of case study is the preparation of materials. Since complete documentation must be available, considerable research may be required. On the other hand, cases are available which fit most of the training situations that can benefit from this approach. These cases are available from the academic sources in which the method originated and has been used for several years. As off-the-shelf items, cases are relatively inexpensive, and when necessary, changes can be made with the permission of the original authors. Few aids and materials are needed for the implementation of the case study other than the printed cases themselves, and no special facilities are needed for presentation. In fact, most of the case work can be done in the participants' homes, offices, or work areas. Where training facilities are lacking, the case approach is often the only effective method which can be employed.

Incident process

The incident process, originated by Paul H. Pigors, is essentially a variation of the case method. Unlike the case method, where the participant is given all of the documentation needed to analyze and solve a problem, the participant in the incident process is given only a crisis or "critical incident" in the development of the problem. This may be a presentation in the form of a script, or, in the industrial situation, a tape recording of a dialogue between individuals involved in a problem. It may also be a published memorandum or document highlighting a critical problem. The participants must then seek out the facts they need to direct investigation. Usually the investigation is carried out by asking questions of the instructor, who gives factual answers. The participants are given only the information they actually seek, and they themselves must develop the documentation needed to bring about an adequate solution. Behavioral criteria can be as well established as for a case study, with the advantage that the learning process more closely approximates the real job environment. In the job situation, after all, the trainee does indeed have to find the facts, talk to people, sift out personal points of view, probe for information which may not always be in the open or readily available, and balance individual opinions. The learning experience is an active one, requiring interaction with other participants in the training group and the instructor, permitting immediate feed-back to both trainee and instructor, and allowing the conference leader to give immediate reinforcement to the trainee for answers to questions as they are asked.

Although the incident process approximates the real job environment more closely than some others do, because of its compression the character of the process tends toward a certain degree of artificiality. A high degree of instructor skill is required, since the instructor must be able to structure answers to evoke a maxi-mum effort from participants, but must not make the process more difficult than is necessary for the learning experience to take place. In other words, the instruc-tor must not withhold information so strictly as to frustrate the efforts of the participants.

The cost elements of the incident process are quite similar to those of the case method, except, of course, that in presentation, classroom facilities and an instruc-tor must be available. The development of incident materials is similar to the devel-opment of case materials, and, like them, incident materials are readily available from commercial and academic sources. Presentation costs are about the same as for a structured discussion session, with the same restraints placed on the number of participants.

Role-play

Role-playing can be described in two ways: first as an extension of the incident process, and second as a kind of psychodrama. As an extension of the incident pro-cess, the critical situation is structured to specified roles for the participants. They are then put face to face and are required to undergo learning experiences in a live interaction. From a psychological point of view, role-plays may be considered a form of psychodrama. The learning experience is primarily interactive, with partici-pants assuming relatively unstructured roles in the interaction. In either case, the learning experience comes about through the live interactive quality of the role-play. Careful structuring of the roles of the individual participants and the critical incident in which they will interact permits clear establishment of the behavioral criteria. The responses brought about in the role-play can be predicted and the con-ditions in which they take place clearly structured. Standards can also be estab-lished, although not as easily, by the group undergoing the training or by careful analysis of the environment from which the groups are taken. A high degree of pre-dictability in the types of behavior brought about by role-playing can be seen, as, for example, in the role-play cases of N. R. F. Maier of the University of Michigan.

Between Maier's highly structured role-play cases and the totally unstructured role-interface of psychodrama, there are many shades and styles of role-play which can be effectively used as training media. A sales demonstration either before a group or in conjunction with audio or audiovisual recording equipment is essen-tially a role-playing approach. Often a form of role-play is used in conjunction with incident process when one of the participants advances a solution and the instructor asks for a demonstration—to show the group "how." Role-play provides an excellent means for trainees to receive immediate response to their actions, since the feedback is from other participants in the role-play activity. Success or failure in accomplishing ends acts as a strong reinforcer of successful behavior and a rapid corrector of unsuccessful behavior. The instructor or designer of the role-plays has a continual opportunity to measure personal effectiveness by the immediate response change observable in the role-play groups. The instructor's role in presenting this approach to behavior change requires various skills, depending on the extent of structuring the designer of the role-plays has put into the actual roles. If they have been highly structured and validated, few instructor skills are needed; the instructor has only to distribute roles, give instructions, and record results. Participants carry on the entire learning activity. If the roles are relatively unstructured, however, a high level of skill may be needed, since the instructor will frequently have to act as a moderating influence, or at least as a communications feedback source, for the role-playing participants.

One of the main attractions of role-playing as an approach to training is that it more closely approximates the job than do many other methods. Participants tend to be totally involved in what is going on and have little time to rationalize or analyze their actions as they take place, but must operate as in the actual job environment. Real analysis begins after completion of the role. The success a participant obtains in role-play has a high degree of transfer to the actual job environment. Accounting for trainee differences in learning rate or attitude within the role-play structure requires a high degree of instructor skill or program-design skill. As in most training methods, reinforcement of learned behavior comes through success. The participant who lags behind the rest of the role-play participants because of learning ability or poor attitude toward either the process or the training experience is unlikely to be successful. This in turn tends to reduce the possibility for a successful learning experience.

Costs for utilization of role-play closely approximate those for the incident process, although additional costs will be incurred in development because real-life tests of material must be made to ensure that the role-play structuring will elicit the required behavior. Once the role-play has commenced, there is less opportunity for control than in the incident process, where the instructor can vary the presentation of the incident or change the way in which the participant group is provided information. Once the role-playing process begins, the participants themselves control the outcome. This means that several validation tests must be run with groups closely approximating the participants for whom the training is being prepared.

Behavior modeling

Behavior modeling is based on the concept that an individual can effectively acquire new behavior by observing and imitating the behavior of a master performer. The correct performance is demonstrated and described; the trainee then tries out the behavior. This is often followed with an opportunity for the trainee to compare his or her trial efforts against the correct behavior and then to modify it in repeated trials.

Behavior modeling is highly adaptable to a wide range of training criteria and can be designed with frequent opportunity for trainee response and feedback. The instructional design requirements of behavior modeling are quite high, but where skilled instructors and master performers are used, it provides considerable instructor feedback. Approximation to the job varies, but this method closely approaches the closeness of job approximation offered by role-playing. Its adaptability to trainee differences is also dependent on design and the manner in which the program units are delivered. Much of behavior-modeling instruction is delivered through electronic media, which tends to reduce its adaptability. Development costs for behavior modeling are relatively high; delivery costs are totally dependent on the media used for delivery.

In-basket exercise

If the materials that make up a case were put back into the business documents from which they came, there would be the beginnings of an in-basket exercise. As its name implies, the in-basket exercise places in the participants' in-basket a body of material intended to lead to the desired learning response. These materials may be in the form of correspondence, reports, and memos—some of which may be important to the case or process under study and some of which may be extraneous. The material may be placed in the in-basket all at once or in installments, as it would normally. The participant examines the materials and takes the actions necessary to get them into his or her out-basket. The exercises may be used to train managers in making high-order decisions or to train a processing clerk in the sequence of entries required in the course of a day's work. Because of the high degree to which in-basket materials can be structured, the conditions under which the responses are to be elicited can be controlled. A series of in-basket exercises can range from very simple to very difficult. Training responses can be observed in the handling of materials and a continuous record kept, since the actions require actual processing of materials. Unless the instructor can take immediate action to provide the trainee with feedback to responses, much of the benefit of immediate reinforcement of correct action is lost. However, if in-basket exercises are broken into short enough units, this ceases to be a problem. Instructor feedback is in the form of finished materials from the out-basket, and there is a good opportunity to evaluate the effectiveness of the instructional method.

Since the major effort involved in preparing in-basket exercises is the development of the materials, the required instructor skills are not difficult to acquire. The instructor usually distributes the materials at the proper times and then acts as tutor or consultant to the participants. If familiar with the in-basket materials and with the processes or skills being taught, the instructor can usually be quite effective. When the in-basket materials are drawn from the actual organization in which the individuals work, a close approximation to the job can be created. This is particularly true when the skills being trained are essentially clerical in nature. The participant undergoes the learning experience with the actual documents processed on the job. If the in-basket exercises are carried out by individual participants rather than groups, each participant can complete the exercise at his or her own rate, depending on ability.

The cost for the in-basket exercise varies greatly, depending on the types of materials used. The major cost element is the preparation of the materials themselves, particularly if large quantities are required. Printing will be needed, and collating services, since the order of presentation in this exercise is of extreme importance. Presentation costs are rather low, since the instructor-to-participant ratio is high. Like the incident process, however, this is normally a small-group training method.

Simulation

Simulation attempts to recreate the job environment in controllable form. In its simplest form, it is an extension of the in-basket exercise, with the participants sitting at desks, receiving information, processing it, and passing it on in the same way they would in the actual job environment. They can use a telephone to communicate with other participants or with "control." Demands are made on them over the phone or in person by other participants or by the instructor, controllers, etc.

In its more complex form, simulation may require the reconstruction of a submarine or a heavy bomber. Most of us are familiar with the link trainer used to instruct pilots in instrument flying. This has been one of the most successful simulators used. It is perhaps in the use of flight simulators that simulation as a method has been brought to its highest level of sophistication.

The keys to simulation are two: first, replication of the actual working environment; and second, ability to control that environment to bring about the conditions under which the responses are elicited. Control may be by human instructors who put additional pieces of correspondence into the participants' "mail" or by a digital computer, as in a modern flight simulator. Because it closely approximates the job and accurately controls input information, simulation is a powerful training tool. The trainee receives direct feedback to responses, and the stimuli presented after each response or series of responses can be further controlled to reinforce correct responses or extinguish incorrect ones. In most cases the trainee receives very immediate and quite direct feedback regarding the adequacy of responses, particularly when the simulation is interactive with others in the group dependent on the responses. In the same way, the instructor/controller receives a continuous feedback from participants and can usually change response conditions to conform with both the participants' learning speeds and the changing needs of the simulation problem.

Simulation requires a real time; i.e., training must take place in a period of time commensurate with the time it would take to carry out the same processes in the real job situation. Therefore, considerable investment in instructor time and necessary facilities must be made. Of course, where immediate true approximation to the job environment must be duplicated, this cost can be paid. But where other methods are available and the immediacy of this method is not an absolute criterion, the cost is usually prohibitive.

Costs for simulation as a training method can vary too greatly for simple description. Obviously the creation of a full flight simulator utilizing a high-speed digital computer can be astronomical. One feature of simulation, however, regardless of simplicity, is that a facility must be available for use during the entire period of simulation, and it must be isolated from any intervening environment. Another expensive requirement is the continuous attention of the instructor/controller, whether human or computer. Usually the ratio of participants to instructors is quite low. This expense can be an important consideration in the decision to use simulation as a training method.

Management games

This training method utilizes a model of a business situation. The participants, individually or as teams, represent the management of competing organizations. They make the same kind of operating and policy decisions they might make in real life. Generally, the game uses a model with a set of mathematical relationships built in. The decisions of the participating teams are processed to produce a series of performance reports. These decisions and reports pertain to a specific time period in the day, week, or month. The participants are then informed of the results of their actions and make new decisions for the next period of time. This is again processed, reports prepared, and the new results reported. Participant performance is compared and critiqued. In most management games competition among participants or participating groups is used to measure performance. Frequently the teams operate against each other; that is, team A, in successfully marketing a company product, does so at the expense of teams B and C.

Unlike simulation, which works in a real time, management games compress time so that an entire year or perhaps even five years of a company's existence may be shortened into a few hours. Gaming seems to have its real value today in training management personnel in utilizing and evaluating information and in making valid judgments and decisions based on that data. The game may be a paper-and-pencil operation involving competitive bidding on construction contracts with only three variables—bid price, cost of material, and cost of labor—or it may be an operation using a high-speed digital computer in which decisions are made on the total operation of the firm, from purchase of raw materials to marketing and delivery of a product in several market areas. In some instances the game becomes far more than a training device; it can become a predictive mathematical model of the actual enterprise, permitting the management group to try out decisions and plans and learn the results they would obtain if these decisions were put into effect in real life.

As a training device, gaming provides immediate feedback to the participants because the reports they receive show the results of their decisions. In the same way, these reports show the instructor how well the trained behaviors are being learned and how well the model approximates the actual job environment. It closely approximates the process the participants must go through in arriving at on-the-job judgments and decisions. The types of data they use are the same. The two essential differences from the actual job are in the compression of time and the fact that the participants are aware that they are operating in a unique, laboratory-type situation. Although they participate fully in the game, they still recognize that it is separate and distinct from their jobs.

Of all of the available training methods, simulation and management gaming are the two most expensive. Unlike simulation, however, management games are available off the shelf. A number of computerized marketing and production games can be obtained from commercial and academic sources. Perhaps the most famous management game in use today is the Harvard Andlinger Game, the software for which can be obtained for use on the IBM 1460 or 7090 computers. Games are available for almost every type of situation, and several consulting organizations will modify existing games or create new games for application in a specific corporation.

One cost-ceiling element of the management game is that participating teams can operate it on off-line schedules. Short periods of time can be used, and, in fact, the training process itself can take place with several groups almost simultaneously, so that the game can be economically applied to train large numbers of people.

Programed instruction

Programed instruction is usually characterized by the presentation of material in relatively short steps, each requiring the trainee to respond and check his or her response against a correct answer, the process continuing until the desired behaviors are reached. However, it might be more accurate to describe programed instruction as a system for bringing about behavior change with an extremely high degree of training feedback and response measurement. Whether instruction is presented by an electrically operated machine and checked and fed back to the participant by computer, or whether the program is structured as a text using a sliding mask or is a combination of audio and visual material, the basic system remains the same: carefully controlled stimuli are used in sequence to elicit predetermined responses. The body of instructional material is validated to make sure that the elicited responses will indeed lead to the behaviors planned. Programed instruction may be essentially *linear,* a form in which each step requires a structured response and proceeds in a straight line toward the terminal behavior, with test stimuli along the way to ensure that the presented data is indeed learned. It may also be *intrinsic* (or *branching*), in which case the instructional information is presented and questions are asked about it to which the participant responds as in a multiple-choice test. Wrong answers lead to additional sources of information or additional instruction to teach the correct response. The arguments regarding the merits of these two approaches to programed instruction will probably go on for a number of years. Both work and either can be a complete failure. From the point of view of a manager of training systems, it does not matter which form of programed instruction one uses, so long as the desired trained behaviors can be brought about.

Preparation and development costs for programed instruction are relatively high. This is primarily due to the extensive research that must be done into the specific behaviors to be obtained and the cost of validating the various programs to ensure attainment of these behaviors. But regardless of the training method used, this investment in development must be made if the training system is to achieve the desired behaviors. Therefore, it is this author's contention that the element of cost should not be the overriding consideration in comparing programed instruction over some other medium.

One part of the development cost to be considered is validation. Since programed instruction is usually used without an instructor who could change materials or presentation to suit individual participants, sufficient validation must be made to give the trainer some assurance that the trained behaviors will be obtained in a large enough percentage of participants to make the attempt worthwhile. This means using large test groups and revising materials until the test groups perform satisfactorily. The other cost involved, preparation of materials, etc., would be about the same as for an in-basket or case study presentation.

In most programed instruction, the participant works independently on a program. Unless more elaborate electronically controlled programs are used, few facilities are necessary and work time need not be lost, since participants can usually study the program on their own time.

DECIDING ON THE TRAINING STRATEGY

The analysis of training needs has developed answers to the three most critical questions asked in the selection of a method or strategy:

> What is the trained behavior, and how will we know when we have it?

> What will it be worth to the organization to have this behavior present?

> When is the behavior required? How soon must the training be carried out?

With answers to these questions, the individuals responsible for developing the training action can recommend the best strategy for meeting the requirements. This recommendation, then, becomes part of the training plan offered for management approval. In recommending alternative strategies for consideration, the development element evaluates each available method in the terms described above. The end result of this evaluation is a recommendation that includes an estimation of the cost to either develop an instructional design based on the chosen strategy or buy an instructional design from an outside source. It is, however, incumbent on the development element to provide a competent recommendation. The element can rely on its prior experience and the experience of others in arriving at a decision.

The portion of costing and scheduling done by the development element will be for the actual development of the training action and will probably not include cost considerations for facilities or for presentation of the training action to trainees. This limitation is suggested so that full consideration can be given to uses of available facilities and so that further make-or-buy decisions can be based on the separation of instructional design from production and presentation. For example, it may be economically effective to carry out the instructional design *in-house* and to hire instructors from a nearby university, or possibly the training subsystem may wish to use in-house instructors, but have an outside source produce specific materials. This is particularly so in the application of programed instruction; individual program writers might be hired on a project or task basis. In this kind of situation the development element will act as a coordinator of the outside resources. The systemization of the training action in this way often permits production of a highly effective training action at a cost lower than might be possible if an early decision is made to produce the program in-house and compromises are made within the system in the requirements to produce the training action, despite possible lack of competence, capability, or increased costs.

From the development point of view, selection of a training method depends on:

> training criteria

> trainee response and feedback

> instructor skill level and feedback

> approximation to the job

> adaptability to trainee differences

> cost

Selection should also consider the needs of the delivery. How easily can the instruction be delivered in terms of logistical and scheduling problems? How easily can the quality of instruction be maintained using the method? How acceptable is the method to the trainees and to the "clients"? This last consideration is essential; innovative methods are often too radical to be accepted, leading to learning ineffectiveness; conversely, a "tried and true" method may not be applicable to the problem at hand.

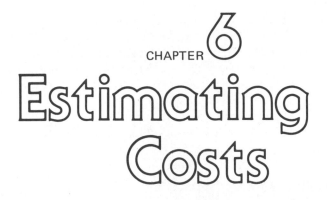

CHAPTER 6

Estimating Costs

COST MANAGEMENT FOR TRAINING

Nearly all organizations expect a training manager to itemize the cost of training actions. Most organizations go further; they expect the training manager to provide a reasonably accurate cost estimate of future training actions. A few also expect an estimate of return on dollar investment in training.

Providing this data is part of the training system's mission. The operations element must develop the means to accurately answer management's questions: "What did it cost? What will it cost? Was it worth it?" But providing accurate data is not enough; the data must also be in terms useful to the organization. The trainer who reports the value of training programs in terms of final tests is not likely to be telling management much about its return on investment. Rather, the results must relate to a unit of measure understandable to the organization. In the same way, an estimate of wage-hours to be spent in training has little real use if the trainees are overhead employees whose time is not computed for their assignments.

THE COSTING SYSTEM

Each training manager will need to develop a data system to conform to the organization's requirements. The first step in developing cost items for inclusion in an accounting-budgeting report is the establishment of a costing system which fits the training system. Costs for support should be separated from costs for individual training actions so that each training action can be measured on its own merits. Thus programs with strong support and good results will not be forced to carry less useful ones. Sound business thinking prohibits loading costs into successful programs simply because they can afford them. For the same reason, costs to support training overhead must be either shared equitably by all training actions or assigned to a separate cost item or account.

SOURCES FOR COST DATA

The second step is to identify data sources and formats. Information about actual expenditures must be made available on a regular basis, and this information will have to be meaningful as accounting data. If trainee time is to be accounted for, the dollar cost of trainee time spent in a training action must be available somewhere. In an organization that does not account normally for paid time by task assignment, it is an arduous process to set up a special accounting system for only training. Even where such a system exists, as in defense contracting, the organization may have a system applying to only part of its labor force. Further, if this is to be a cost item, a decision must be made about the type of cost to be included. The cost of trainee time might include wages or salary for actual time spent. It might also include down time, total time away from the regular assignment. It might exclude fringe costs. The decision whether or not to use trainee time as a cost item, and the form it will take if it is used, is up to each organization. If the decision is negative, the problem is solved. But if this is to be a cost item, the training manager must define its form and find a data source.

A valid data source has four characteristics:

1. It must be readily available—ideally, from an existing system, such as payroll records, time cards, purchase orders, expense records, etc.

2. It must provide the data in a form consistent with other sources reporting similar data; if time-card data reported for personnel budgeting does not utilize fringe costs, it would be useless to include these costs in training actions.

3. It must provide complete data; all transactions must be included in the system. Thus if trainee time is to be an item, there must be some assurance that time will be reported on all participants. Or, in another situation, if purchases of software are included, they should account for all items, even those bought out of petty cash.

4. It must be able to control the inputs it receives and maintain records from which meaningful reports can be compiled. Lack of backup records usually results in missing information. Without all necessary data, measures of training cost will continue to be estimates at best and creative writing at worst. With data sources identified, a record system can be structured which will identify the cost item, allocate it to a specific program or action, record it, and provide for camparison of estimates.

BUDGET CATEGORIES

In answering management's questions about return on investment, the training manager will need data on the value to the company of the training actions under-taken, on the actual costs of specific training actions, and on the support costs of training actions. A number of cost items for training cannot be directly applied to specific actions. Research, for example, applies generally to all actions, as does initial-needs analysis and administration of the training function. In the same way, some training aids and materials are considered a capital outlay having long-range service over many training actions. It would be difficult to allocate the cost of these to individual programs. Therefore, in establishing a costing system, two budget categories will be required—one for general support and another for specific training actions. Together they will provide overall costing data for the training system.

SUPPORT COSTS

Staff

The major cost item for general support will, of course, be staffing. The actual cost item will consider how the dollar cost of labor-hours is broken into research, analysis, and administration. Labor costs for staffing fall into technical and clerical categories. The training manager would be carried as a support cost except for that time devoted to development or presentation of specific training actions. Most technical labor-hours would be allocated to specific programs, except for the time spent analyzing future training needs. Clerical expenses would be considered largely support except for such activities as preparation of training materials for a specific program. The staffing cost item can easily be divided to separate labor expenditures for each kind of activity. The decision might be made, for example, that all time spent in the evaluation of specific programs be carried as a support cost rather than allocated to specific training actions.

Unless a time card is used to provide data for staffing costs, the most likely data source for this item would be a system of work reports based on time audits. It might also be useful to develop a system designating time spent to accomplish specific objectives, such as the "management by objectives" program quoted earlier. At this point a decision must be made on the type of costing data to be collected: Should only actual salaries be used, or should allocations be made for fringe benefits? It would probably be most cost effective to carry actual salary hours spent, allotting other forms of reimbursement to a general overhead expense item. The cost estimates for budget planning may be based on the prior year's experience, using either the actual dollar cost per training hour or the number of hours per unit of employee population. For example, in a given year, 25,000 training-staff hours were spent for a total of 5000 trainee hours. This ratio of 1:5 would be multiplied by the number of planned training hours for the coming year to give an estimate of staff cost. Such a standard estimating base could be multiplied by planned sales dollars for expected employee population. In actual practice, the cost base would probably be employee population, since budget planning is usually carried out before training plans are made. However, the decision on the base to be used would depend partially on the total company budget.

Special materials

The second budget item for support would include expenditures for special materials used in preparation of program aids. Included are inventory items that cannot be charged to specific training actions, such as drafting materials, drawing paper for preparation of art dummies, various minor items of paint, ink, brushes, lettering stencils, etc., as well as general photographic equipment if the training function carries out its own processing. Minor inventory items in the equipment cabinet of the functioning training department would also be included: pointers, transparencies, mounts, storage trays, slide cabinets, placecard holders, badges, etc. These items are included as materials in the support element because they are normal inventory, usually purchased in quantity and seldom worth breaking down by cost per training action. For example, a $7.00 purchase of name tags might be allocated over 23 programs. However, sufficient expenditures are usually made so that some accounting must be maintained. Charges for these items are usually made via a petty cash system, so that a file of vouchers must be maintained. Or if a central accounting report system is used, a special account or code number must be assigned to petty cash. If the organization allows it, of course, a separate petty cash fund can be put aside for the purchase of these materials. No specific accounting would be made in this case, but a general expenditure account would be kept for materials purchased. Estimates of expenditures for the next budget period can be based on prior year's expenditures per trainee hour, as discussed above, or on some other base figure.

Equipment

The third item to be included in costing support of the training function consists of equipment expenditures. In most cases this equipment would consist of audio and visual aids used in training actions. Some organizations might, however, include such expenditures for training facilities as actual betterment and improvement of the buildings, e.g., interior decoration, furnishings, built-in screens and boards, etc. These items could just as easily be carried as expenses for general facilities and not included in training accounts or budgets. The accounting data for current expenditures are most easily obtained from actual purchase requisitions or similar sources. Estimates of future costs would be based on actual expenditures for justifiable needs. It might also be important to the organization that these major purchases be carried as depreciating items for tax purposes. If so, the system of depreciation would have to be consistent with that used by the organization in its tax reporting. The purchase of these items will probably comprise the largest single expenditure outside of consulting fees. Therefore, it must be decided whether the most cost-effective means of acquiring equipment is by outright purchase or by short- or long-term rental. Experience has demonstrated that in the long run, aside from the minor tax advantages involved, outright purchase of the equipment is most cost effective even for such major outlays as closed-circuit television. The decision must be based on the trade-off between cost and utilization. If this is to be the basis for the rent-or-buy decision, the operations element of the training subsystem will have to do some long-range planning. In order to justify extensive purchase of equipment or facilities, a reasonable prediction of usage must be made. This means that there will have to be long-range forecasting of the kinds of training the organization will be doing, the numbers of trainees to be involved, and the general strategies or training methods to be used in the future.

Budgeting for equipment must also include a planned allocation for maintenance fees. Major equipment for maintenance and supplies will probably be paid for by petty cash vouchers, and the training manager may wish to set up a single petty cash fund for these and the minor materials expenditures previously mentioned.

In planning the acquisition of audiovisual equipment and training facilities, it will be important to consider future needs. For example, it might be advantageous to purchase two compatible 35mm slide projectors which can at a later time be coupled into a single control system. Even if both are not purchased at one time, the one obtained first could still be compatible to a single control system. Similarly, if an expenditure is made for videotape equipment, long-range needs should be considered in deciding among tape widths, editing, mixing, and playback compatibilities so that equipment bought today can be expanded in the future and used in conjunction with new developments in the equipment field. For example, can black-and-white television equipment be modified for color applications? If best use is to be made of the training dollar in equipment purchases, it is obvious that some effort must be made to research new developments in this area and to predict at least the near-future state of the manufacturing arts involved.

Travel expenses

Another item to be considered is travel expenses for staff members. This item includes interlocation expenses as well as the travel necessary to meet with resource people: trips to local educational sources, universities, etc., as well as trips to audit specific training programs and to attend professional meetings. Accounting for this travel will necessitate recording expenses via the normal expense reporting system of the organization or by the medium of petty cash vouchers. Since travel expense is a common item processed through the organizational accounting system, it may be necessary to have a specific account number assigned for training function travel so that this data can be reported to the training function for budget purposes. Estimates for future periods would be based on present expenses, with special attention paid to travel planned for the coming budget period. If considerable travel is to be expected, this is necessary for budgeting not only costs, but also staff time.

Consulting fees

Consulting fees are another cost item. Normally, consultants will be used in the development and/or presentation of training actions, but they may also be used for specific projects such as needs analyses, evaluations, consultations in the utilization of audiovisual media, etc. Records of these expenses could be obtained from the organizational purchase requisition system; or, if this is not feasible, the training function could maintain records of actual payments to estimate future expenditures, basing budgets on specific project plans rather than prior expenditures. When long-range planning is carried out, use of consultants should be carefully considered against permanent staffing. It will often be found that the expense of maintaining a staff specialist is lower than continually bringing in consultants on similar projects or series of projects.

State-of-the-art expenses

Another support item is expenditures for training programs for the training function itself. Into this category go specific training actions to prepare in-house instructors to act as conference leaders or trainers in specific training programs. In this case the individuals being trained are acting as part of the training function, and therefore that function would bear the cost. However, once these individuals were trained and serving as instructors, etc., their cost would be charged to the training action in which they were serving. Other expenditures in this category include attendance by training staff members at state-of-the-arts programs, conventions, institutes, etc.; attendance by the individual responsible for instructional design and development at a university program on audiovisual aids techniques; and participation by a member of the training staff in a course in linear programed instruction. Expenses to be accounted for would include tuition fees and charges and living expenses. Possibly charges for travel for these activities would be charged under this item rather than under a separate travel item. From the point of view of a cost accountant, it makes little difference whether an expenditure is charged under one cost item or another. The decision is important, however, in making estimates of future expenditures. In preparing a budget for staff training, it is usually useful to be able to present general management with the total cost of an action rather than reporting costs peicemeal. The source of accounting data would be the normal expense-accounting records of the organization, e.g., purchase orders, requisitions, and/or other documents used to process payment to accounts, etc. In the case of in-house training actions for instructor training, the data would be obtained from records of expenses for specific in-house training actions. These expenses and their accounting will be discussed below.

The expense item for staff training might also include expenditures for dues and subscriptions to professional societies and publications. This, again, could be carried as a separate expenditure or included in another item such as library expenses. The library item would include permanent materials for reference or for use with specific training programs, and state-of-the-art materials. These expenses would be accounted for through either petty cash or purchase requisitions. Further expenditures would be based, for example, on planned society memberships or planned acquisitions of library materials.

Guidelines for support costs

It would be impossible to present here a magic formula setting forth the exact budgets that should be allocated for the support of training actions, but it is possible to present ranges for these expenditures. Few contemporary organizations having training functions identifiable as such maintain a total accounting system for that training function, and fewer still separate out expenses for support elements of that function. However, interrogation of several organizations has provided ranges for these accounts, and the author's direct experience with several organizations provides further data.

There are two sets of constraints that can be used in recommending expenditure ranges. The first is based on a percentage of total training dollars to be spent within the organization. This gives a ratio of support expenses to expenditures for specific training actions, providing a measurable return. The second uses dollars per trainee as its base and is perhaps a more useful set of figures. Using total training dollars as a base, the minimum support cost should not be less than 10% of the total training dollars spent in the organization. (The maximum sample did not go beyond 25% of these training dollars.) Therefore, if the total training budget were $10,000, one could expect budget allocation for support expenses to range from $1000 to $2500. Using dollars per employee as a base, the minimum observed was $6 per employee, and the maximum $45. These ranges can be further broken down by the individual cost items in the support element; staffing costs for hours devoted to purely support functions range from $2 to $5.25 per employee. The latter figure, though apparently high, includes considerable expenditures for organization analysis and research into supervisory techniques and skills. In a 4000-person organization, this amounts to $21,000 and supports a full-time personnel researcher as well as the part-time efforts of a training manager, two training specialists, and two clerical staff.

The item with the greatest range is equipment and facilities. One relatively stable organization with a well-established training function budgets slightly under 70 cents per employee per year for replacing and updating its training facilities. At the other extreme, an organization in the process of establishing a major training effort spends $30 per employee as an investment in training facilities. This wide cost range is understandable when we consider that in a single year a 5000-person organization with a training function in the process of outfitting a vestibule operation can spend more than $1 per employee for furniture alone. This does not include audiovisual equipment, programed 35mm projection equipment, or closed-circuit television; in fact, it does not even count the investment in such basic materials as tools, machines, and related equipment.

Remaining expense items fall within narrower ranges. Materials expense ranges from 50 to 80 cents per employee, as does training-staff travel. Consulting fees for support functions range from only 50 cents to $2 per employee, staff training from 20 cents to $1, and outlays for library and professional memberships from 30 cents to $1.25 per employee.

With staffing costs and training aids and facilities—the two major items of support expense—together accounting for 50% or more of the total support dollar, it may be useful to explore further the ranges for these expenditures. How much of the budget should be allocated to staffing costs, not only for support of the training system but for specific training actions as well? Taking the total number of individuals in the organization, the range appears to be extremely broad. The lowest ratio found was 1 professional staff member for each 500 employees; the highest ratio, 1:4000. Further analysis shows, however, that in a stable organization without marked change in numbers or operations, the range narrows to from 1:800 to 1:1200. Both the low- and high-range extremes cited existed in organizations that were in the process of establishing training systems. In planning the staffing of the training system, it can be anticipated that the organization will reach a steady-state situation at about 1 professional training-staff member to each 1000 employees.

Without attempting to establish salary brackets for professional trainers, this range of ratios represents from $10 to $25 per employee for professional staffing. Considering the percentage of time allocated to support functions by the professional staff, the range of $2 to $4.75 per employee would seem reasonably representative. The amount of time the professional staffer will devote to the support function varies considerably. Obviously, where there is only one professional in an organization, the major portion of his or her time, once basic systems have been established and basic analysis and research carried out, will be spent in the development and presentation of specific training actions. The problem of economic effectiveness of the professional trainer is one that each organization must decide for itself. The trade-off between the immediate gains of specific training actions and the long-range gain from organizational research and analysis must be weighed against the cost of acquiring additional staff members to carry out these responsibilities. Addition of professional staff requires new allocations for management of the system itself. The manager of the training function must then take on supervisory responsibilities, which means an added support cost.

More difficult, perhaps, is the development of guidelines for equipment and facilities. The nature of these items so depends on the types of training to be done that it is almost impossible to present concrete guides to acquisition; however, some examples may help. The most dependent variable is facilities. If skill training is to be carried out and a separate or vestibule training facility established, the size and cost of the facility is directly dependent on the number of individuals to be trained, rather than on the specific training actions to be carried out. The exception to this rule is apprentice training. The maximum space requirement for training of job skills seems to be approximately one bench position for each 100 employees in the classification. Thus if the organization has 500 individuals doing soldering work, the vestibule facility will need space for training at least five persons at a time. If the total labor force in the family is 2000, 20 spaces will be required. But the individual organization can more accurately determine the number of spaces required from its own turnover records. Normal growth plus turnover should give the exact number of spaces needed in a vestibule. The cost of equipping such a facility is wholly dependent on the type of training carried out, and no guidelines can be given. The equipment used will have to approximate on-the-job machinery, and costs should easily be determined by expenditures made for the production equipment.

It is interesting to note at this point that training facilities often receive castoff equipment from the line. This is an interesting approach, since the trainee who is least able to handle inadequate equipment is actually trained on it. From the trainer's point of view, this is a particular challenge, since line standards will be almost impossible to meet in the training facility due to the inadequacy of the machinery!

Other training facilities to be considered have an environment more like that of a classroom. These facilities can range from a borrowed conference room to a separate, fully equipped building. The only guideline that can be provided here is that the individual responsible for training facilities should plan acquisitions for at least a ten-year period. In this way the tables and chairs that go into the borrowed conference room will be chosen for future use in a more elaborate facility. If cost is not a consideration, each training room should be planned solely for utility. Then if the training actions include formal lectures, the room should accommodate an audience and have a speaker's podium, blackboards, movie screen, etc. If a conference approach is to be used, there must be tables; if role-play is to be part of the action, the tables should be separable so that participants can be organized into small groups. If in-basket exercises are to be used, the tables must be further separated, possibly with partitions to divide individuals or work groups. The variety of potential problems is endless, as is the amount of money that can be spent on the training facility.

Audiovisual equipment requirements, again, depend on the type of training planned. However, some general guidelines can be given for equipment needed in or easily available to the training function. Four pieces of equipment are basic wherever audiovisual aids are to be used. Most important today, perhaps, is the overhead projector with an $8'' \times 10''$ capacity. With this projector, the training function will need the means for producing its own transparencies. Next is a 35mm strip film projector with its own sound system; third, a 35mm magazine projector compatible with programming units and a tape sound system. The fourth item in this basic inventory is a portable monaural tape recorder with at least five watts output so that it can double as an amplifying system. It goes without saying that a motion picture screen should be included in this inventory and that each piece of equipment should be chosen on the basis of not only cost, but also durability.

(At the beginning of my career in training, I was told that the best way to choose a tape recorder, for example, was to bounce each sample down a flight of stairs and pick the one that was still playing at the end. Although this is not a bad piece of advice, a service contract would probably be a more reasonable substitute to this approach!)

This basic inventory must all be portable; it must be easily moved from one location to another, since most of the equipment will have to serve double and triple duty. Lightness of weight and ease of operation become criteria for choice.

The next group of equipment in order of frequency of use includes a 16mm sound motion-picture projector and a battery-operated tape recorder for use in on-the-job recording during needs analysis and case development. If large groups are to be instructed, a 4" × 5" magic-lantern type of projector should be available because of its long focal length and brilliant image. An opaque projector is useful where transparencies are not available, but because of its severe light limitations and general noisiness must be considered as primarily for special applications.

As needs grow and new techniques are added to the training-function repertory, a second 35mm magazine slide projector with programming equipment can be added to the first projector. Additional sound equipment can be acquired if feasible and the organization can afford it. Programed-instruction equipment can be obtained, although this purchase is critically dependent on the type of instruction to be given. Once a piece of equipment is acquired, the training function will usually find itself constrained to use programed material adaptable specifically to that machine. Many of the formats for programed instruction are extremely valuable, but this author has not had sufficient experience with any one machine system to recommend it over others.

One of the most valuable acquisitions a training function can make is equipment and facilities to produce its own audiovisual software—for example, a 35mm camera with copystand and copy lights, 16mm sound motion picture camera equipment, tape on tape sound equipment, etc. These acquisitions depend largely on technical capabilities within the organization, as well as the cost of having this work done on a fee basis by a professional laboratory.

COSTING TRAINING ACTIONS

Completion of the definition and development of costing for the support segment of the training system leaves from 75% to 90% of the accounting and budgeting for the training function still remaining. These are the dollar allocations for specific training actions. Since we have treated the support aspects of the training system as a subsystem, it may be best to continue the same pattern for specific training actions and discuss cost items for each element in them: analysis, development, operations, and evaluation.

Analysis costs: Task-hour expenses

Beginning with the analysis element, the first cost item is again allocation for labor-hours. Hours spent by individuals staffing the training function are relatively simple to allocate from the points of view of both data capture and assignment to a specific training action. However, complications arise in the costing of specific training actions when accounting for task-hour expenditures of management personnel, subject-matter experts, and line personnel within the system or subsystem for which the training action is being designed. These system personnel will be interrogated and will assist in the investigation of training needs and in development of criteria for the training actions. If the decision is made not to charge these hours to the training action or the training function, there is no problem. If, however, organizational management decides that these costs must be budgeted and accounted for, data capture must be considered. Most individuals in these categories are considered indirect or overhead expense labor; time cards are not kept for them, nor is the time they spend in their usual duties accounted for. At first glance, the time investment of these individuals would appear to be low, but in the analysis of a major training effort, experience shows that as much time will be devoted to the training action by line personnel as by training staff members, possibly more. In any training action, one of the major hidden expenses is this cost of indirect or overhead labor.

In addition to these individuals, there is another category of labor that may or may not be chargeable: the cost of trainee labor. A given training action may require that personnel to be trained participate in the analysis to provide data for the development of the training action. For example, in the case of skill training, the professional trainer and the subject-matter expert may want to observe the potential trainee in action to identify the specific parts of the job in which the substandard behaviors are exhibited. This kind of investigation may call for pulling potential trainees off line in order to isolate various parts of the individual's job. If time cards are maintained, a separate account can be set up for training to record time spent by the trainee in any part of the training action. If a history of cost data is required to estimate the cost of future training actions, however, there must be a way of allocating this trainee labor cost to each element: analysis, development, operations, and evaluation. It is only in providing a matrix of costs for each of the training elements that estimating becomes practical. The reason for this is that in estimating the cost for a training action, it will be important for the estimator to cost each element, basing the estimates on prior experience. Usually it will be found that analysis costs remain fairly constant, varying only with the relative complexity of the training content. Thus the cost of needs analysis for a machine operation will be fairly constant regardless of the kind of machine under consideration, and the cost of needs analysis for supervisor training programs will remain relatively constant regardless of the type of shop supervised. This relative constancy is true only within an organization. Good estimating within that organization will depend on the data collected on line.

In summary, the major decision to be made regarding the allocation of labor-hours is whether the training function shall account for the hours expended by individuals outside of the training function. If these costs are to be part of the accounting budget, it is necessary to seek a system for data capture. Care must be exercised to ensure that the training function is not thereby making demands on the organization for data not otherwise required, or the expense of data collecting may exceed its value!

One other labor expense that may accrue to the analysis element is for instructors. If in-house instructors are to be used, it is possible that they will have an active role in the analysis of training needs. Where instructors are drawn from the training function, they have already been included in other account items. There are occasions, however, when these instructors come from other systems of the organization, and if the organization maintains a chargeback system, it must be decided who will be billed for their services—the function undergoing analysis or the training function. Where chargebacks do not exist, the potential instructors would probably be accounted for according to their classification as expense or direct labor.

It is not intended to overcomplicate the situation; it simply is a fact that once the decision is made to account for the usually hidden costs of training, data has to be collected in an orderly and consistent manner. For this reason alone, the individual responsible for collecting data for accounting and budgeting will have to meet these problems of hidden labor costs and find a system for solving them.

Analysis costs: Aids and materials

One cost item to be considered for each element is that of aids and materials. From a purely systems point of view, the label attached to this classification might more properly be "software." When we discussed support of the training function, materials noted included various articles used to produce this software, and the aids themselves included such software as printed material, visual aids, films, filmstrips, slides, and audio material. The applications to the elements involved in the training action are somewhat broader. In addition to the materials used in presentation, they include such things as materials for testing and recording, used in both analysis and evaluation of training. The aids and materials used in the analysis element are primarily those of testing or investigatory nature. Aptitude and ability tests, for example, will have to be purchased, and this cost would be included in this item. Motion pictures might be taken to sample the behavior of the machine operator so that the task process can be broken down movement by movement in the development of visual program material. Audio tapes might be acquired for interviewing and maintained as permanent record, negating the possibility of reuse or other application of the tapes.

Analysis costs: Consulting fees

A major cost item frequently required for analysis is consulting fees. Consultants can be used in any of the four elements of the training function, and their use in the analysis of training needs may range from a few hours of employment for specialized advice on analysis techniques to weeks or months of involvement in an entire organizational analysis. However, consulting fees in the analysis element are most frequently allocated for specialized advice on the use of testing or the purchase of testing services. Consultants are also frequently used in analysis to obtain special-ized technical knowledge in the functions or tasks undergoing analysis. Employing expertise from outside the function or organization being serviced is often the only cost-effective means of discovering and identifying training requirements. This may be especially true where what appears to be a training problem is really a system deficiency, and the inside training specialist is not in a position to fully pursue analysis because of the organizational interface situation or where the necessary technical expertise is not available within the organization, as, for example, in the investigation of a potential training need to update the state of the art of an en-gineering group. The very fact that a training need exists may be an indication that the precise parameters of the necessary training are unknown to the organization. An outside specialist in the field can often recommend required subject areas, some of which might be critical prerequisites to the technical area to be pursued. In one case, for example, a training program developed to prepare a group of electronics engineers in the utilization of integrated circuits came near to failure when it was discovered that participants did not have sufficient precourse knowledge of ad-vanced logic techniques. The analysis resulting from this discovery led to a series of tutorials in mathematical fields which might not otherwise have been covered.

Analysis costs: Special equipment

The final cost item to be considered under the analysis element is that for spe-cialized equipment. Purchase of major equipment will usually be allocated to the support system because of the spread of applications over many training actions. There have been situations, however, in which specialized equipment usable in only one training action (or at the most in a series of related training actions) was re-quired. The only expenditures made for this item in the analysis element in the experience of this writer have been for temporary rental of equipment for testing purposes. It may be expected, however, that expenditures will be made in this cate-gory in the development element, particularly for acquisition of special tools or possible lease or purchase of programed instruction equipment called for in the in-structional design.

Another item that might be accounted for under specific training actions, de-pending on the organization, is staff travel. This is a consideration only for multi-location organizations or where travel is necessary to audit training actions in other firms or investigate resources which might be used in part of the training action.

In summary, the major cost items to be considered for each of the elements involved in the training action are labor-hours for training staff, system manage-ment, and trainees; aids and materials; fees for consultants; equipment; and travel.

Development costs: Staff

The greatest expenditure for staffing will usually occur in the development element. The expenses for time actually spent in instructional design and development of the training action are charged to this element. It can be expected that additional costs for hours devoted to the structuring of course content will be required from the system being served. It is in the development element that the greatest use is made of subject-matter experts, from either within or outside the organization. Trainee time can also be expected in the preparation of segments of the program to test criteria and possibly to retest it after revisions of pilot runs. If special instructors from within the organization are to be used, their time will also be required to assist in the development of the materials which they will use in the operations element.

Development costs: Aids and materials

Major expenditures can be expected in the development element for aids and materials. It is in this element that the actual software of the training actions will be produced. The cost of copy production—the actual writing of material—will probably be allocated to staff labor-hour expenses, but art and photographic work, printing, and duplication will usually be chargeable items. Even where the training staff includes technical specialists in the production of aids and materials (a highly unlikely event), there will still be expenses for laboratory work and printing. Even when materials are printed within the organization, there will be chargebacks for the service. Minor make-or-buy decisions will have to be made regarding aids and materials, case materials, in-basket exercises, perhaps programs for management games, and it may be desirable to purchase them as off-the-shelf items from training sources. These would be included in the budget for aids and materials for specific training actions and would be allocated to the development element.

Development costs: Consulting fees

Consulting fees budgeted in the development element would include such items as the hire of technical specialists for production of specific materials for a training action. Paying a specialist to produce programed instruction, for example, might be an expenditure based on a specific fee per hour, or an entire program might be produced on a flat-fee basis. Specialists in the field of audiovisual productions might be retained to produce motion pictures or to set up and advise on the production of videotapes. The possibilities are unlimited. This is the particular area in which an outside specialist can be of most use. The allocation of equipment expenditures to the development element is unlikely. It might be possible to lease equipment necessary to produce films, for example, but if such action is undertaken, it is likely that the equipment would be purchased.

Delivery costs: Trainees

Trainee time would probably be the greatest expense in the delivery element. Instruction time, or staff time, would be relatively minor, since we can assume that the ratio of instructors to trainees will be comparatively small. A note of warning is appropriate here, however: Instructor time or staff time should also include the time required to set up and prepare for each individual training session and to clean up after the session. In accounting for trainee time, the total of actual paid time should be included. Thus the calculations to be made are not simply the number of training hours multiplied by the number of trainees, but this number multiplied by the trainees' hourly wage or salary. The computation ought to include wages or salary expenditures to get the trainee to the place of training and back to the job again. For a training session lasting one hour, this could mean doubling the actual trainee time expense (a half hour to get there and a half hour to return).

Another point to consider is the unique problem of after-hours training actions. The obvious cost saving makes this an attractive alternative. Under current wage and salary laws, the saving is available only for exempt personnel. Those not exempted from the laws' application must be paid, often at a premium rate. The law also requires that in the case of nonexempt personnel, the cost of transportation, if any, must be paid. The possible saving results from the preservation of productive time on the job. In any case, where an individual is removed from his or her regular job there will be, in all likelihood, a loss of production. In many cases a temporary replacement is necessary. In situations in which the loss of productive time prohibits release of trainees from the job, the after-hours action may be the only possibility.

The decision to pay or not pay for these extra hours will depend on the organization. Some companies do and some don't. Firms taking an after-hours approach to setting training schedules generally experience some problems. Trainees' attitudes are often negative and are sometimes expressed in strong terms. Seldom is participation in these programs purely voluntary, and most people have negative feelings about giving additional time to their jobs unless there is a particular payoff for them. More important, however, training performance in off-time programs is not as satisfactory as performance in the same programs run on-time. This may be due to attitudes, or it could be due simply to fatigue on the part of the trainees, considering the long hours they are putting in. Possibly fatigue or boredom on the part of the instructors is a factor. Another cause could be inadequacy of the technology itself for the job of after-hours training. The design of the instruction or the method employed may require differences for off-time and on-time actions.

Delivery costs: Trainee materials

The allocation for aids and materials is low compared to that for development. In the case of text materials and visuals, costs are for finished copy and prints, respectively. The greatest expenditures for these materials will have been in their development: the cost for makeup, artwork, etc. The decision to charge materials produced outside the organization to development was an arbitrary one. Off-the-shelf or purchased special materials could be charged to the delivery element. The reason for this choice is that when actual cost data are used to estimate future budgets, it will be more convenient to have the cost to develop aids and materials in one class. In this way, make-or-buy decisions will be better based on data. Data about beans will not be compared with data about bananas, so to speak.

The decision to separate fees to outside sources for aids and materials from other consulting fees is another arbitrary one. This separation also is made for improvement of cost effectiveness in the make-or-buy decisions. Separating consulting costs from development costs more clearly delineates the expenditures for the training materials themselves. Thus, calling in an outside specialist to assist in the development of training aids and materials would probably be an outside-fee cost, but if the development of the materials themselves were farmed to an outside source, it would probably be more appropriate to allocate this cost item to aids and materials.

Delivery costs: Single-use equipment

The delivery element would probably bear two major costs for equipment. First would be the purchase or rental of special single-use equipment, such as programed instruction machinery, motion-picture projection equipment, special audio equipment, etc., if such needed equipment is not presently in the training system inventory. The second expense is for the temporary use of special facilities to hold the training action. The most obvious such expenses would be the rental of meeting rooms and possibly provisions for meals (including coffee breaks, without which no training program can be run!).

Evaluation costs: Labor

Following the same pattern of cost-item classification in the evaluation element, the first item is wage and salary for staff expenses. The primary expense, of course, will be staff hours to carry out whatever evaluations are necessary: testing, interviewing, observation. Additional time can be expected from management in the organizational system being served and perhaps from the trainees, if a special testing effort is made. The problems of evaluation will be covered in detail in a later chapter.

Evaluation costs: Aids and materials, etc.

Aids and materials expenses for evaluation tend to be minimal, as do equipment expenses. Fees for outside specialists may be needed in evaluation. Again, this expense may be part of a consulting arrangement package or may be incurred specifically for the evaluation.

ALLOCATING COSTS WITHIN THE TRAINING SYSTEM

The first step in estimating costs for specific training actions is to break down costs within the system. A benchmark division can be established by allocating 70% of the budgeted dollars for a training action to the development and operations elements, approximately 35% each. Of the remaining 30%, about 20% goes to analysis and 10% to evaluation. The greatest variance will occur in the division between the development and operations elements. As the number of trainees undergoing the action grows, the percentage of the allocation to the operations element will increase proportionately. The 35% allotment to each of the two major elements seems to hold for most training actions, however, and until actual expenditure data are collected for estimating purposes, it does provide a reasonably accurate benchmark.

USING COST EXPERIENCE FOR COST ESTIMATING

Once experience has provided an expenditure breakdown system in which the training manager has confidence, this breakdown can be used for estimating future actions. As soon as the analysis element has completed its outputs, reasonable estimates can be provided for the balance of the action. Thus if data show that in past training actions for supervisory training, for example, 20% of the training investment is taken in analysis, it is a simple matter to project an additional $4 for each dollar already spent to complete the action. The ratio may change for other kinds of training actions and may even differ by location or by system within the organization. This is further reason for collecting accounting data by element in as great detail as possible.

Further refinement in the use of the estimating base can be made once data have been collected on differences in expenditures for different training methods. Actual experience with programed instruction, for example, will provide an accurate basis for estimating costs for further programed instruction applications. These estimates could be made in the very first steps by the analysis element as soon as a decision is made to consider programed instruction as a medium. Data on costs, the bases for estimating, vary according to the organization in which the training actions are to be taken. There is no quick and easy formula for cost estimating specific training actions. This does not mean that estimates cannot be made, only that the training manager must carefully account for on-line expenditures and analyze them to seek out viable estimating costs.

COST WORKSHEET

Project _____   *Client* _____

1. Overhead allocation elements
   a) Overhead (G & A, space, utilities, etc., per task hour   _____
   b) Management cost per task hour   _____
   c) Equipment allocation per task hour   _____
   d) Other costs (R & D, administration, etc.)   _____
      Total overhead allocation per task hour   _____

2. Analysis
   a) Assigned to ＿＿＿＿＿＿ @ ＿＿＿/task hour
   b) Support by ＿＿＿＿＿＿ @ ＿＿＿/task hour
   c) Estimated professional hours ＿＿＿
   d) Estimated support hours ＿＿＿
   e) Estimated professional cost [(a) × (c)]   ＿＿＿＿
   f) Estimated support cost [(b) × (d)]   ＿＿＿＿
   g) Travel expenses   ＿＿＿＿
   h) Aids and materials   ＿＿＿＿
   i) Consulting costs   ＿＿＿＿
   j) Other expenses   ＿＿＿＿
      Total estimated analysis costs   ＿＿＿＿

3. Development
   a) Assigned to ＿＿＿＿＿＿ @ ＿＿＿/task hour   ＿＿＿＿
   b) Support by ＿＿＿＿＿＿ @ ＿＿＿/task hour
   c) Estimated professional hours ＿＿＿
   d) Estimated support hours ＿＿＿
   e) Estimated professional costs [(a) × (c)]   ＿＿＿＿
   f) Estimated support costs [(b) × (d)]   ＿＿＿＿
   g) Aids and materials   ＿＿＿＿
   h) Consulting costs   ＿＿＿＿
   i) Other expenses   ＿＿＿＿
      Total estimated development costs   ＿＿＿＿

4. Delivery
   a) Coordination by ＿＿＿＿＿＿ @ ＿＿＿/task hour
   b) Estimated coordination task hours ＿＿＿
   c) Instruction by ＿＿＿＿＿＿ @ ＿＿＿/task hour
   d) Estimated instruction hours ＿＿＿
   e) Support by ＿＿＿＿＿＿ @ ＿＿＿/task hour
   f) Estimated support hours ＿＿＿
   g) Estimated coordination costs [(a) × (b)]   ＿＿＿＿
   h) Estimated instruction cost [(c) × (d)]   ＿＿＿＿
   i) Estimated support cost [(e) × (f)]   ＿＿＿＿
   j) Trainee materials   ＿＿＿＿

k) Staff travel/expense   _____

l) Facilities expense   _____

m) Equipment expense   _____

     Total estimated delivery expense   _____

n) Delivery—trainee costs

     (1) Numbers of trainees (1st year) _____

     (2) Average trainee hourly cost _____

     (3) Estimated instructional hours _____

     (4) Estimated trainee cost 1st year $[(a) \times (b) \times (c)]$ _____

     (5) Trainee travel 1st year   _____

     Total trainee costs 1st year   _____

5. Evaluation

     a) Assigned to _____ @ _____/task hour

     b) Support by _____ @ _____/task hour

     c) Estimated professional hours _____

     d) Estimated support hours _____

     e) Estimated professional cost $[(a) \times (c)]$ _____

     f) Estimated support cost $[(b) \times (d)]$ _____

     g) Travel expense   _____

     h) Aids and materials   _____

     i) Consulting costs   _____

     Total estimated evaluation cost   _____

6. Summary

     a) Total professional task hours _____ $[2(c) + 3(c) + 4(b) + 4(d) + 5(c)]$

     b) Overhead allocation $[(a) \times 1(total)]$ _____

     c) Estimated analysis costs (2 total)   _____

     d) Estimated development costs (3 total)   _____

     e) Estimated delivery costs (4 total)   _____

     f) Estimated evaluation costs (5 total)   _____

     g) Estimated total project cost   _____

     h) Cost per trainee $[(g) \div (n)]$ _____

     i) 1st year trainee cost $[4A(d) + 4A(e)]$ _____

     j) Total cost of project   _____

CHAPTER 7

Instructional Design

FROM STRATEGY TO DESIGN

The design and production of the training action began when the development element, working with the analysis element, completed the training plan for management approval. An important part of this plan was the selection of the general strategy that would be used in the training action. Recommendations were based on a preliminary analysis of the kinds of instruction or other learning experiences that would be most effective in obtaining the behavior described in the training plan. Recommendation of the method is the first step in instructional design, but selection of method or strategy does not necessarily mean that instructional design will be carried out by an in-house action; it could mean the purchase of outside services. Although the function of any element in the training subsystem can be performed by a system outside the organization in which the training is to take place, the most frequent use of consulting services is for the development and presentation of the training action.

THE CONSULTANT'S ROLE

The proper role of the consultant who is not involved in the analysis or preparation of the training plan itself begins only after the trained behaviors have been identified. Some function within the organization should be responsible for defining these behaviors and making a selection of general training strategies on the basis of its own experience with the organization. If the consulting services include the analysis element, then it will be up to the consultant to create the training plan and gain management approval. Looking at the role of the consultant in this way has two very specific benefits to the organization. First, it prevents the purchase of instructional design and training materials which will not obtain the required behavior changes; second, it protects the consultant from designing a program without all data necessary to produce effective behavior change.

CHOOSING A CONSULTANT: THE "BUY" DECISION

The make-or-buy decision involves three considerations: competence, capability, and cost. These are the same three constraints used to locate each element of the training subsystem within the organization. Thus a decision to put supervisory training into the production line itself takes the same approach as is used to hire an outside source to produce a specific training program.

Competence defines the technical ability to bring about the required behavior change. If the training function within the organization sees a series of in-basket exercises as the best way to bring about a particular trained behavior, it must first ask whether it has the technical ability to produce such a series of exercises. If it does not and no alternative method seems as effective, then the training function must seek an outside source with the competence to produce the exercises. It can evaluate this competence by looking at what the outside source has done using this technology, by questioning organizations which have used the source for their in-basket exercises, and by discussing with the outside source the kind of in-basket design it proposes.

The second test is that of capability. This is essentially a staff and scheduling test. Even supposing that the training function within the organization has the competence to create the instructional design needed, can it have such a program completed within an acceptable period of time? The training manager who accepts in-house program development beyond the capability of the available personnel is often forced to select training methods for their simplicity and ease of design rather than for their effectiveness. It is difficult to see how a manager of training can be embarrassed to simply say that he or she does not have the capability to perform a particular job. No organizational management would expect an efficient production system to produce beyond its machine and staff capability. But the capability of the outside source must also be tested. Does it have a reputation for producing what it says it will in the time limit it accepts? Again, a check of other organizations which have used the source is likely to reveal its capabilities.

The third test is one of cost. Will producing a particular training action in-house be less expensive than going outside? In making this kind of evaluation, it is critically important that the actual cost of in-house staffing for the project be known so that a valid cost comparison can be made.

EVALUATING AN OUTSIDE RESOURCE—A CHECKLIST

1. Has the resource *demonstrated* its ability to apply the proposed technology or method?

2. Has the application been demonstrated in *similar situations*: similar problem, similar organization, similar training population?

3. Will the resource specify training objectives and *measurable performance criteria*?

4. Can the resource demonstrate that it *has met measurable criteria* in past projects?
5. Can the resource provide a *time and action calendar* for the project?
6. Has the resource demonstrated its *ability to meet target dates and milestones*?
7. Can the resource provide a *quality-control plan*?
8. Has the resource demonstrated the ability to *interface smoothly with client personnel* at all contact points?
9. Can the resource *relate costs to specific actions, milestones, and outputs*?
10. Has the resource demonstrated its ability to *meet cost objectives*?

IN-HOUSE DEVELOPMENT: THE "MAKE" DECISION

If, after three-point evaluation of competence, capability, and cost, the decision is to make rather than to buy, instructional design begins. Following the decision to design and produce a training action in-house, the constraints within which the instruction will be carried out must be defined. Definition of these constraints requires a careful look at the conditions under which the training actions will be implemented. The training plan provides a number of knowns which can be used in defining these constraints. They include the trained behaviors to be sought, the trainees, the general strategy to be used, including the method, and the training criteria established for evaluation of the expected behavior change. Using this information and that gained from the system in which the training is to take place, the development element can define its constraints of instruction, scheduling, and location.

DECIDING ON THE TRAINING METHOD

The instructional constraints are imposed by the "what, who, and how" of the design, and the first line of questioning centers on the training method itself, with the instructional designer asking what limitations will be placed on this training action by the method selected. For example, if programed instruction is to be used, what media are available for the presentation of the programed material to the participants? Will the presentation be limited to paper-and-pencil media, or are audiovisual aids in the form of slides and tapes available? If they are, can random selection be employed, or do they operate only within a given sequence? In terms of the audiovisual media available, how can the responses of the participants be recorded?

The constraints imposed by programed instruction are pretty obvious, but suppose the selected method is case study. Here the process is the same, for the instructional designer must find out whether suitable case material is available in-house, whether it must be purchased "off the shelf" from an outside source, or whether an outside source will be hired to develop it. If the designer must go outside, the availability and suitability of the outside material must be questioned. No matter what method is to be employed, the instructional designer will discover that resource availability will place constraints on the finished product. Even after choosing the method suitable for the training action, there are a number of trade-offs required to make the method operable in a specific system. Questioning the "what" of the method will include these aspects:

What materials will be required to implement the training action by this method? The designer wants to know what modifications are necessary in the instructional approaches to conform to the organization's capability to produce these materials.

What media will be used to present the materials? The designer wants to know whether the equipment or facilities for producing the required materials are available.

What specialized knowledge or expertise is required by the method? Here the instructional designer wants to know if there are resources to develop the materials planned. This includes the availability of content or subject-matter experts as well as knowledge of the instructional technologies needed.

What will be the effect of this method and these materials on the participants? The instructional designer wants to know whether the approach must be modified to conform to the expectations of the trainees as well as to their learning capacities as indicated by their entry behaviors. Will the trainees in this particular situation be able to learn efficiently from the materials and method selected? At this stage it can be expected that modifications will be required, but that the method will not need to change radically. The investigation of these four lines of inquiry will provide the instructional designer with information about the kinds of limitations placed on the training design by the system in which the training action is to be implemented.

INSTRUCTOR SELECTION AND TRAINING

The second line of investigation in defining constraints is to decide who will do the training. This question looks forward to the presentation of the training action, and asks: Who will be the instructors? Will they be individuals drawn from the training system, or will they be line personnel in the subsystem being trained? Will they be in-house people, or will it be feasible to go outside the organization to hire them? If in-house instructors are to be used, does the method to be employed impose the additional requirement of training the trainers? If so, can this be accomplished with the instructors selected? Do they have the time to undergo training, and, indeed, is it feasible to train them? If line people are selected as instructors, will it be possible to have them participate in the instructional design and development?

The instructional designer must then identify those constraints imposed on the training action by the organization's approach to the presentation of the action: How will the training action be handled in the organization when the finished product is finally presented? How will it be coordinated? Who will be responsible for evaluating the project and for seeing that the right things and people get to the right place at the right time? At this point the instructional designer should have a clear idea of the limitations placed on the training action by the organization. Those areas in which modifications will be necessary and special actions must be taken are now identified, as in the case of trainer training or in the modification of programed-instruction techniques.

SCHEDULING THE TRAINING ACTION

With this knowledge, the designer must then question the scheduling of the training action. The line of questioning centers on the three kinds of constraint, the first of which concerns the amount of time required for the learning experience to bring about the behavior change. How much time will the participant spend in the training action before one can reasonably expect that the trained behaviors have been obtained? The instructional designer is in the process of discovering the constraints placed on the proposed action by the trainees themselves. Now certain questions arise: Given the requirement of 45 hours of trainee participation, can these people be kept in the training action for 45 hours? Do the demands of productivity prohibit their release to the training action for that long? When can time allocations be made? Will the program have to be broken into smaller units? Will it have to be run after or before regular work hours? What will be the effect of the time of day or length of each unit on the participants? Will the problem of fatigue arise? Can the participants be kept in a training situation without interruptions from a ringing telephone or a sudden production problem? Unless the instructional designer considers these kinds of constraints, even a well-designed program may not be implemented. Typically, the instructional designer or instructor does not consider these constraints, but there seems little reason not to predict the possibilities and effects of these constraints on the training action.

Another time-imposed constraint on the training action is that arising from the instructional design and development of materials. Here the instructional designer must determine how his or her own working schedule will affect this particular training action. When can the job be done? Is there the time to work on it? What are the probable stumbling blocks in producing required materials? Is there likely to be an overload in the print shop when text materials are ready for reproduction? Will the art work have to be farmed out? If so, what kind of a schedule can be expected for production? The instructional designer needs to determine how his or her own use of time will be affected by the method chosen.

The third set of constraints imposed on the training action is geographic. The instructional designer must identify those constraints imposed by the physical training plant and the physical location of the participants. What are the minimum and maximum group sizes allowed the training methods selected? Can an instructor handle that particular group size? Is there a training room? Are the participants so widely dispersed that they will have to come to central training points to meet optimum group size? Will it be more efficient for the training action and instructors to go to the participants, or for the participants to come to the trainers? What is the difference in cost? What is the feasibility of each alternative? What are the logistics required to bring the trainees and the training action together? Do equipment constraints identified earlier affect the portability of the training action? The organization's geography can impose a large variety of constraints on the training action, and it is important that the instructional designer investigate these carefully. Otherwise, the training package may not be usable within the physical confines of the organization.

BLOCKING OUT THE DESIGN

Careful identification of the limitations imposed on the training action permits the instructional designer to approach the next step with some confidence that the product is usable. This next step is blocking out the instruction. In doing this, the instructional designer first arranges the trained behaviors and training criteria in the best order. Tasks or behaviors that reinforce one another can be arranged together, and tasks that require specific sequencing can be appropriately arranged. The idea is to gain the greatest possible economy of instructor and participant time and energy. The instructional designer can expect to spend some time in analyzing the trained behaviors to arrive at the best order for the learning experience. In the same way, the criteria to be used for test items will have to be analyzed and grouped for effective testing and feedback.

With an instructional order in mind, the designer would break the instruction into teaching units for each trained behavior or group of behaviors. Here it is extremely important that constraints be carefully considered, for the amount of time the participants will spend on each training or learning-experience unit must be determined. In making this determination, time availability, location of the participants, and the instructional media to be used must be considered. Each learning unit must not only include instructional material (the content), but also provide for participant and trainer feedback, behavioral reinforcement, and criteria testing. The instructional designer will also have to consider the problems of participant fatigue and boredom; if an instructional unit lasts for several hours or days, breaks or changes in the pattern of the learning experience will have to be provided.

When this blocking is finished the instructional designer should have a fairly complete model of the training action. It may be convenient to use a flow sheet as the model-visualizing medium or possibly a blocking outline describing step-by-step coverage of each of the points: behavior, criteria, content, feedback, reinforcement, and testing. For each instructional unit, the use of necessary equipment or materials must be noted, as well as the logistics of securing them at the training facility when they are needed for that particular training action.

Design block example

Project Consulting Skills for Staff Personnel

Training objective Objective #3: Participants should be able to identify problems from users' point of view.

Criterion #3.2: Given a request for staff help, the participant will use a question-restatement guide to elicit a usable problem specification from the user. The question-restatement guide will be provided in the training action. Problem specifications will be obtained for each attempt.

Content The process of using a question-restatement approach to getting a user to state a problem in his or her own frame of reference forms the primary content. The participant will already be able to describe the advantages of this approach and will be able to demonstrate the use of summary statements and commitment questions.

Method

1. Instruction team will demonstrate process.
2. Question-restatement guide will be discussed by instruction team and participants.
3. Instruction team will demonstrate process a second time.
4. Participants will be divided into triads to rotate as staff consultant, user, and observer.
5. Observers will be furnished with feedback instrument.
6. Triad will complete first simulation.
7. Observer will furnish feedback to staff consultant.
8. User will provide staff consultant with positive reinforcement verbally on correct or helpful behavior.
9. Steps 6–8 will be repeated with a role shift.
10. Steps 6–8 will be repeated with a role shift.

Materials

1. Question-restatement guide.
2. Observer feedback instrument.
3. Two instructor team simulations.
4. Three participant simulations.
5. Participant evaluation instrument.

Facilities Provide for triad break-off.

Logistics Block should take two hours at most. Will need to sequence after problem-definition block. Will have to ensure repetition of process in all later blocks where new problems are introduced.

PREPARING THE INSTRUCTION

After the design has been blocked out, the development work on the training action can begin. The next step depends on the method selected. If human instructors are to be used, leaders' guides and the necessary case material must now be written. Visual aids must be dummied and readied for production. If slide films or motion pictures are to be produced, scenarios and story lines must be plotted.

One of the major problems in producing instruction arises when line personnel are to be used as instructors. Their use brings up a number of questions; their experience, competence, and capability certainly act as constraints on the type of instructional instruments to be produced. If the instructional designer is wise, and if it is feasible, he or she will bring these instructors into the development of the training action. They will participate in the writing of the instructional instruments they will use; or, if this is not possible, a separate training action to train these instructors in the media selected for the training action may be necessary. As a last resort, instructors' guides might be produced to explicitly lead them through every step of the learning experience. The instructors' competence and capability will also affect the types of aids incorporated into the training action. The less capable the instructor, the more reliance there may have to be on an audiovisual system. The instructional designer in this case may choose to prerecord portions of the instruction, using the temporary instructor only for feedback and testing functions. In sum, where human instructors are required, their capability and competence must be carefully considered in the development of the instructional materials. The instructional designer must be cognizant of who is to do the teaching.

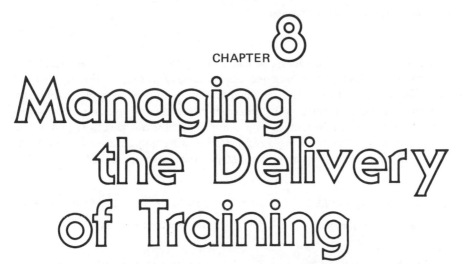

CHAPTER 8

Managing the Delivery of Training

This chapter addresses two issues: (1) how performance change can be managed so that it takes place consistently, as planned, and so that training processes are implemented as designed; and (2) how performance, once obtained, can be maintained.

Training or other performance change strategies are often mandated and developed centrally in organizations which have decentralized operations. From a technical point of view, this permits a concentration of specialized abilities to ensure a high-quality product. From a management point of view, however, control of the product is removed from the users, reducing their commitment and support to the goals of the function which created the training.

It is often not economical for a centralized training function to participate in training delivery to the degree necessary to maintain quality control of the performance change processes. The larger the organization, the less likely it is that a centralized training function can affect the consistency and quality of training in the decentralized units. Frequently, the users have sufficient autonomy to accept or reject training programs or to modify them in ways which critically impair their effectiveness. Without the continuous participation of the centralized function, and with the ability of the users to reject or change programs, quality control and consistency become extremely difficult.

If it is difficult for the training function to participate sufficiently in the actual training process, it is nearly impossible for it to directly influence maintenance of trained behaviors once a training program has been completed. Performance-maintenance processes are almost always in the control of the users. Although posttraining evaluation is done by the training function, the day-to-day performance environment is controlled within the user unit.

Given that the training function is not able to influence activity in a user unit at a level which will ensure quality training or maintenance of performance after training, we need to look at the factors which influence both these aspects. There are three critical influence sets: first, the trainees' managers, who in effect are the real clients of the training function; second, the trainees themselves; and, third, the managers' bosses.

Before we can detail an approach to managing the delivery of training, it may be useful to first look at the consequences of training to each of the members of these influence sets. From the training function's point of view, it is often assumed that all the consequences for implementing a training process or a behavior-maintenance process are beneficial. This point of view is not always shared by the other influence sets involved. A general list of positive and negative consequences for each influence set might look something like that shown in Table 1.

TABLE 1   CONSEQUENCES OF A TRAINING PROCESS ON THREE INFLUENCE SETS

Positive Consequences	Negative Consequences
Managers	
Reduction in costs due to nonstandard performance	Increase in operating costs of unit
Reduction in training	Loss of control of employees
Reduction in turnover	Loss of autonomy in unit
Reduction in criticism from second-tier managers	Increase in "nonproductive" administrative activity
Increase in self-esteem from being perceived as a good manager	
Increase in productivity of unit	
Trainees	
Retention as employee	Labeling as "trainee"
Potential increased compensation	Possible negative comments from boss and/or peers
Potential promotion	Possible negative consequences for failure in the training situation
Recognition for performing to standard	
Pleasure of acquiring new skills	Lost time from work
Opportunity for new experience	Aversive reinforcements in the learning process
Managers' bosses	
Improved unit performance	Increase in overhead
Potential increased compensation	Increase in administrative duties
	Negative comments from managers

Ensuring positive consequences for members of each influence set and eliminating or reducing negative consequences must be central concerns in an effectively managed performance system. Training, then, is a performance system to be managed in the same manner as any other performance system. The performance-management model described in Chapter 1 is an effective tool for examining the problems of delivery.

Five factors are to be considered:

1. clear performance expectations
2. timely and usable feedback
3. positive consequences for desired performance
4. effective job design
5. appropriate training.

Expectations establish all the standards of required performances relating to training actions and to posttraining performances. They include training criteria, training-program objectives, performance standards or descriptions, and, if possible, related expectations coming from other processes in the work environment, be they administrative procedures, cultural values, or "rules of the game." The process for setting and communicating expectations is as important in managing performance as the clarity and measurability of the expectations themselves. Both the performers and those who will control consequences for the performers need to be involved. In addition, managers' bosses and managers should be involved in setting expectations for the managers. Managers and trainees too need to be involved in setting expectations for the trainees.

The processes used to communicate expectations should be such that expectations and consequences are communicated together. Communication of expectations should be as much a part of the consequence-management process as possible. This means that the best way to communicate expectations is through the individuals who manage consequences for the performer.

Communication of expectations should comprise three parts: first, it should state the results expected; second, it should describe how the performance against those results will be measured; and third, it should describe the roles, that is, the activities expected, including responsibilities of the performer. A strategy for communicating expectations is best completed along with the training plan but prior to instructional design. In other words, the communication of expectations should be part of a needs-analysis process to ensure that whatever training takes place will be realistic in terms of the possible consequences to each of the influence sets.

The second factor to be considered in an approach to managing the training-delivery system is feedback. A feedback process will need to be designed for each influence set, just as expectations are set for them. Feedback is focused on specific performance information to provide the performers with information about how they are performing.

There are four elements in an effective feedback system. First, content must be considered to determine the specific information to be communicated and to ensure that this information is related to a given performance. Second, the medium for the feedback must be considered to identify the feedback processes—whether individual or administrative, internal or external. Third, control of the feedback must be considered in order to determine who will manage the feedback process.

Finally, the frequency of feedback and its timeliness must be considered to ensure that the information given to the performer is usable by him or her.

Whatever process is used, the feedback must relate current performance to desired performance and, if possible, to prior performance in order to give the performer an indication of progress toward expected results. Feedback must also be neutral or provide a positive consequence to the receiver so that it will not be rejected. It might be noted here that the best controller of feedback is the receiver of this information. The more the performers are able to call for feedback as they see the need, the more impact it will have on their performance.

The third factor in building a performance-management system is consequence management. We have already looked at some of the consequences to the members of the three influence sets, and an actual examination in a given situation would probably generate others. The basic rules for consequence management are the same as those for feedback design: consequences must be managed for each influence set, must focus on specific performances, and must be concerned with the same four elements of content, medium, control, and frequency.

Managers need to determine consequences in three areas of performance: participant performance in the training process itself, posttraining performance, and their own performance related to the training process and performance maintenance. The focus here is on the manager as a standard setter, feedback controller, consequence manager, job designer, and trainer.

The training responsibility performances to be managed for the manager are integrated into the training design itself. For those performances relating to performance maintenance, integration is with other management subsystems: performance appraisal, performance reporting, etc.

Two performance areas should be considered for the participants in the training process: those centering on training criteria and those relating to posttraining performance standards. For each of these areas there are two sets of consequences to be managed: those that will be integrated within the training processes and those that will be integrated into the job environment. The means must be provided to manage consequences for the trainees for all important performances, both training and on the job, and these consequences should be as similar as possible in both situations. A number of consequence managers might be considered: the manager, the manager's boss, the central training function, the trainees' peers within the user units, and any significant others in the job or home environment.

For managers' bosses, the focus of consequence management centers on managers and their performances, especially in the management of the training process and in the areas of trainee turnover and productivity. There must also be focus on the managers' boss as standard setter, feedback controller, consequence manager, job designer, and trainer for managers. The central training function might properly be directly involved in the consequence management at this level, whereas it has no opportunity to directly influence the other two sets.

The fourth factor in building an effective management system for training delivery is job design. This approach considers the training process or program to be in itself a job design, setting and meeting criteria in the following areas:

1. performer knowledge—all influence sets must be provided with objectives, criteria, process design, feedback plans, etc., relating to the training process.
2. information—all data required for satisfying the training criteria must be provided: input information, feedback data, external information, etc.
3. task sequencing—the training tasks need to be ordered for most efficient accomplishment of the criteria, not for ease of training or administration.
4. task congruency—task interferences must be eliminated or neutralized.
5. tools—the tools needed by the trainee to perform both within the training process and in the posttraining environment must be provided.
6. materials—the same considerations apply to providing materials as to providing tools.
7. interface congruency—all those who come into contact with the trainees need to be congruent with the training process so that there is no task interference. The training process must be supportive of trainee performance requirements; their roles and the consequences should be known and interpersonal issues caused by training reduced or neutralized.
8. performance feedback—feedback relating directly to training criteria must be provided as an integral part of the training process.

Instructional effectiveness also needs to be considered as part of the job design. The form the instruction takes must be acceptable to the trainees; that is, it must be at their level and the method used must be one with which they are comfortable and familiar. If the instructional approach is not that expected by the trainees, a transition must be built from the known to the new.

The instructional approach also needs to be congruent with the working environment so that there is enough similarity between the training and the work environment to facilitate transfer of new knowledge and skills. Instruction, of course, must be relevant to posttraining performance requirements so that positive consequences will accrue to the trainees and the other influence sets.

The final factor in building a performance-management system is training. The knowledge and skills under consideration here are those that apply to the management of training and posttraining performance. Each influence set needs to "know how" to manage the performance system around the training process. A process for gaining this knowledge and skill must be implemented for each influence set and is desirable for all interfaces.

The basic premise of this approach is that a training program is a performance system and needs to be managed as such. The performance-management system considers five elements of the management process: expectations, feedback, consequences, job design, and training. Each influence set that impacts on trainee performance is treated as part of the performance system, and the consequences to members of each influence set are a central concern of the training function.

DELIVERY–MANAGEMENT GUIDE

1. Preparation
    a) Specify influence sets
        (1) Managers
        (2) Participants
        (3) Managers' bosses
    b) Qualify influence sets for each influence set
        (1) Actions required of each set
        (2) Potential resistance in each set
        (3) Potential drive in each set
        (4) Constraints for each set: timing, location, politics
    c) List potential consequences for each influence set
        (1) All possible consequences
        (2) Consequences controlled or influenced by training unit

2. Planning
    a) Set expectations for each influence set
        (1) Participants
            (a) training program objectives
            (b) in-training/end-of-training performance criteria
            (c) posttraining performance criteria or standards
        (2) Managers
            (a) roles and responsibilities related to trainees
            (b) performance criteria or standards dependent on trainee performance
        (3) Managers' bosses
            (a) roles and responsibilities related to trainee performance
            (b) performance criteria or standards dependent on training in user units
    b) Prepare feedback processes for each influence set
        (1) Specify information to be communicated
            (a) related directly to expectations in 2a
            (b) selected on basis of cost and practicality
        (2) Specify feedback media
            (a) using existing administrative media
            (b) using indicators in training or job settings

  (c) to be built into training or job settings
  (d) using special media—people or specific communication processes
(3) Specify feedback controls

  (a) controlled by receivers
  (b) controlled by administrative systems
  (c) controlled by superiors
  (d) controlled by peers
  (e) controlled by subordinates
  (f) controlled by central training function

c) Prepare consequence management plan for participants

(1) From 1c identify consequences relating to

  (a) training criteria
  (b) posttraining performance criteria

(2) For each consequence, identify those to be integrated with

  (a) training activities
  (b) job environment

(3) Identify individuals who will manage consequences

  (a) manager
  (b) manager's boss
  (c) central training function
  (d) peers within user unit
  (e) participants' "significant others"

(4) Set consequence management priorities

  (a) cost
  (b) practicality
  (c) impact

d) Prepare consequence management plan for unit managers

(1) From 1c identify consequences relating to

  (a) participant performance in training process
  (b) unit performance dependent on posttraining performances
  (c) unit manager performance dependent on management
       relationship with trainees

(2) Identify consequences to be integrated with

  (a) training activities
  (b) posttraining performance maintenance

(3) Specify individuals who will manage consequences

  (a) trainees
  (b) subordinates

        (c) managers' bosses
        (d) central training function
        (e) managers' "significant others"

    (4) Set priorities

        (a) cost
        (b) practicality
        (c) impact

e) Prepare consequence management plan for managers' bosses

    (1) From 1c identify consequences relating to

        (a) unit manager's management of the training process
        (b) unit performance dependent on posttraining performances

    (2) Identify consequences to be integrated with

        (a) unit performance requirements
        (b) manager's career development

    (3) Specify individuals who will manage consequences

        (a) central training function
        (b) managers' bosses' supervisors
        (c) peers
        (d) subordinates—managers

    (4) Set priorities

        (a) cost
        (b) practicality
        (c) impact

f) Review training process for job-design effectiveness

    (1) Trainee knowledge of objectives, criteria, method, etc., assured
    (2) Trainee provided with all information needed to meet criteria
    (3) Tasks sequenced to accomplish criteria
    (4) Task interference minimized or eliminated
    (5) Tools and materials available at correct time and place
    (6) All trainee interfaces supportive or neutral
    (7) Performance feedback part of training task sequence for
        each criterion
    (8) Instruction form and content within acceptable range of trainees
    (9) Instructional approach is congruent with work environment

g) Review training process for relevance to posttraining performance
   requirements

    (1) Posttraining performance requirements approximate training
        criteria

      (a) transfer plan to reduce differences

   (2) Review job design

      (a) performer knowledge
      (b) information
      (c) task sequencing
      (d) task congruency
      (e) tools and materials
      (f) interface congruency
      (g) performance feedback

h) Prepare training required to manage delivery

   (1) Identify trainee population

      (a) managers' bosses
      (b) managers
      (c) participants
      (d) participants' interfaces

   (2) Prepare training design

3. Implementation

  a) Prepare time and action calendars
  b) Complete training actions from 2h
  c) Complete feedback systems from 2b
  d) Complete required job-design changes from 2f
  e) Implement training processes
  f) Implement consequence management plans from 2c, 2d, 2e.

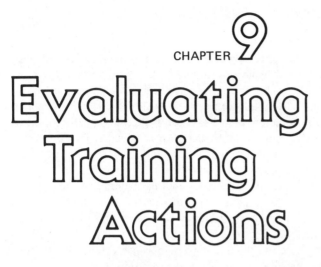

CHAPTER 9

Evaluating Training Actions

EVALUATION: IN TRAINING AND ON THE JOB

In discussing a player with a colleague, the coach of a tennis team described the youngster's fine form, power, control, and great concentration. In sum, the youngster was "a great player by anyone's standards." "Not by mine," replied the other, "not someone who always gets beaten." From a trainer's point of view, the coach was evaluating the training program. The trainee demonstrated the behavior which the coach looked for during the training action. The coach's colleague was evaluating behavior resulting from training actions in terms of on-the-job performance.

Evaluation of training actions is in fact a double problem. Training must be measured in terms of both the training action itself and behavior outside the training situation. In the process of analyzing a job or function to identify training needs, the desired behaviors have been specified. These on-the-job behaviors are then translated into behaviors expected in the training situation. Criteria are established detailing the behavior, the conditions under which it will occur, and the standards which it will meet. At this point the means for measuring the behavior or comparing it to the standard have not been established.

Measurements will be needed to solve both parts of the double problem—and both parts *must* be solved. For the organization served by the training function, the only measurement required is on-the-job performance. This measures the return to the organization for its investment in training actions. The manager of the training function, however, needs to gauge the effectiveness of the training actions themselves and must measure performance within the training situation. This provides the feedback which will indicate the need for revising the training. If the instructional design fails to bring about the behavior changes planned, the actions must be revised. Beyond the requirement for internal feedback, the training manager needs an immediate, accurate forecast of the trainee's on-the-job behavior. Without it, dangerous problems may arise. Evaluation of the trainee's performance on the job may show that the trained behaviors are inappropriate for the real world. For example, a worker may now be extremely accurate, but too slow. On-the-job evaluation may show that the trained behaviors are incomplete, that the trainee is not meeting all task requirements, as in the case of an insurance-claim clerk who can record accident descriptions with great accuracy, but still fails to get the policy number right. Still another possible problem can occur if the trained behavior is not supported on the job, as in the case of an inspection task which is felt to be overdone or inimical to the interests of the trainee's fellow workers or supervisors.

Of course, none of these problems should occur after a well-prepared training action. In the real world, however, there are too few opportunities to achieve the required degree of perfection without making revisions, and these revisions use data fed back from evaluation. Three kinds of evaluation are needed to provide the data needed to revise training actions and to measure their quality and value. Each of these facets of evaluation operates on the training action as feedback to the training function and on the trained behaviors as a measure of the action.

EVALUATION DURING THE TRAINING ACTION

The initial evaluation is a process that takes place within the training action. This assessment tests each step of the action to determine whether the behavior change predicted has been achieved. In programed instruction, testing is easy to describe though arduous in discipline. Each segment leading to a test item is tried out to determine precisely how many of a test group will respond to the item as predicted. If the results are not acceptable, the segment is revised and tested on another group. This evaluation/revision process is repeated until the ratio of correct responses is acceptable.

Applying this discipline to other training methods and to other kinds of training action is not only possible but also necessary if the form and content of the training are to be evaluated. In the brief description of evaluation of programed instruction during the preparatory stages, it can be seen the approach is simply one of trial and error. The writer of the program calculates the kind of content and format that will obtain the required responses and then tries it out. If successful, he or she is ready to go on to the next segment of the program. If the section fails, the program designer corrects errors, revises, and tries again.

Suppose, however, that the instructional designer chooses a nonstructured conference approach to the training problem. There is now a live situation in which the only method of evaluation is observing the performance of the participants through a complete session. As in programed instruction, a sample group must be tested. However, it may be more difficult to choose a sample group, here, because the type of learning experience presented is likely to be more complex than programed instruction. The answer to the problem, of course, is to define the measurement criteria or describe the expected behaviors just as strictly and narrowly as programed instruction does. Assuming that the instructional designer is to use an unstructured approach to the training action, there will already have been developed some degree of consistency or homogeneity in the training group, and these be-havioral criteria may not be as difficult to set as they might first appear. With prior structuring through other training media, the instructional designer can reasonably expect that a certain kind of behavior will take place in the unstructured confer-ence. He or she will then be able to test the training action internally by observing the performance of individuals who have had the same prior structuring. This kind of internal measurement is highly predictive; it is one application of the doctrine of similarity. The evaluator assumes that given the same conditions, similar groups will behave in the same way. Statistically this is very likely, but it is not inevitable.

It is the position of this writer that internal evaluation of the training action must be attempted to obtain the feedback for improving the training approach. To say that a method cannot be evaluated and therefore should not be used or that a training method cannot be evaluated and therefore no evaluation should be at-tempted is to beg the issue. The action can still be evaluated on the line, as it were, by observing the performance of the trainee and breaking the criteria into small pieces so that revisions can be made on the spot. As an example, let us suppose that the instructional designer has decided to use an unstructured conference in an ori-entation program for new college hires. The trained behavior has been described as a positively expressed acceptance of the organization's profit-sharing program as a suitable long-term performance security. The unstructured conference has been chosen because it allows a high degree of mutual reinforcement within the group of new hires without generating feelings that they are being coerced into this behavior or brainwashed in the formation of their attitudes. Prior to the unstructured ses-sions, the instructional designer plans to use an audiovisual program to train the group to respond to profit sharing in terms of content, definition, and relation to other forms of long-range security programs. A structured discussion is designed to lead the group to the desired responses on the profit-sharing program and to rein-force these responses. The programed materials are to be tested on available popu-lation groups, as is the structured part of the program. The trainer must now consider how to evaluate the responses obtained in the unstructured session when statements are made about the profit-sharing program or when problems involved in it are introduced to the group, keeping in mind that this session is meant not as a test of the participants' knowledge of the program, but as a learning experience. For measurement criteria the group's responses to two questions and a case prob-lem are chosen. The first question is: "How can we as an organization improve our program for providing long-range security to our employees?" In their responses, the group members are expected to formulate minor changes in the plan, demonstrating their knowledge of the plan's content. It can also be expected that the group's re-sponses will develop a more or less homogeneous attitude toward the plan in the interchange of individual ideas.

The second measurement criterion will be based on the group's solution to a case problem involving a retiring employee of a defined marital status and health condition in which the retiree requests the group's help in developing an option to best utilize the proceeds from the plan for retirement. The instructional designer will expect the group members' responses to this problem to demonstrate both their knowledge of the plan and their facility in applying the various potential options to a specific situation.

For the third criterion, the instructional designer asks the group, "Why do you believe this company has chosen this profit-sharing plan as an alternative to the various types of insurance and other pension plans available?" Here it is anticipated that the responses developed in the group's discussion will reveal the participants' willingness to accept the program and their affirmation of the idea that the company has supplied them with a superior security program.

After the first two segments of the program, with the criteria tests for those segments successfully passed, the designer brings the group together for the unstructured session. As required by the approach, the designer presents the two questions and the problem and withdraws from group participation until the successful completion of each problem, when he or she reinforces the participants' responses by saying that they have done a good job. During the process the designer observes the group to determine whether the responses of the participants indicate that the trained behaviors have indeed been reached. If all goes well, and it probably will, it may be predictively assumed that this approach is valid for the next group of college hires in an orientation program.

However, let us suppose that in the response to the third criterion question the group decides that the present profit-sharing plan isn't all that good and that the company selected the plan to secure a cost advantage to the detriment of the employees. For this particular instructional design, the method obviously has failed. If this were a test group, the instructional designer would go back and either shift the method or provide more prior reinforcement. Since the individuals are employees of the organization, the designer is not without stake in their future performance. An immediate action to recover must be taken. This poses no great problem for the experienced trainer, who can easily and smoothly shift into a more structured discussion, either moving the group into a new topic or providing structured leadership to revise the group's decision into a desirable and acceptable pattern which can be reinforced. The point here is that for an experienced trainer, on-sight evaluation and immediate revision are not wholly implausible. A less experienced conference leader may find it necessary to develop alternatives in the instructional design so that a new approach may be selected from an available repertoire. This is somewhat analogous to the use of looping or branching in programed instruction.

In training action such as that described in this example, a number of rather complex behaviors are being sought. The initial in-process evaluations fulfill a single function: to give the instructional designer data on the effectiveness of the methods being used to bring about the desired behaviors. The intention is to evaluate not the trainees, but the instructional design itself. Each definable behavior is tested in terms of its criteria for the training action. It is as if the builder of the program were attempting to evaluate the building blocks in the total action to determine whether each segment performed its required part in obtaining the trained behavior.

The example given probably represents the most difficult method for which this kind of evaluation will be made. In most other methods, the building blocks are more clearly defined, and they are usually used to obtain less complex behaviors. The instructional designer can, for example, set up and test complete in-basket exercises and reasonably expect that the exercises will be performed in the same way by future groups. The same is true for written cases, critical incidents, and role-plays. The instructional designer might extend this initial evaluation if the sum of the building blocks seemed such that the total program should be tested for possible revision. Usually this is not necessary and often it is impractical; if the evaluation of the program segments has been carefully carried out, the probability of success in obtaining the sum behaviors is extremely high. However, evaluation of the entire program may be fruitful when many of the building blocks (cases, role-plays, etc.) are drawn from the instructional designer's experience repertory; that is, they were tested in other situations, and similar results are expected in a new situation. In such instances pilot programs can save a great deal of time and effort.

At any rate, whether testing is done in small steps or on a whole, the unit of action, the use of the pilot program, is the same: to determine whether or not the planned training action will indeed achieve the responses for which it was designed. Regardless of the methods to be used, the steps for making a pilot evaluation are the same. First, the instructional designer defines the behavior to be verified in terms of criteria tests. Second, the point in the training action at which the criteria can be tested is identified—in other words, those points at which the desired behavior will occur. Third, the designer identifies the beginning and end of the training block or module to delineate precisely the segment of the training action under evaluation. Fourth, a pilot group is selected, with participants chosen on the basis of their similarity to the population to be trained. This may be done in a laboratory situation by bringing in a pilot group, or the evaluation may be carried out on-line with the first real training group. Fifth, the training module is completed and the pilot group's behavior compared with specific test criteria or with a predicted behavior pattern. Finally, a decision is made as to whether or not a high enough percentage of the pilot group demonstrated the behaviors sought. If the percentage of success is high enough, the designer is ready to go on to the next step; if not, the program must be revised.

In the case of programed instruction, the expectation of successful performance will normally run above 95%, and the program writer will revise until such a mark is achieved. For other training methods, the expected success may be as low as 75%, depending on the complexity of the required behaviors. Proposed attitude changes and very heterogeneous training groups can definitely be expected to wind up at the lower end of the scale. However, given reasonable amounts of time, money, and expertise on the part of the instructional designer, it is not too much to expect that the usual success area should be above 90%. The organizational function for which the training is being carried out must determine the percentage of success it needs and the amount of time and money it can invest to obtain such success. A good time to discuss this problem is just prior to pilot studies. It should be done by showing the system management how the training action will be implemented and advising on the expected percentage of success within the given constraints of time and cost. This kind of fair and open discussion can usually bring about reasonable agreement on the extent of behavior change really required. If the system management can also participate in the evaluation, so much the better. Then they will be in a position to better evaluate their own expectations. It is often at this stage of revision that the greatest effectual change in the training action will take place, as system managers examine and analyze the behavior change they have requested. They will often be ready to accept suggestions for systems changes or other nontraining solutions to their problems. It is important, however, that management be prepared for what will happen in a pilot program. Management must realize that the function of such a pilot is to identify needs for revision and that it is not the purpose of such a program to "sell" training ideas or to entertain.

EVALUATION AT THE END OF THE TRAINING ACTION

Having made revisions and completed the design and development of the training action, the trainer looks forward to the second evaluation, the one made at the end of each presentation. This is the training program evaluation, and it has three functions. The first is to score the training action itself—to tell the trainer and functional management how good the training program is, whether it did indeed bring about the planned behaviors. It is at this point that the training criteria so carefully established and defined are used to measure the performance of the participants. The second function is to provide data needed by the trainer to predict the performance of the participants on the job. The third function is to score the participants themselves. This will permit the trainer and functional management to plan further training actions for the 10% to 15% of individuals who were not successful. A higher percentage might need further training if partial successes were observed and recycling or reinforcement of training is necessary. In programed instruction this evaluation is made through a postcourse test; for other training methods, various performance tests might be devised. The essential difference between this evaluation and the initial in-process evaluation is that the trainer is now evaluating *the results that the participants obtain* in the solution of specific problems, the completion of specific tasks, or answers to specific questions, *rather than the processes* by which the trainees obtain the performance results.

When the instructional designer began the development of the training action, management was told that the training would result in certain specific behaviors. These promises are now being evaluated. The key to this level of evaluation rests in the ability of the trainer to tell management with some degree of precision what is to be measured and how and to obtain the agreement of management on both points. At this second step of evaluation, it is the *performance of individuals* in the training program which is being measured, not the overall effect of the training action on the organization. For example, the overall training objectives in a sales-training program may be to improve sales for the sales force, in terms of either dollars or new customers. But at this stage of the evaluation, it is the performance of the individual sales trainee which is being measured. A determination must be made as to how well the salesperson can carry out the actions (behaviors) that sales management and the trainer have agreed will produce the desired sales improvement. Going back to the anecdote about the tennis coach, at this stage we are evaluating form, concentration, power, and control, not the ability of the player to win games; that can be done only in match play. What we are doing here is controlling the conditions in which the player demonstrates performance. We are not putting him or her up against an unknown opponent; that must be left for the next stage of the evaluation. Like the tennis coach—and properly so—we are evaluating the individual player by certain standards of performance. From performance within these restricted conditions (the training program), the coach or trainer can predict how the player will perform in a match, and the trainer can predict how the sales trainee will perform in the field. As knowledge grows of how this behavior is applied under field conditions, the trainer will be able to make more and more accurate predictions, given the cooperation and understanding of system management. As the field conditions are closely simulated within the training action, predictions will become highly accurate.

Here is should be pointed out that it is quite important for the trainer to be open with management about any ignorance of field conditions. For example, if the instructional designer developing the sales-training program does not know the sales market, techniques applicable to the product or service, etc., he or she must work with sales management to effectively simulate the actual working environment. Otherwise, there is little hope that the program will pass the third and most crucial evaluation: that which occurs on the job. The second evaluation, if successful, may not even be pertinent, for if the simulated conditions are invalid, the validity of the training criteria and standards of performance may also be called into question.

EVALUATION ON THE JOB

The third evaluation rates the performance of the trainee on the job, in the field, in the match. It is at this point that the training action's contribution to the organization is evaluated. The key to this evaluation is the same as that for the second: the clear understanding and agreement of functional management about the performance to be evaluated and the measures to be used.

The evaluation of performance on the job involves three critical problems: (1) What behavior is to be measured? (2) Who is to do the measuring? (3) When is measurement to be made? The first item is the most critical. When the trainee's performance is evaluated at the close of a training program, most of the conditions under which the measurement is made are controlled. The behavior to be evaluated is isolated, and conditions within the training program are usually structured so that a limited repertory of responses take place. Interference by other stimuli or conditions is not normally allowed. The entire structure of the training action is built in such a way that the trainee is led only to a certain small group of desired responses. This, after all, is the simplest and usually the best way to structure a training program. The trainer carefully builds a repertory of desired responses which will comprise the trained behavior.

On the job, however, the situation is usually quite different. Conditions are usually quite complex, and it is extremely difficult to isolate the desired behaviors to be evaluated. The problem is similar to that of the student geologist who easily identifies a wide variety of minerals in the classroom, but finds that it is extremely difficult to sort out specimens on a field trip when they exist under a wide variety of conditions. Separating one mineral specimen from several hundred in the immediate vicinity is sometimes difficult; identifying a diamond among the other pebbles in a dry stream bed is, I am told, almost impossible except for an expert. The problem the trainer faces, however, is even more difficult than that of the student geologist. The object of evaluation is often fleeting in time and must be discriminated not only from other objects, but also in diverse locations and conditions. The solution to the problem lies in a careful definition of what is to be observed. Not only the behavior, but also the conditions in which it will exist must be carefully defined. Further, the trainer should be in a position to identify conditions that might interfere with his or her findings. It must be remembered that because the process of evaluation may itself be an interference, it must be carried out in such a manner that either the interference is measurable or the trainee being evaluated is not aware of it.

Ideally, the behavior to be evaluated will be isolated. This means that the trained performance forms a large enough part of the overall behavior to be identified as separate from other elements of an individual's performance. If the performance of, say, a punch press operator is to be evaluated, there is a relatively limited behavior repertory. A sequence of operations within the task can be followed and measured against a fairly specific standard. The operator can also be evaluated in terms of results by counting scrap and finished pieces. However, if a supervisor must be evaluated, the problem becomes quite different. The total performance of a supervisor may not be so easy to relate to any specific training received. Further, how can the trainer attempt to measure such a wide complex of behaviors when in order to do a complete job, the supervisor must be observed in action over a long period of time? After all, the supervisor may not have the opportunity to demonstrate every element of his or her behavior repertory in one hour, or, for that matter, in one week. It is far more likely that a single element will be evaluated, e.g., the manner in which the supervisor handles discipline.

Here is a very good example of the complexity of the trainer's problem in carrying out the on-the-job performance evaluation. Assuming that discipline is the subject of a training action, what is the criterion used for measurement? Should it be a limited number of discipline cases going into grievance? If this is to be the criterion, the supervisor who takes no disciplinary action will be just as successful as, or more successful than, the one who settles descipline cases by using a well-developed skill in human relations. Well, then, the trainer could evaluate the manner in which the supervisor carries out the disciplinary action. If this is to be the approach, the evaluator will have to establish a rather complex set of standards against which to measure. And what, after all, is being measured? It is basically an interpersonal-relations skill, and the ability to carry out disciplinary actions may be only one small part of that complex order of behavior. Along with counting cases that go to grievance, the trainer may have to select a broad range of criteria, such as absenteeism, tardiness, turnover, attitude survey results, etc. It is the ability to find alternative criteria that makes it at all possible to evaluate complex behaviors by means of on-the-job performance. A solution to the trainer's first problem of on-the-job evaluation, then, is to identify the measurable aspects of the behavior to be evaluated and to seek out as many meaningful alternative criteria as possible.

The second problem the trainer faces is that of who is to do the evaluation. It is in the on-the-job part of the evaluation system that the line manager plays the most important role. This is the behavior that counts; it is the performance by which the individual trained will be appraised in the normal course of affairs. The trainer must, however, make sure that the line manager is considering the training responsibility in evaluating performance. The manager must understand exactly what the changed behaviors brought about by training are and how they are to be applied on the job. Going back to the insurance clerk, if management had agreed that success was the ability of a similar clerk to read and act on the claim form filed by the trainee, and if the manager was checking spelling and grammar, the training system and the claims system would never communicate.

It is also up to the trainer to obtain feedback on this performance evaluation from the line manager so that additional training actions can be developed and current training actions revised to meet on-the-job requirements. Since this evaluation may take place some time after the training action has been completed, the conditions on the job will probably have changed; further, the requirements for standard performance may also have changed.

The third problem is timing. This problem breaks down into two parts. First, at what point after the completion of the training action should the evaluation be made? Second, should the evaluation process be repeated? Ideally, sufficient time should have elapsed between the completion of training and performance evaluation to have established the trained behaviors as a normal part of the trainee's on-the-job behavior; that is, enough time should have passed so that the trainee's responses to conditions on the job are distinguishable from his or her responses to conditions in the training program. This would seem to be a function of the training action's similarity to the job. If, indeed, the training situation were identical to the job, the evaluation could be made at any time without the danger of limiting the responses only to the structured training situation. There is a dilemma here: The longer the trainer waits to make an evaluation, the more chance there is for the trained behavior to be extinguished by job conditions. If this happens, the opportunity to reinforce desired behaviors or to take additional training actions to correct behaviors is lost. The answer seems to be to begin on-the-job performance evaluation shortly after the training action is completed and to repeat the evaluation periodically until the desired performance has become part of the trained individual's standard behavior.

CHAPTER 10

Industrial
Skill Training

APPLICATIONS OF THE GENERAL MODEL

In applying the concepts we have been discussing to a specific organization or system, we must first carefully define the missions or objectives to be imposed. We will want the system to produce training actions which will obtain the behavior changes required by the organization served. It is clearly impossible to develop on these pages a specific training system for every possible variety of organization. We can, however, turn our attention to several specific areas of training and examine problems of behavior change and their potential solutions.

APPROACHES TO INDUSTRIAL TRAINING

The field of training that has traditionally been given most attention and through which the most trainees have passed is industrial skill training. The subjects here are usually hourly paid "blue collar" workers associated with an industrial manufacturing facility, the human resources of our contemporary mass-production systems.[*] This area encompasses the training of machine operators, inspectors, maintenance workers, and other groups of people associated with processing systems.

In our general model, the training system mission was described as the bringing about of planned and predefined behavior changes. The mission of a training system in industrial skill training can be adequately defined only after the organization determines the framework within which it looks at individual performance. Industrial systems can look at worker performance in a number of ways, but basically they look at it from the point of view of the job, the task, the skill, or some combination of the three.

---

[*] Although the trade skills are a part of this system, they are not usually considered under industrial skill training. The traditional apprentice-journeyman training systems will, therefore, be considered separately here.

PERFORMANCE IN TERMS OF JOB

If performance is defined in terms of the job, the behaviors required are defined in terms of a job description or pay grade. In systems taking this approach, individual performance is usually described as a large number of specific behaviors. It deals with a family or group of tasks which have been judged of equal difficulty or complexity. In this system an employee may be set to work at various work stations, as in an automobile assembly line. The behaviors to be changed by training are defined in terms of the entire system's requirements. Thus the training operation is asked to train a specified number of machine operators who, when certified as fully qualified, may be assigned to any one of a number of specific machines and machine tasks. Performance standards in such a system are usually qualitative rather than quantitative, since the performance requirements may vary depending on the trained operators' assignments and, in fact, may vary from day to day as they are assigned to new machines or work stations. The standards are usually established by an industrial engineering function and are set in terms of production requirements for a group of operations. Often these standards are interpreted by the personnel function responsible for employment, which determines the entry behaviors with which the training system will deal. Because of the range of assignments possible within the job description grade or classification, quantity or quality standards are rarely stipulated. The broadest example of this approach is the "general labor" classification in a manufacturing plant. An individual hired in this classification can be assigned to jobs ranging in complexity from placing stampings on a conveyor to running a lift truck. The entry requirements are arbitrarily grouped together, usually to fit the least complicated job.

In a system utilizing a job approach to performance, the training system's mission will have to be defined in terms of on-line productivity standards. In other words, the system mission is the development and maintenance of an acceptable level of unit production where that production is controlled by human operators. The number of units, an acceptable quality level, and the operator group can all be fairly closely defined. The aspect of operator control can also be defined and indeed must be if the analysts who identify training needs are to have the freedom to also identify changes needed in the system.

PERFORMANCE IN TERMS OF TASKS

The second way of looking at performance is in terms of tasks. Here the organization is no longer looking at a generalized job description or wage classification, but rather at the specific activities of the operators. This brings performance to the level of a specific machine and machine setup or a single work station. The behaviors dealt with are less complex than those defined by a job description. They are delineated by the specific task at hand. From this organization point of view, the standards established are defined in terms of what the operator does and the inputs and outputs involved. Standards here are established by industrial engineering, but are often redefined by the operator's immediate supervisor. In this situation a different performance is expected for each assignment or for each task change. Often this approach is taken where the system deals with a "job shop" kind of production with relatively short and changeable unit runs.

From the trainer's point of view, an important distinction can be made between an approach to performance based on the job and one based on the task. If the task is the central performance definer, the training system's mission centers on the operator's behavior rather than on system productivity. The mission can be stated as the development and maintenance of the behaviors required to meet specified standards for task performance. Attention shifts from total system requirements to individual performance. In the task approach the trainer may deal not with electronic rack assembly, for example, but with the operation of Pines press #12, job 90.

PERFORMANCE IN TERMS OF SKILLS

In the third general approach to industrial training, performance is described and measured in terms of skills. In the industrial setting skill is closely related to the approaches used in job orientation. Skills or skill areas are usually classified by job type or wage grade. The primary distinction is that in a job-centered approach, system performance is primary; in a skills approach, human operator performance is primary. A machine operator can be described in terms of skills or of the stations to be filled on a continuous line. Instead of talking about these stations in a classification family, however, we now turn to the actual behavioral skills required to carry out a group of related tasks. Machine operator behaviors are defined in terms of the skills required to carry out necessary operations in the family of tasks. For example, we can look at the milling machine from the viewpoint of the physical or motor skills needed to operate it. With these skills the operator would be able to operate any milling machine, as well as a number of related machining units. In an electronic assembly situation, the trainer deals not with wiring operations on a specific job, but rather with soldering, wire wrapping, etc.

The skill approach is essentially one used in apprenticeship training in which the apprentice/trainee is trained to perform a number of related tasks traditionally included in the particular trade. Thus the sheet-metal worker is trained to read blueprints, operate brakes, manipulate a scriber, etc. The expectation is that at the end of training, he or she will be able to make decisions as to the proper way of applying the family of skills to specific tasks. In many extended skill training programs the trainee's final exam consists of exactly this kind of independent selection of skills in a task. The sheet-metal worker, for example, is given a blueprint and is expected to produce a finished piece.

THE MISSION OF INDUSTRIAL TRAINING

The mission statement for a skill-oriented training system might be given as the development of behaviors to meet specified standards which define or describe the skills required in a production system. This approach requires sufficient generalization of the standards for consistency within the organization. Thus the electronics assembler in one part of the organization would be transferable, in theory, to another part of the organization which required the same skills. In the same way, the training and experience gained by the machine assembler in Corporation A should eliminate the need for skill training when the assembler resigns and moves on to Corporation B.

The discussion of these three general approaches to industrial skills is not merely a semantic one; the distinctions made have an important impact on the organization of the training function as well as on the ways in which that training function handles specific problems of quality and quantity as measures of operator performance. In a job-training situation a new operator enters a system through assignment to a shop, line, or work area. Depending on job classification, the operator may be assigned to any one of a number of tasks in that shop or line. The range of tasks he or she will perform may or may not be related in terms of skills or standards applied for a particular station or task. This can be easily visualized in the situation of an automobile assembly line, in which a single operator may be assigned to such varied tasks as fitting an instrument panel, operating an automatic screw driver, fastening seat brackets, using an impact wrench to tighten a steering column, etc. The work positions vary, the skills vary, but most important, the standards vary. Often there is little need to bring performance standards to a very high level, since the system usually has sufficient built-in redundancies to correct operator errors. In fact, there may be no way to identify the specific operator committing the error (or, rather, exhibiting substandard performance), since he or she may have been moved three times before the error is caught 30 minutes later 20 yards down the line.

Actually, one could almost say that this is an ideal training situation, since training problems as such never arise. The management of such a productive system seldom regards the behavior of an individual human operator as worthy of economic consideration in the design, development, and maintenance of a system. It must be noted, however, that this system is *machine-paced;* that is, the machine subsystems control the job and provide the constraints for the human operators. The human operators themselves have little opportunity to develop behavioral skills, nor have they any motivation for so doing. Not even the most cynical person could disagree with the automobile factory old-timer whose advice to a newcomer was, "To do this job, you've got to check your brains at the door!"

The villains of the piece, however, are not machine-paced systems or automotive assembly lines or indeed the automotive industry itself. The real villain appears to be failure to consider the requirements of a job-centered approach in the first place. Most glaring, perhaps, is the failure of the organization to consider the human operator requirements of the system or the behaviors required for those operators to function within the system. This, in turn, seems to result from the failure to establish measurable standards—indeed, the failure to provide standards meaningful to the people actually making the performance measurements.

At first glance, this seems difficult to understand. After all, when the assembly subsystem is designed, the human operators' tasks are considered in the design. When the machine pace is established, operator requirements are analyzed and tested. In fact, each time a change is made in the system, human operator requirements are studied. A number of staff specialists are involved in the design and modification of the system, none of whom is directly involved with operator performance. However, line supervision, in-process inspection, work leaders, etc.— those who interface with the machine system or who could provide immediate feedback to the human operators—are not involved in the design or modification process. When substandard performance does occur, it is not related back to the human operator but rather to the machine system alone. Thus the operator is not usually trained for a job, but rather is attached to it by a tool. He or she receives no feedback on performance, and those in a position to provide feedback are not in a position to relate output quality or quantity to the performance of a human operator. Offhand, this kind of a production system bears no requirement for operator training. There is sufficient profitability in the process involved so that enough redundancy can be built into the system to correct substandard operator performance.

Other frequent constraints on the use of training to increase system effectiveness are the positions taken by a bargaining unit to which the human operators belong in unionized organizations. The limits within which management is permitted to utilize behavior change agents or training actions is rigidly limited, and through one cause or another, management has abdicated or been deprived of its responsibility for bringing about an economical standard of performance by human operators. It is also true, however, that in many organizations utilizing the job approach to operator performance, standards can be established and change actions taken to bring human operator performance up to those standards. Many organizations do not have the high profitability which allows redundancy for error correction and instead seek to make their products right the first time. It is in this kind of organization that a training subsystem can be designed and maintained to make sure the operators in the system can and do meet established standards.

A very basic "go-to-hell" decision has to be made in an organization taking a job approach to its workers. Shall the human operators in that system be accountable for meeting productivity and/or quality standards? If the decision is negative, then there is no economic value in creating or maintaining a function to train industrial skills. Without some reason for behavior change other than the punishment of suspension or termination, training requires more effort and expense than most organizations can afford. If the human being to be trained is not accountable for the results of his or her actions, he or she has no real reason to learn. However, if such accountability is to be assigned to the people in the system, then it becomes useful to organize an operating system for behavior change. There is, of course, another, more general, constraint on this decision: Is it possible for the human operators in such a system to control the quality and quantity of their performance? If they have no possibility of affecting their outputs—that is, if their effort or lack of effort, efficiency or lack of efficiency, really has no effect on the outputs of the system—then training can serve little purpose.

ASSIGNING THE ANALYSIS ELEMENT

In discussing a general model for training, five elements were described: research, analysis, development, delivery, and evaluation. Starting from scratch, the analysis element needs to be considered first. The first problem to be faced is the establishment of standards and the examination of required and present performance. Since we are confronted by a system in which any standards set are established for the system as a whole, the most effective interface for the analysis element will be at the juncture or point at which the standards are set. Step one, then, is to determine exactly where this takes place; step two is to identify those people who make the decisions about the standards. Therefore, the quality control or quality assurance subsystem will have to be part of the analysis element, as will the production control or production scheduling system, which establishes the quantity standards for the system under investigation. This procedure will permit the establishment of standards and the measurement of results.

Quality control and production control will also be the best available sources of information about the present performance levels of the system. Logically, then, it would seem practical to assign individuals from these two functions to the analysis element. But this element will also be accountable for developing the behavioral descriptions and criteria for use in any training actions. Since the system under examination includes a number of operators with a given range of behaviors, there would be some advantage in assigning a training specialist here. This would be especially true if the job class covers more than one supervisory assignment. In other words, in situations in which the quality and quantity measures are at the end of a number of processes or in which the product flow moves through a number of sections or departments, it is more effective to assign a behavioral specialist to the analysis element than a line supervisor who may or may not be in a position to analyze behaviors all along the line. Thus where a number of supervisory responsibilities are involved (several sections or departments), and particularly where separate operator behaviors are involved, the specialized knowledge and experience of a professional trainer with unique competencies and capabilities become effective.

In some organizations it would also be useful to add at this point a specialist in work methods, so that the human/machine relationships can be effectively analyzed and systematically standardized. However, if such an action is taken—that is, if the industrial engineering function is added to the analysis element—it will, from a training point of view, become critically important that a specialist in behavior change participate. The industrial engineering view tends to restrict actions to "efficient" human/machine relationships and to exclude from consideration some important human aspects of the job, whereas data from current research into human/machine relationships would indicate that the motivational aspects of these relationships must be considered in the development of any training actions.

Four aspects, then, need to be included in the analysis of industrial skills training from a job or job class approach: quality standardization and measurement, quantity standardization and measurement, behavioral analysis, and work-methods analysis.

ASSIGNING THE DEVELOPMENT ELEMENT

The development element poses a different kind of problem. The nature of the system under investigation is such that once training actions have been designed to meet the system's standards, changes in these actions will not need to be structured unless there is a radical change in the human/machine relationships within the system or marked changes in the quality and quantity standards. The assumption here is that entry behaviors of the human operators entering the system will remain relatively constant. This, of course, is controlled by the selection function in the organization, whose members presumably hire according to fairly rigid, unchanging standards. In this case development can be assigned to a training specialist, who will be working with a training population large enough to make the assignment economically feasible. Also, instructional design, once completed, will remain usable for a relatively long period in the life of the industrial organization. This provides an excellent example of the applicability of a consulting organization in the development element, whether the consultants are in-house or are hired on a contract basis.

ASSIGNING THE DELIVERY ELEMENT

The delivery element can be based on similar considerations: a large number of human operators to be trained over the life of the training action and criteria and standards that, once established, are invariable. We now go into a numbers game. For example, if there are enough operators to be trained to establish a separate system such as a vestibule, this could be considered an approach. It is important to note, however, that the behaviors to be trained are usually not going to be very complex. Training each individual operator is not likely to take more than a few hours or a few days at most, and with careful planning, this training can often be done on the production line itself. Economically, this on-line training can take place if no more than one out of every 20 operators is a trainee and if the instructional medium permits it. This reservation about media usually involves a human factor: whether or not a trainer will be available to implement the training action as designed.

Most likely the trainers will be drawn from three functional areas: first-line supervision, industrial engineering, or a separate training operation. As with other decisions in the establishment of training-system elements, this one will be based on competence, capability, and cost. Capability will be the major hurdle. Few industrial situations call for a full-time trainer/instructor, so accountability for training operations will be a part-time assignment. Therefore, specific goals and objectives will have to be very clearly assigned to whoever undertakes the job. The easiest solution, purely from the point of view of staff, would be part-time assignment of a training specialist, one with other duties, but the part-time specialist, like the part-time supervisor/trainer, will be able to perform effectively only if there is some guarantee that other job demands will not be so great as to prevent effectiveness in the training role. If the trainer is drawn from industrial engineering or supervisory functions, time will also have to be devoted to training the individual for the new role and to maintaining his or her effectiveness as a trainer in the future. It is assumed that the person will be supplied with instructional materials to do the job, but he or she will still have to be trained to use these materials properly. Of course, if it is feasible in terms of available facilities and numbers of trainees to create and maintain a vestibule for training operators, it will probably also be appropriate to assign a full-time trainer to the operation of this vestibule. Experience would indicate that at least a 50% time utilization is required to break even in a vestibule operation if the equipment contained in it is to be kept up to date. With this utilization a full-time trainer is almost universally required.

A frequently useful approach is the combination of vestibule and on-line training. If this is a possibility, the vestibule can best be applied to those parts of the human operator function which can be generalized as skills. In other words, the vestibule will be used to bring about trained behaviors applicable to a number of on-line operator positions. When the partially trained operator moves from the vestibule to the line position, he or she undergoes additional training in those tasks and/or operations not generalized in the vestibule.

This approach requires a careful breakdown, from the industrial engineering viewpoint, of all operator tasks and skills used in the system: an analysis of tools, motions, and materials. Enough data will have to be gathered to determine which tasks can be generalized within the job classification and which parts of tasks must be generalized in terms of operator skill requirements. In the case of the electronics assembly worker, for example, an operator can be trained in the use of a specific wire-wrapping tool in a vestibule, with the task performed on a generalized rack and the operator completing this rack to standard. The operator can then be placed on the line and trained in the use of the wire-wrap tool at a specific production station. If the operator's station is changed, additional time is required to train him or her in the specific requirements of that station, etc. The wire-wrap tool itself and its application are taught in the vestibule, and the specialized operation is taught on-line by an individual trained and assigned to this kind of work.

This modularizing approach requires considerable preparation, particularly in the area of standard. One of the clearest dangers of such an approach is that line supervisors, as well as quality-control people, sometimes forget that the operator transferred from the vestibule into the line situation is not a fully trained operator, but rather one who needs additional training. Where on-the-job training is not clearly defined, the additional specialized training is often neglected, and one hears the complaint that the training operation is not doing its job, that the operators put on an operating station are unable to carry the load. It would be useful if we could hang a sign around partially trained people: "I am not yet at the top of the learning curve; I need additional training." The solution to this, of course, is for a partially trained operator to be immediately taken in hand by someone specifically designated to carry out the on-the-job portion of the training module.

ASSIGNING THE EVALUATION ELEMENT

The evaluation element in a job-classification approach is really a matter of identifying feedback points. Since such a system is normally evaluated at the output end after a number of operations have been completed, it does not lend itself to the immediate feedback needed in a well-designed training action. Still, this end point will be the first and foremost feedback junction. However, regardless of the inspection process for quality or production checks, the message of performance must get back to the trainee and eventually to the trainer. A regular schedule for this feedback should be provided, as well as a formalized system for feedback on operator performance at each station. There is a clear conflict between production requirements and training requirements in such a system: Pulling out a partially finished unit for quality or quantity inspection in a machine-paced operation is a potential difficulty. This can cause a slowdown in the entire production system. Yet provisions must be made if only for a visual count and inspection. Means must be found to feed back operator performance to both the trainer and the operator. Without this feedback, it is impossible to determine whether any training is taking place and, if it is, how good it is. Since one of the keys to behavior change is the immediacy of this feedback, provision for it is crucial.

Most problems found in the job approach to the human operator are absent from the task-based approach. The analysis element, while still requiring participation by whatever functions establish and control quality and quantity standards, is likely to be effectively assigned to direct supervision. There are a number of reasons for this. The most important, perhaps, is that the supervisor is in a position to evaluate the output of each task. Further, he or she normally has a great deal of control over the operator's assignment to the task and training for it. Standards of performance can easily be established for each task, and the outputs are immediately available for comparison to the established standards. Part of the supervisor's job is to perform all of these functions, and so it would seem appropriate that he or she play an important role in training analysis at this point. A task approach is uniquely suitable for the participation of first-line supervision. Where standards are established and controlled by staff specialists, performance still acts as a very direct link between the staff functions and the operator, and whether or not it is formally recognized, the supervisor usually controls assignment and evaluation of the operators.

Another general characteristic of task systems reinforces the direct control of the first-line supervisor—application of various incentives or piecework rates to the operators. Whether a manual counting system or an electronic technique is used, there is a fairly direct measurement of the output in terms of both quality and quantity for each assigned task. Substandard performance, operator- or machine-caused, is quickly brought to the supervisor's attention.

The behavioral analysis in arriving at criteria will make use of the specialized expertise of industrial engineering. This is as true as in the job approach, in which industrial engineering establishes work methods for the tasks. In other types of operations this might not be true, since industrial engineering is seldom called on to evaluate the work methods of an operation such as a punch press. However, in most machine operations and in operations such as maintenance or housekeeping, various indirect work measurements and standards will have been established.

THE ROLE OF THE SUPERVISOR

The application of a licensed work measurement system like Work Factors or Master Standard Data will provide data for the establishment of performance criteria. In the analysis element, then, using a task approach, the key person is the first-line supervisor. He or she will have available the technical expertise of the industrial engineering specialist, if one is involved, and should also have a staff training specialist to train him or her in analysis and then to provide technical help in behavioral analysis. Again, the problem of capability must be solved; other work demands on the first-line supervisor must not be so great or have so superior a reward that he or she cannot devote the necessary time and energy to the training analysis. This is not as serious a problem in a task-oriented system as in a job-oriented one, since the supervisor is usually held more directly responsible for the outputs of operators reporting to him or her.

The development of training actions in a task system can also be assigned as part of a supervisor's job. It is the factor of control of the task, nonexistent in a job-centered approach, that makes the supervisor important in developing instruction in a task-centered system. What is needed in such a situation is a generalized pattern for the trainer, much as a generalized skill was sought for the operator-trainee in a job-approach system. This essentially is the departure taken in the famed JIT (Job Instruction Training) program of World War II, in which analysis, development, and operations were combined and a generalized approach defined which had clear universal applications for industrial-task training. It is in this kind of situation that on-the-job training becomes most effective. The supervisor/ trainer or operator/trainer in many cases becomes intimately acquainted with the behaviors required to perform the task. He or she learns it first and then is helped by specialists to analyze his or her own performance against specified criteria. Following an established method of operation, the trained person works with the trainee/operator to bring the new worker up to this same level of performance. By providing a supervisor/trainer or operator/trainer with expert help from a training specialist, a fairly high level of trainer skills can be acquired. Of course, the process must be repeated as the tasks change, and where a supervisor is responsible for a great many tasks, work leaders or operator/trainers must be developed to keep the system at a high level of proficiency. Even in a task-oriented system modularization is possible using the same approach as that used in a job-oriented situation: The generalized skills are transferred to a vestibule, and the specialized skills used in specific tasks are trained on the job.

The evaluation element can also be assigned to the supervisor if he or she is normally responsible for performance measurement. All that is needed for the feedback aspect is to formalize the system normally used to count and inspect the task outputs. The trainee must have access to the evaluative information. The entire approach recommended here depends on one factor: that the first-line supervisor be in a position to control operator outputs.

TRAINING THE TRAINER

Frequently, when assigning a supervisor or a master performer as a part-time trainer, we assume that he or she is able to train others simply because that person is able to do the job well. Sometimes this is true; often it is not. The knowledge and skill required to complete a task are quite different from those required to transfer that knowledge or skill to another person. The effectiveness of on-the-job training can be enormously improved if the part-time trainer has been prepared for this new task.

The on-the-job trainer needs to be able to do five kinds of things: (1) set and clearly communicate standards of performance; (2) model or demonstrate the correct performance; (3) observe the performance of another person; (4) provide timely and usable feedback; and (5) give appropriate reinforcements to the trainee. If an instructional designer has been involved in the training task, criteria have probably been established which can be used as training-performance standards. If not, the part-time trainer will need to learn how to set these "minimum" standards. Care must be taken to ensure that the standards set by the part-time trainer are based not on what he or she is able to do, but rather against a level of performance that will indicate that the trainee has completed the training process. As noted above, this level of performance is not the same as that reached by an experienced practitioner.

A similar problem relates to modeling or demonstrating. The part-time trainer needs to learn how to model a performance not to demonstrate his or her own competence, but rather to provide a model that the trainee can easily and comfortably duplicate. The part-time trainer will need to know how to break down the performance into distinct subtasks and to get the trainee to describe what is being done.

The most critical piece for the part-time trainer to learn is how to observe the trainee demonstrating a task and using that observation to provide the trainee with immediate feedback and correction and to provide step-by-step encouragement as correct performance is being approximated.

A small investment in trainer training can have extremely high payoff for both the organization and the trainer.

PROBLEMS OF "SKILL" TRAINING

In a skills-training approach, the problem of analysis becomes both more simple and more complex than in job or task approaches: simpler because the criteria used for testing skill proficiency themselves become standards against which performance is measured; more difficult because the establishment of those criteria actually defines the skill to be trained. The degree of difficulty is quickly recognized if one examines the problems involved in testing a candidate for transition between apprenticeship and journeymanship in a traditional skilled trade. Where there are examinations, tremendous collective effort must be made to obtain test criteria satisfactory to the various forces impacting on the given skilled-trade program. Licensed masters (if licensing is the practice), members of the state education system, business representatives, labor representatives, and so on—all these forces must reach a collective agreement on standards. Often the development of standard test criteria is so difficult that the parties involved abandon the idea of testing and instead develop a course content and establish a time span, accepting anyone who has completed the prescribed course content and followed the program for the established period of time as *ipso facto* a skilled tradesperson.

The complexity of the problem seems to stem from two sources. First, "skill" has a very broad definition; that is, it is the sum of a number of trained behaviors which could in themselves be defined as skills, as a sheet-metal worker learns the "skills" of blueprint reading, layout, machine operation, finishing, measurement, etc. In the trade system this complexity leads to a minimization of the standards required for the trainee to be labeled "skilled." Compromise standards are dropped to a level acceptable to all parties concerned. This is especially true of the academic areas of skill training, at least in the trade schools themselves. However, when a trainee begins on-the-job training as an apprentice working for a journeyman or master, an opposite effect impacts: The already "initiated" journeyman or master tends to maximize the requirements to fit in with his or her own views of the necessary skills. The on-the-job trainer frequently tends to idealize the standards training must meet, perhaps to increase personal stature. This is a natural outgrowth of the "I-went-through-it-the-hard-way" school of thought. In the industrial setting, however, these skilled-trade standards cannot be effectively implemented. The varied definitions of "trade" and the increasing need for skilled people make traditional approaches inadequate. The toolmaker of a generation ago could probably claim competence in a dozen or so skilled trades today. However, the approach is much the same. Somehow, experts define skills by establishing a set of criteria against which the trainee is tested. On passing this test, the trainee is admitted as a skilled practitioner and is assigned to tasks applying these skills.

To effectively carry out skills training, then, the analysis element must first seek out someone in the organization to establish the criteria. Training analysis begins with a member of line management at an organizational level high enough to identify those in the work force who qualify as experts in the skill or skills to be trained. This manager (or group of managers) says in effect: "These are the best people known in this organization in this skill area. They will establish the test criteria to define the skills to be trained." This breadth is required for two reasons. First, there must be a commitment that the criteria finally chosen are acceptable to management in that they meet the quality and quantity requirements expected when the trainee is finally placed into the task or job situation. In other words, because of their arbitrariness and abstraction, the criteria chosen need management commitment. The second reason is that in this case we are dealing with a trainee not in terms of trained behaviors directly related to on-the-line tasks, but rather to those related to generalized skills. An unusual example of this approach is to be found in an electronics organization that has developed the concept of an engineering board for training and examining technicians who, though not degreed engineers, are being qualified as engineers. In this particular organization, a group of senior engineering specialists and engineering managers is assigned the task of examining the technician/engineering candidates and certifying them. Membership on this board varies, but is always based on management's high evaluation of the skills and abilities of the board's members. This certainly hearkens back to the ancient masters' examinations, in which a journeyman tradesperson had to pass a board of masters before becoming a member of their ranks.

If such a committee approach is not possible, a skilled trainer must analyze a given cut of the work force to determine the skills inherent in tasks performed and from this analysis to establish the criteria. Thus if an organization wanted to train people in skills involving hydraulics for the purpose of carrying out machine-repair tasks, the training analyst would have to take two kinds of action: (1) determine the assumed technical requirements for hydraulic trouble shooting and repairing, and (2) observe experienced, qualified repairers in the process of trouble shooting and repairing hydraulic failures. These analyses would be the basis of a list of typical tasks performed, and from this list a set of skill criteria would be developed.

The development of the standards or the set of defining tasks becomes particularly crucial in a skill approach to training. If the skills are defined at too generalized a level, extensive on-line training will be required to successfully accomplish any assigned jobs or tasks. On the other hand, insufficient generalization means that the analyst must break down skills within limitations that will often require a large number of individual training actions. Thus the skill approach becomes a task approach and must be considered as such, with the same constraints. There are then the common limitations of retraining the operator for each assignment because skill proficiency is not transferable from assignment to assignment.

When working with government-supported skill training, this problem of overgeneralization, together with the problem of minimal skills, can so hamper the trainer's objectives that the training becomes totally unusable. In fact, the trainer will often discover that the restrictions placed on the setting of specific standards for performance in the utilization of such sponsored programs as MDTA dissuade this form of assistance. The formalization of institutionally sponsored "apprentice-type" training programs may actually deter the hiring of individuals "certified" by such a program. The quasi-skilled person so certified cannot be expected to transfer the obtained skills to a job situation, so the trainer cannot assume any level of proficiency and must work with this kind of new hire as with an untrained one. Yet the trainer is expected to treat the public program graduate as indeed able to meet the skill standards the organization has established.

Perhaps the clearest warning to the manager of an organization's industrial skill–training system is that the new hire from such institutional training cannot be expected to have the designated skills. The manager must instead prepare some series of entry tests to determine exact performance levels and then develop in-house skill training accordingly. In some circumstances labor contracts forbid such testing and in fact often prevent carrying out the necessary training action to bring the individual's skills to the required standards. In this situation it might be wise to consider having union representation participate in the establishment of these skill standards and in the development of a new way of looking at such a partially skilled individual. Although this particular kind of problem is not insurmountable, the real world tells us that with the limitations imposed by union agreements and the traditional ways of handling contract definitions of skilled personnel, the application of a form of task training may be the only way to achieve the required standard of performance.

THE MODULAR SOLUTION: SKILL TO TASK

A possible answer to this dilemma is again to modularize the training actions, developing an individual instructional system to cover those areas of the individuals' skills not meeting the organization's standards. This means carrying a "skilled" person at the full pay rate during task or vestibule training. In any case, a skill approach to training will permit the development of training actions for use with a large number of trainees over a long period of time without the necessity of a rapid change in content, format, or criteria. This is perhaps one of the greatest advantages of having individual operators participate in a series of specific skill-training actions and then placing those individuals in the work environment for individual or specific task training.

The economic feasibility of such an approach really depends on the number of trainees and the degree of generalization required for the skills. When the number of trainees is large enough and the range of skills to be learned is narrow enough, such training can be extremely economical, for then training actions can be developed which are suitable to vestibule training or to a formal classroom approach for a good part of the training. Then only those specific differences involved in either the job situation or the task situation need be trained on the job. Again, the on-line or on-the-job trainers must become an important part of the development of such a training system. They must be aware of the degree to which trainees are limited in their ability to generalize the skills learned before going on the line. They must realize that the training period extends beyond the classroom or the vestibule for a period on the line where individual task instruction must be given. Thus fairly generalized skill training is combined with very specific task training approaches.

With the separation of the general and the specific, evaluation of the general skills achieved becomes relatively easy. The criteria test for typical tasks to be performed can be established and scored for a large number of people, and the specific task portion of the training can be evaluated just as task training is when the total system is done on line; that is, the on-line trainer will use established quality/quantity and time standards for the task to measure trainee achievement.

ENTRY BEHAVIOR

In this discussion we have been considering generalized approaches to industrial skill-training situations. This is a primary consideration in the management of an effective training system. However, an equally important consideration, since it governs the training system's development of any given training action, is the trainee's entry behavior. In industrial skill training there are usually two kinds of entry behaviors: those of the new hire and those of the substandard performer. A third kind which might also be considered is that of the trainee who has a behavioral problem which must be solved before he or she can become a new hire. This person might be called a "pretrainee," one who for whatever reason must be given some fundamental skills before in-house training can become effective. The functional illiterate may be a case in point. Another is the culturally deprived individual whose motivation is such that in-house training cannot be effective.

The entry behaviors most common in the industrial skill–training situation are those of the new hire. From the trainer's point of view, there are two kinds of new hires: those with experience at a given level of skill or in a given series of tasks the same as, or similar to, those in the organization—the person who has had "experience" in another organization—and those whose skills have not yet been assessed at any point or whose skills or past tasks were quite different from those being considered.

In a job approach the training analyst's first task will be to get together with informants who can provide the information needed to break down the job classification into required skills and discriminating tasks. As a simple example, we can look at the job assignment title of "press operator." The new hire is to be assigned to a press shop to operate any one of a number of machines. The first information source for the training specialist will probably be the industrial engineering department's time-and-motion studies of the operations. With the help of the industrial engineer and the shop supervisor, the training analyst will go through the time studies to find out what skill areas can be generalized for all or most operations in the shop. In this particular case the first skill might be the accurate reading of a job slip, required when the operator is assigned to an operation and has to get stock. Some assignments in this shop are group operations, so the skill of identifying the proper job slip may not be required of all operators. However, it is a skill that can be generalized throughout the shop for most operations.

A second skill that might be generalized is the movement of stock from the dolly or bin into the jig of the press. Placement against the posts or blocks of the jig will generally be appropriate regardless of the assignment. The next skill is starting the machine. Some machines will be operated by foot and others by button. This may seem a relatively simple operation, but the training analyst will have to be very wary of the safety precautions required. Thus the safe starting of the machine could be considered a generalized skill in this situation. Finally, the operator will have to remove the finished blank or, on an automatic machine, stop the operation. The operator will then have to complete the job ticket, particularly where incentives are involved, in order to prepare the output material for the next operation.

This seems to be a relatively simple set of skills and indeed it is. It is unlikely that a vestibule is needed in this situation, but a training press should be made available, one that will enable the operator to utilize each of these skills and enable the trainer or supervisor assigned to training to ensure that these skills are performed to a specified standard. The training press may be on the line and have an assigned rate. It is not necessary to make this a nonproduction assignment; the only requirement is that the training press assignment make use of all the criteria skills.

Once the skills have been identified, the supervisor, the training analyst, and probably the industrial engineer will set up standards for each of them. Standards will be set, of course, in the same way as most other training standards: in terms of time, quality, and unit production. Then the new hire will be brought in and placed on the training press, where a JIT approach can be used until the five criteria standards are met. The new hire might be assigned to this machine and asked a critical question, such as: "Can you operate a punch press?" If the answer is yes, the supervisor/trainer will let the trainee go ahead. If the basic skill standards are met, then the new hire is ready for task training on a regular assignment. If not, he or she will be held on the machine until those standards are met.

This done, the training analyst will go on to the discriminating tasks of the other operations. Then the trainer and the supervisor will look at each press operation to find out how they differ from the operations on the training press, and it is only for these differences that standards will be set as criteria for further training. The entire training sequence of the new hire from training press through first task assignment will probably take no more than 45 minutes to one hour, but with standards established and criteria tests set up, the supervisor/trainer would have a job aid to ensure that training standards are met.

Let us now suppose that our press operator has been on the job for a few months and has bid into a machine shop. As far as the machine shop is concerned, this operator is a new hire and an unskilled one. The training analyst must now deal with a far more complex set of skills and a much larger number of specific tasks. The analysis process, however, will be the same as for the press room. A fourth member may now have to be added to the analysis team, since quality would be an important criterion. This would be especially important in dealing with operator inspection and even more important if one of the inspection tasks were visual, with no use of instruments, for now the trainee would have to be taught the skill of discriminating flaws without aids. In this case vestibule or classroom training would be appropriate, for each of these skills can be trained separately, many without the need of machine applications. In the case of visual inspections, for example, the trainee can be taught the skills of discrimination without ever going near a machine, simply by looking at scores of finished pieces and picking out those not meeting quality standards. Rejects will certainly be available, and a programed instruction approach might well be considered, for this discrimination skill is uniquely suited to it. Instruction skills using instruments such as gauge blocks or other devices could be taught in a similar manner, again without the necessity of going down onto the machine floor.

The sequence of events in the analysis and development of training actions is the same for almost all industrial-skill situations: first, to examine the job classification and determine which skills can be generalized for the job; second, to establish performance standards for those skills; third, to develop typical behaviors or tasks for use in measuring performance; and, fourth, to develop a criteria test for use in determining completion of training and evaluating entry behaviors of the new hire. Once this is completed, performance standards for the discriminating tasks may be determined, and measurements in terms of the task can be established. These will be followed by criteria tests to evaluate trained performance and to determine whether or not a person is trained.

TASK TRAINING

The development of task training usually follows the pattern of a JIT program and is done most effectively on line. Skill training must be analyzed further to isolate those skill areas effectively taught through group media or a specialized training system. The decision to use a vestibule form of programed instruction or a type of formal group training will depend on two criteria: first, the suitability of the method for the particular skill area; second, the number of trainees expected to pass through the program.

RETRAINING AND CORRECTIVE ACTIONS

The retraining situation is quite different. The basic approach is one of problem-solving. In the retraining situation the trainer is called in because something is wrong. The first job is to identify the existing problem. Assuming that performance standards have been established, the first step is identification of the measurable variance. What is the variance? What is considered substandard in this case? How substandard is it? Usually this is stated in terms of a finished operation: too much scrap, too much rework, or too slow an operator. Now the analyst must determine when the variance was first noticed and what differences began to occur then. Is the problem widespread, or are only one or two operators involved? If the problem is widespread, perhaps the situation cannot be controlled by the operators. The training analyst may then have to look elsewhere in the system: a difference in stock, perhaps, or in machine setting or work arrangement. None of these things would be under the control of the operator, and training would make little difference in performance. Is it a nontask situation, that is, some other circumstance of the work change? Perhaps it is a piecework change or a union problem or any one of a number of situations which, again, falls outside the industrial skill training area. True, many of these things could require training, but they are not considered job-task-skill problems.

Suppose that after a complete analysis of inputs, outputs, process changes, feedbacks to the operator, and other environmental changes, the analyst discovers that indeed this is a training problem and that changes in any of these other variables will not affect operator performance. Now the analyst and his or her associates—the supervisor, the quality control person, and the industrial engineer—must observe the tasks in process to find out where the variances occur. This may be carried out through an inspection process, going through each step of the operator's sequence of tasks. Is the output at standard? Usually, following the process from input through output identifies the problem very quickly. In most cases only a single operator needs retraining. Since the standards exist, the supervisor/trainer or whoever is assigned the training responsibility can take the operator through a JIT process to correct substandard behavior and reinforce proper behavior. Checking back after a few hours or a few days to further reinforce standard behavior will usually take care of the problem.

There is a considerable difference between the problems involved in taking an operator who is no longer meeting a standard and retraining him or her on a machine or at a worker's station and those involved in transferring an operator from one station or machine to another. In the first case we are attempting to correct a substandard variance and reinforce the proper behavior. In the second, we are dealing with the same kind of situation we ran into in taking the new hire from skill training to task training, for we are really training a worker new to the task. A popular fallacy which has caused many a training manager heartburn is the assumption that because an operator has done a similar job, he or she can without further training be assigned to a task which does have differences—in standards, in process, in input material, or in output quality or quantity requirements. Let the operator then be returned to the former task for job assignment. He or she will be in the same situation as the experienced operator hired from the outside; before being expected to fully carry out the job, the "new" operator must be tested against the job criteria. When a worker is placed in a new task situation, particularly one similar to the old one, many old skills will be extinguished, and retraining will have to be considered as a new event, not as a correction of substandard behavior.

THE USE OF ON-THE-JOB TRAINING

In most industrial skill situations we will be dealing with an on-the-job training process. Development of such training has four requirements. (1) Both trainer and trainee must be able to identify and understand the standards. (2) The trainer must have clear responsibility for the training assignment and a time allocation within his or her job scope for this function. (3) There must be a formalized feedback system in the form of job aids or procedures which the trainer can use to ascertain that progress is being made. (4) A control system outside of the training environment must be available to test criteria to make sure that the industrial skills being developed meet the requirements of the job in changing situations. Viable standards can be developed from the training analysis, given the time and resources for a rational approach to the training problem.

Trainer preparation is crucial. Whoever is assigned this responsibility must be trained for it. The trainer must not only be a subject-matter expert (proficient in

Instruction Guide   Blanking Press No. 16, Job No. 26

Trainee Sam Williams # 1907   Trainer J. C. Jacobs
                                                                      Date   1/3/67

	Subtask	Criteria	Checked
1.	Obtains production card.	Obtains from Dept. 3 foreman; checks for Press no. and Job no. and informs trainer that he has a card for Press no. 16, Job no. 21. Identifies number of parts to be produced and informs trainer. Clocks card according to station procedure.	JCJ 7:45
2.	Makes stock request.	Checks machine station for stock box. Matches production card to job card. Given a no-stock situation he calls foreman and requests stock. Given a wrong-job-card situation he calls foreman to advise him of status. Checks station for empty output box; if none, informs foreman.	JCJ 8:15
3.	Positions stock.	Obtains piece from box and places in jig correctly in judgment of trainer. Removes both hands from work area.	JCJ 8:15
4.	Actuates press.	Reaches with left hand for piece of stock, then presses start button.	JCJ 8:15
5.	Removes part.	Removes part with right hand and drops in output box.	JCJ 8:30
6.	Repeats 1–5.	Makes a one-hour run, meeting criteria with continuous observation first 10 minutes and at 10-minute intervals after that.	JCJ 9:45
7.	Clocks out production card.	Completes number of parts given on production card. Clocks card according to station procedure.	JCJ 11:15

Sig.: Sam Williams
      JCJ

Figure 1

the skills and tasks involved), but also be able to demonstrate proper behavior, observe it in the trainee, and then reinforce it at the right times. The simplest recommendation that can be made is that the JIT format be used and that each trainer be given thorough training. Some assurance of adequate performance can be obtained through the use of a job aid or procedural format. This outlines the key tasks the trainee is to perform and the standards to be met for each of them. Then the trainee is put through the process and graded on each key task until the formal procedure is completed. This procedure is the basis of the on-the-job evaluation, for the evaluator can use this very same procedural format to evaluate the trainee's performance on the job against the key task standards.

Figure 1 on p. 167 is a sample procedure based on the press operation discussed above.

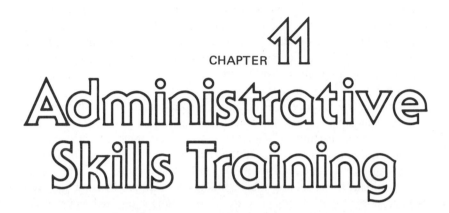

CHAPTER 11

Administrative Skills Training

FUNCTIONS IN ADMINISTRATIVE SKILLS TRAINING

Defining the areas of industrial skills is not too difficult. However, when we turn to what might be called the area of administrative skills, definition becomes more complicated. The former is for the most part limited to the "blue collar," or hourly, employee; the latter includes the salaried, or "white collar," employee, a designation which covers a considerable range of jobs and skills—from messenger or file clerk to the senior staff specialist. Let us define the administrative skills area as including all salaried employees who deal primarily with the administration of the organization, excluding individuals involved in direct sales, supervision, and technical fields requiring specific prehire training in formal accredited programs.

MISSIONS FOR ADMINISTRATIVE TRAINING SYSTEMS

Even with these limitations, the potential missions for a training system or systems in the administrative skills area are quite wide. For example, one potential mission could be to bring about a specified standard of performance for new hires who enter into a job classification without the necessary skills. This would include training actions, such as teller training in a bank or casualty underwriter training in an insurance company. In each case entry skills required for hire are not specific to the job classification itself. In the case of the insurance underwriter, fairly extensive behavior changes will be required before the incumbent can undertake job responsibilities. The underwriter trainee probably has never seen a rate manual or even read the exclusions of a policy. And the person hired as a teller trainee is not likely to have operated the equipment in a teller's cage or, for that matter, to have justified a cash balance.

NEW–HIRE TRAINING AND INCUMBENT TRAINING

A second potential mission for such a training system would be the specific task training of new hires with certain entry skills for a job class such as typist, stenographer, or secretary. On a more complex level, the training of an experienced programmer or systems analyst in a new operation would be of the same order.

A third mission typical of such a system is training employees in the system with a certain level of skills in current assignments to upgrade and prepare them for more complex job assignments. An example of this is the training of keypunch or computer operators as programmers.

Moving away from the new-hire or upgrade situation, other missions might include training personnel to perform to new standards, or, on the same order, retraining operators whose performances are below acceptable standards. Still another possibility for a training mission is the updating of incumbents in a position to exploit technical advances in the systems employed by the organization. The use of automated equipment in accounting subsystems is one example; another very real one is the changeover to an automated system from paper-and-pencil record keeping in, say, a production scheduling operation. The point here is that individuals would be having their own skills updated or changed. There can also be actions to train a whole group of individuals when an entire process is changed or when the system itself is altered to take advantage of new methods, equipment, or systems improvements. All of these missions would be appropriate in different circumstances for the training function accountable for administrative skills training.

If we examine training from the point of view of the trainees—that is, if we concern ourselves with the way employees look at training—we can generalize in terms of two kinds of training action: one for the new hire or upgrade, another for retraining a single incumbent or group of employees within a system. In setting up a training system to act in the case of a new hire or an upgrade, we are operating with a set of problems very much like those of the industrial skill training area. The first step in establishing such a system is to identify standards from which we can define the generalized skills and the subsequent specific task skills to be trained. However, in administrative training skill definition becomes more complex: There are many more given conditions in most cases. Of course, in some cases, such as clerical situations, the method of operation is identical to that of the industrial skill situation: Given a set of entry skills clearly defined by the job classification, only specific task implementation is necessary. For example, when a typist is hired into an organization, the selection process has already determined the skill level. Ability to type 45 words per minute on a given typewriter fairly well defines the competence level of the new-hire trainee. All that remains is the application of this skill in the specific task assignment. Little more is necessary in this fairly simple on-the-job training process than a job aid in the form of a task check-off sheet which the supervisor can use to carry the new employee through the task sequence. Of importance here is the fact that such a job aid can be prepared for the supervisor and specific feedbacks built into the system so that entering trainees can be expected to follow a consistent sequence to its conclusion. The check sheet would list all subtasks of the assignment; as each is completed to standard, the trainee and the supervisor initial the proper space. Subtasks not performed to the standards would be cause for further instruction until the sheet could be completely initialed.

This appears to be the same process followed in hiring an experienced machine operator into the industrial environment: Generalized skills are available; only the specific task must be trained.

ENTRY BEHAVIORS AND SKILL TRAINING

It was wasteful of trainer and supervisor time to go through any task that covers a skill already completed by a particular trainee. Of course, a skill-level test at the selection point is important if a specified standard of performance is expected at a given time. This is the simple side of the situation.

Far more difficult are those administrative job areas in which the skills are not easily defined or discerned in the usual framework of employment testing. The casualty underwriter is an excellent example of such a case: The trainer must grapple with a series of decision-making skills based on a rather complex set of data where the wrong decision can be costly to the organization. Indeed, one might ask whether such training can be effective or whether we must again turn to "experience" to solve the problem of developing a casualty insurance underwriter. Although standards of performance and the means to measure performance against those standards are the most important jobs of training analysis, the system undertaking the training of administrative skills such as underwriter training has an additional project which, though complex and difficult, provides an advantage that the industrial skill training system does not have. This project is the clear definition of selection requirements and establishment thereby of selection standards. The advantage is that entry behaviors of new hires can be much more specifically defined than the behaviors of those discussed in the industrial situation. In the hire of hourly employees the expense of establishing and testing entry behaviors is often more than the expenditure needed when only the most grossly unqualified applicants are eliminated. In administrative skills, however, the situation is somewhat different. Pragmatically, the market is more flexible for such employment, at least at present, and the system can afford to reject a larger percentage of applicants. In this context, the task of defining entry behaviors becomes an important part of establishing training actions.

STANDARDS FOR ENTRY BEHAVIORS

How can such standards for entry behaviors be set, and once set, how does the system measure them? The analysis of these entry behaviors begins with the examination of current employees. From employment records and direct interviews with people now in the jobs, the training analyst collects data on the entry behaviors of these people as new hires. Evaluation of the success and failure of those now in the organization, those who have left the organization, and those rejected on application will enable the analyst to draw a biographical profile with a series of criteria for selection. If possible, the training analyst should expand these data by learning from organizations with similar classifications their experience with various entry behaviors and their evaluation of the successs and failure of employees.

With these data the training analyst might enlist an outside consultant, such as a clinical or industrial psychologist, to infer from the biographical profiles what types of testing are applicable. In most cases, with or without the help of specialists, fairly accurate insights into the kinds of entry behaviors that have a high predictability of success are possible both in the training situation and on the job. One may find, for example, that liberal arts graduates with a given Kuder interest profile toward social service and clerical skills have the highest probability of success. One may also find that other factors—family geographical area, family size, marital status, etc.—sometimes used as selection criteria cannot be validated for this use and that they do not define entry behaviors, although they can predict on-the-job success. With the help of a testing specialist, the training analyst may run the existing work force in the job classification through a series of objective or subjective tests to develop a set of cutting scores that will further define entry behaviors.

With these data about behavior, the analyst can consider the basic structure of the training actions. However, performance standards must still be established as well as the means to measure performance against those standards.

DEFINING PERFORMANCE STANDARDS

Defining performance standards for jobs like those of insurance underwriter or financial analyst or perhaps even employment representative of a personnel department is a fairly tall order. The problem differs from that of the industrial skills situation, since in this case the development of standards can be a matter of "art" rather than of "science." How can we define underwriter, analyst, or interviewer? Probably each position requires a wide range of skills. The standards of measurement probably differ for every organization and may even differ within a single organization from time to time. Further, the means of measurement may themselves be unclear and poorly defined. What, indeed, does a casualty insurance underwriter do? What do we look for in such a person? How do we ever know when an underwriter is fully trained? Management's usual answer is that the person is considered trained when able to carry out the required duties; in other words, when the supervisor can trust the person to make decisions. Pressing further, we could probably get the manager to say that this is a matter of time, of experience, that it is a problem for on-the-job training, and that little formal education is required.

In one typical situation a training analyst asked the employment supervisor what skills an interviewer needed.

"Well, for example, one of the skills is to be able to make good reference checks," replied the supervisor.

"What is a good reference check and how do you recognize it?"

"Well, it's a feeling you have. Some people have it and some haven't."

The real question here is not how to train an employment interviewer to satisfy this particular supervisor, because this can easily be done simply by putting the person through a graduated sequence of reference checks, reinforcing the behavior when the supervisor was satisfied and extinguishing any behavior which did not satisfy the supervisor. The question is: Will this employment interviewer, when transferred to another location with a new supervisor, still be considered a satisfactory performer as far as the reference-checking skill is involved?

EVALUATING PERFORMANCE STANDARDS

The importance of setting clear and realistic performance standards has been one of our major themes. This need is not limited to administrative situations. It has been especially stressed for administrative skills because standards are so often lacking here. This same lack becomes a critical problem in professional and technical situations.

Good performance standards become a foundation for effective training. It may be helpful to look at a checklist for evaluating the quality of performance standards:

1. Does each standard contain a task, activity, or responsibility description?
2. Has an indicator or "measuring stick" been identified for each standard?
3. If it is a quantitative standard, has a way of counting the units been identified?
4. Can the units be counted often enough to provide performance feedback?
5. Does the performer have direct access to the counts?
6. If it is a qualitative standard, does it involve a tangible output?
7. Could the qualitative performance be evaluated by an uninvolved third party?
8. Does the qualitative standard include a calendar of measuring points?
9. Are measuring points frequent enough to provide performance feedback?
10. Does the standard include a consequence for meeting or not meeting it?
11. Does the performer agree that the standard can be met?
12. If the performer meets all standards set and does nothing else, will expectations be met?
13. Does the performer's boss agree to the standard?
14. Does the performer's boss's boss agree to the standard?
15. If there is a tangible output, does the receiver of the output understand and agree to the standard?

DEVELOPING A PERFORMANCE MODEL

One approach seems workable in dealing with the complex set of skills and tasks involved here—developing a model from which performance and performance standards can be described. The objective of such an approach is development of a series of typical tasks which will define the end product: the trained worker. The model to be put together is one which, if it really represented the system, would satisfy all minimum requirements of management for a particular assignment. The stress here is on "minimum" requirements. Again, as in most standard-setting problems, we are looking for the *sine qua non*—the musts—of the training situation.

Creation of such a model requires considerable subject-matter expertise. It is extremely important that the model be built by a team which includes both technical specialists and management. The training analyst's job as such is to assist other members of the team in defining and building this model and, from the model, standards. This is done through the usual process of "If this, then that" interrogation. The analyst begins by asking the experts, "What does this person do when trained?" From a general statement, the analyst continues with: "If that, then what?" For example, in the case of the employment interviewer/trainee, the training analyst may ask the supervisor, "If the trainee makes a direct telephone call to every employer, what then?" "Well, that's good, but, of course, that isn't all that's necessary for a good reference." The training analyst prods, "What else is required?" The reply might be, "Well, the interviewer has to get all the information." The training analyst might ask, "And what is all the information; what do you mean by that? Can you give me an example?" The supervisor might look back introspectively and reply, "The exact starting and termination dates of the person's employment at a particular company." Here the training analyst might ask the key question, "If the reference check produces the starting and termination dates of the candidate, then will it be complete and satisfactory?" The supervisor would probably say, "No," and the training analyst would continue question-by-question until obtaining a complete definition of what a trained employment interviewer does to get a satisfactory reference check. This would then be included in the model of the "trained" employment interviewer.

The same process would be applied in building a model of a trained casualty insurance underwriter, for in this case the manager would be asked precisely what is done by the underwriter, and the supervisor might reply, "Well, one thing is to determine the correct rates for an insurance policy." The training analyst could then say, "What tools are used for this job?" The supervisor would show the training analyst the proper manuals; the analyst could ask the key question, "If the underwriter, using these manuals, correctly rates every policy, would he or she be considered to be performing at standard?" The reply might be that there are certain key decisions in determining the acceptability of a business, and then the training analyst and the subject-matter experts would go through the arduous process of defining precisely the kinds of decisions made by the underwriter and the information needed to make them. But gradually, by careful and patient interrogation of the system, a set of standards based on a model could be developed.

The creation of this model by the training analyst and the subject-matter experts is only the beginning. The next step is to test the relevance of the model in the real world of the job. The analyst and his or her associates must now find out whether or not the underwriters in the organization who are considered to be trained meet enough of the model standards to demonstrate its relevancy. What will probably happen is that the model will be modified in terms of the actual standards being met. Eventually a usable model will be built if care is taken.

So far the model is one only of standards, more or less a picture of the end results expected of an experienced underwriter. The training analyst now enters the next stage: the careful observation and interrogation of underwriters who approximate the model. What are their minute-by-minute activities? How do they obtain the end results which meet the standard? What skills do they demonstrate, and to what degree? What specific tasks do they perform? All of these things must be described and defined in the process of preparing for the development of an appropriate training action. The objective in observing the underwriters' activities is, as it was in the industrial skill situation, the identification of skill areas which can be generalized and tasks which delineate differences in assignments. It may be found, for example, that the process the underwriter goes through in deciding the acceptability of a risk is essentially a skill performance, just as is the operation of a milling machine for a machine operator. The process or series of discriminations which the underwriter makes in reaching these decisions are the subject matter used in training people to make decisions. It may be that the series of discriminations which go into making the decision are relatively clear and logical and that they can be based on some sort of decision-tree pattern. It may also be that the series of discriminations are broader and that an element of chance, which is narrowed through experience, enters into it. If this is true, the more important discriminations can be taught to the new trainee as generalized skills, and the elements of guess or experience may be considered task skills, paralleling industrial training. In other words, part of the decision making—comparison of the application with available manual data and existing risks on the books—may be part of a formalized training program, whereas new risk areas and other considerations may be trained on the job. From this structure, a training approach can be used to bring about the desired standards of behavior.

IDENTIFYING NEEDS BY IDENTIFYING BEHAVIOR

In all of this, the primary job of the training analyst is to assist the subject-matter expert in examining the system to identify the required standards and behaviors. In most cases involving the more complex administrative skills, development is largely a matter of researching available material. Most of the skills, such as the discrimination-decision-making process of the underwriter, have a fairly wide application, and often existing program material can be adapted to the purpose at hand. Appropriate programs and materials can be examined and tried in order to find out what modifications might be required to make them applicable to the present situation. The selection of a training system here is a matter of economic feasibility: If a large enough number of individuals are to be trained in enough skills and tasks, we can afford to make extensive modifications in existing material or, perhaps, to develop completely new material. On the other hand, if a relatively small number are to be trained, or if training is to be developed for an extremely complex skill and task area such as systems analysis in a computer operation, we may have to consider all of the training actions as task actions and handle them on an apprentice basis. This, of course, depends on the time available for this kind of training. To develop a systems analyst capable of handling relatively complex problems could take a number of years on an OJT basis, even if the trainee begins with the basic computer knowledge. The systems analyst will still have to be taught to operate in a new system. Indeed, this is an excellent example of a training action for a small number of people which requires a very careful combination of classroom experience or formal training and on-the-job instruction. The new college graduate hire may find his or her time split in thirds, with one part spent on graduate studies in systems, another as an instructor of computer technology and advanced programming, and the last as a trainee systems analyst or senior programmer. The entire process of training such a person may take one or two years.

The general model (Fig. 1) for a system to develop new hires for administrative positions is composed of the following four elements:

Definition element With the help of a training analyst, management and technical specialists in the field would establish the kinds of functions the training job incumbent will carry out. The output would probably be a functional job description of the various classes of actions the incumbent will take.

Standard-setting element These same individuals would establish specific performance standards generally applicable to everyone in the particular job classification or function defined by the functional job description. The output would be a set of standards for measuring behavior.

Evaluation element These standards would be tested against actual performance of incumbents in the jobs defined by functional descriptions. An important input at this stage would be management's separation of incumbents performing to standard from those who are not. The output would be a set of performance standards relevant to the real organization.

FLOW MODEL

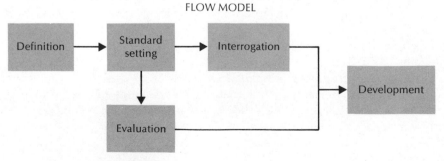

Figure 1

Interrogation and observation element The training analyst would examine the day-by-day activities of the successful incumbents to discover what they do in order to meet standards.

TRAINING BASED ON THE MODEL

Now program development is possible. The training analyst, the subject-matter experts, and the successful incumbents began to generalize the behavior demonstrated in those activities important to the meeting of standards. From these generalizations skill applications can be defined; where generalization is not possible, it will be necessary to consider task approaches. From the skills can be built a general model of the trained incumbent. Understanding that a number of task elements have been left out, those responsible for development of the training action will plan, realizing that the full job of training is not done when the trained behaviors meet all aspects of the general model. Training will still be necessary for those tasks which do not generalize from incumbent to incumbent. Special attention must be given to this problem in the process of training: Both management and the incumbents must be committed to the idea that although standards established by the training actions are met, further training may still be necessary for some aspects of the jobs. Some action will have to be taken to provide a normal experience cycle.

The general model must now be tested. The training analyst and the trainer will now have to return to the system to observe and compare incumbents against the model. Are the activities described in the model performed? Are they common to the job family? Are they generally consistent within that group of incumbents who are considered successful?

IDENTIFYING KEY ACTIVITIES AS A BASIS FOR TRAINING

From this investigation, key activities will be discovered that separate successful performers from marginal or unsuccessful performers. These key differences are the important measuring points of the training process. The trainer's directive is to bring about successful performance, and the keys to successful performance can be discovered only by analyzing the general model in relation to the actual organization. When the general model is judged valid, training actions can be developed. We already know a great deal about what is to be trained: the output behaviors of any training actions. What is needed now is the means to obtain the required behavior changes. A number of varied and complex trained behaviors are sought, and a number of training methods will be utilized.

A most practical approach to method choice is to find out from successful performers the specific kinds of tasks and/or skills they use on the job. The person responsible for training development is acting as a feedback source for the recognized subject-matter experts. This requires taking the very crucial role of interpreting the experts' points of view into specific action plans, and the trainer will probably find that many successful incumbents think in terms of either having the trainee watch a successful performer at work or having the successful performer tell the trainee how to do it. In pursuing these predicted responses, the training specialist must determine exactly what the trainee will be told and shown. From this a flow of training actions can be conceived, utilizing a number of specific cases, problems, or simulated tasks through which the trainee can be moved over a period of time.

TRAINING ACTIONS

A workable structure now appears; training actions begin to separate into three kinds of activities. First, there are the fairly formal structured approaches which develop concept or vocabulary to enable the trainee to talk about what is expected of him or her. Then the trainee is moved into a second kind of process in which these concepts are structured into individual or group exercises, with the trainer or subject-matter expert available to provide immediate feedback and reinforcement when successful behavior is demonstrated. Last, the trainee is placed on the job as an assistant or apprentice and tests the generalized exercises in real-work situations, with assignments limited to the exercise tasks. Thus the trainee moves from the instruction to the exercise or simulation to the job, skill area by skill area. As the trainee completes the general model processes, more and more time can be given to the experience phase of the training action, and those unique tasks not included in the general model can be started.

Once training activities in the general model process are completed, on-the-job training occupies 100% of the trainee's working time. The trainer's job is to provide the trainee with timely feedback about on-the-job performance. The trainer is now the voice of experience, telling the trainee, "Hey, you're doing pretty well" or "You made a mistake there; what other alternatives do you have? What else should you try?"

The length of time required for this process is directly dependent on the complexity of the administrative functions to be learned and the amount of generalization possible in the job. The more it is possible to generalize skills that are widely applicable and highly consistent for a time span, the greater the number of formal structured training actions that can be carried out; the more structure there is to such a program, the more rapidly the desired behaviors can be acquired. This is true because the structured situation can concentrate on a limited behavioral area without the incursion of job activities directed toward specifically defined performance. On the actual job these incursions are quite frequent, due to rapid·shifts from one job to another. They consist of internal administrative tasks which are in themselves fairly simple and highly repetitious; they tend to be quickly learned and once learned, add nothing to the behavioral repertoire of the trainee. In the formal structured situation, these incursions can be controlled so that they are introduced only when they apply to the specific behavior being trained. The process can then carry a new hire far more rapidly from the point of entry to the point where only those unique tasks which identify individual jobs remain than if the trainee is put on a pure one-to-one apprentice relationship with the subject-matter expert for a period of time.

It might also be noted here that in the trainee/apprentice situation, the master performer often finds it difficult to devote enough energy to the training process. Usually this person is responsible for meeting production standards and is seldom evaluated on ability to produce a trained individual.

Most of the problems of developing a system to train administrators or administrative technicians arise in retraining incumbents when new standards arc introduced or when there are major changes in the job itself. Perhaps the most common example of this is the change in the administrative paper-processing or decision-making process from unautomated to semi- or fully automated systems, as in the introduction of a computer system in warehousing and distribution. Both the introduction of standards and the introduction of a new system can be met by the general model approach. However, this situation differs from one in which individuals are to be trained, for here the training analyst is concerned not with points of individual decision or the decision-makers, but with the flow of material or the process flow for decision-making. In other words, the task in this case is to analyze the system itself.

DEFINING A MODEL FOR ACCEPTABLE PERFORMANCE

The first step in analysis, then, is to build a general model which will answer the kinds of questions raised in Chapter 4 for the analysis of training needs. These questions are now directed toward a system model rather than an individual behavior model:

1. What is the mission or goal in terms of the organization's objectives? What will it be after the change?

2. What is the economic gain if the new goal is met?

3. What is the economic loss if the new goal is not met?

4. Does the difference between the answers to questions 2 and 3 demonstrate an economic worth of the system change?

5. What new outputs will be required?

6. What outputs are presently produced?

7. What differences are there?

8. To whom do the present outputs go? To whom will they go after the change?

9. What will be done with the outputs?

10. How are the outputs evaluated by the system receiving them? How will they be evaluated after the change?

11. Do the outputs of the change system meet the requirements of the receiving system?
12. What inputs will be required to meet the new goal?
13. What inputs are presently received?
14. What differences are there?
15. Who are the input sources? What source changes will there be?
16. What is done with the inputs? What will be done after the change?
17. Do the inputs meet requirements?
18. Are standards or requirements known to the input source? How will they be communicated after the change?
19. What feedback is provided the input source? What feedback will be provided?
20. Who is involved in changing input to output now? Who will be involved after the change?
21. What are their accountabilities now? What will they be afterward?
22. What are their goals in relation to the system mission or goal? What will they be?
23. What outputs are required from each one? What outputs will be required?
24. What standards (dollars, quality, or schedule) are used to evaluate the outputs? What standards will be used?
25. Who receives feedback on outputs? Who will receive it?
26. What form does the feedback take? What form will it take?
27. When does each person receive feedback on outputs? When will it be received after the change?
28. What form does the feedback take? What form will it take?
29. What controls are applied when feedback identifies a variance from standard? What controls are planned?

The answers to these questions for both the old and the new systems will allow the training analyst to define the difference between the two and to develop the new generalized skill requirements for satisfactory performance in the new system. The media and methods used in the development process for this training follow exactly the pattern discussed in the first section of this chapter. Special problems exist in the implementation of such a training program, however, since it usually deals with a one-shot training problem and must include careful consideration of the cost parameters in terms of expected results.

RELATION OF SYSTEM CHANGES TO TRAINING REQUIREMENTS

The more extensive the system changes, in number of both operations affected and possible alternative decisions or flows of material, the more extensive and time-consuming the training will be. It will become more expensive also in terms of training employee-hours and development costs. In most cases, however, the potential costs of nonutilization of the new system outweigh training costs. This is true whether these costs result from ineffectiveness of employees or discontinuation of the system. In this situation the trainer can usually expect strong management support in implementing the change, and the cost parameters will be widened because of the need for training. It can be assumed, further, that cost restrictions will not be so narrow as to necessitate compromise in the training design.

TRAINING FOR SYSTEM CHANGES

Let us look at the type of action and structure required: During the analysis, a model was developed for the new system. This model is not the generalized skill model that was devised in functional training, as for the underwriter or personnel interviewer; rather, it is a very specific model of the new system itself, showing exactly what processes are to be carried out. This system model describes not only the general processes, but also the human operators involved, with their inputs and outputs, and with standards of performance described for each operator. A similar model has also been drawn for the old system. There are some similarities in most cases: Some operations are quite similar in both the new and the old systems; some are quite different. Quite frequently the decision points important in the new system will carry different weights from those in the old.

The objective is not to train skills to individuals so much as it is to train a group of individuals to operate in the system. Training individuals, therefore, may be less effective than training the entire group as a team. The paper model developed in the form of a flow sheet or similar device becomes a model for a simulation exercise or series of exercises. The actual materials, forms, and data to be used on the job in the new system will be simulated in the form of inputs used in the exercise. It is critical at this point for the training specialist to consult with the system designers and managers regarding alternatives which might be fed into the system. What possible problems might be introduced into the real system that could be thought of as tripping key decision tasks? In other words, when this training simulation is utilized, the trainer will want it to introduce step by step, on a graduated scale of difficulty, the problems that the operators will face on the job. The key question that the program developer will ask the subject-matter experts is: "What is the most critical mistake that can be made in handling this particular input? Or, what is the worst thing this person can do in this process as far as the rest of the system is concerned?"

The simulation designed for most internal administrative systems will probably take the form of a series of in-baskets, possibly with calendar-dating and, if necessary, with on-line computer use. Regardless of how complex the real-life system is, the training model must be based on it and the attempt made to simulate it as closely as possible without duplicating tasks. In the process of creating a simulation, areas common within the new system and those common in both the new and old systems need not be included except to reinforce successful performances. Also, in the exercises themselves, the extraneous data of the real-life situation are eliminated. Thus the individuals being trained will be able to concentrate on the particular tasks involved in the simulation without being distracted by other operations required in their jobs. At each critical decision point throughout the system, the trainer will have to detail a method of obtaining feedback to determine the quality of performance of each incumbent. This task might be accomplished by beginning training with those individuals closest to the output end of the system, providing them with partially processed inputs adequate in all respects for the job—that is, error-free inputs. As these operators are able to perform to standard, errors will be introduced into their inputs gradually until they are able to recognize them. They will then be expected to discriminate between acceptable and unacceptable inputs.

Then training can begin for the individuals who provide inputs for the operators mentioned above, who in turn will provide the new trainees with feedback on the adequacy of their behaviors. Thus those previously taught to identify errors in inputs will now feed back any errors to the person furnishing that input. Training can thus proceed back through the system until each member can correctly feed back data to the preceding member. Finally, the entire human system can be given problems that begin at the first input, and the trainer will have only to observe the final outputs to be assured that the entire system is at standard. This approach to this particular training problem will probably be quite satisfactory to management, since the entire operation is not pulled off the job at once. In fact, in this way it may be possible to introduce the new system element by element rather than all at once.

Administrative training, then, introduces a new aspect into the creation of the training action: *constructive modeling*. Whether the model is of a complex function or of a system with many human members, its creation will enable the trainer to formulate behavior changes against preset standards and to test those standards in real life. The development of a constructive model will find increasing application as the complexity of the training problem increases. It would seem that this approach is the only effective one in dealing with system training, the training of a number of individuals to work together each in his or her own portion of the total system.

CHAPTER 12

Sales Training

MISSIONS FOR SALES-TRAINING SYSTEMS

Four kinds of behavior-change mission can be used to define sales-training systems. The first is the development and maintenance of a system to train individuals who have never performed as "sales persons" to carry out such behaviors as constitute satisfactory sales performance. This is another way of saying that the mission is to take people who have never sold and make them into people who can sell, but such an approach is necessary, if only to make one point: Many kinds of people are designated by the word "salesperson" or a word like it, and each organization defines and classifies its sales personnel in different ways. A sales-training system could deal with any group, from inside sales correspondents to order takers to retail clerks to account servicers to cold-canvass salespeople. The behaviors required at one point in this broad range differ markedly from the others.

The second probable mission is the development and maintenance of a system to train individuals who are presently performing below standard in a sales capacity to meet performance standards. This kind of system can deal with such specific problems as territory change, market change, rehabilitation of salespersons whose productivity has been substandard, etc.

A third mission is to carry out new-product training through what may be a continuing cycle of one-shot training actions.

A fourth mission, one not usually considered part of sales training but that shares more characteristics with sales training than with any other kind, is training a salesperson to be a sales manager. This transition process is more logically considered a form of sales training than a form of management training, since most organizations require more selling activities than managerial actions from lower-level sales managers.

SELECTION CRITERIA AND PERFORMANCE
REQUIREMENTS FOR SALES TRAINEES

In developing a system for training insurance underwriters, the two critical problems were selection criteria and standards. In sales training these problems are even more critical because of the multiple meanings of the word "salesperson." Considering the new-hire problem first, step one in the development of a sales-training system is to seek a working definition of the word "salesperson." What is the salesperson really expected to do? What are the organization's expectations of him or her at various career points? At first glance, this is a fairly simple question. Standards are quite clear: Salespersons are to produce a given quota in volume, dollars, and mix, or perhaps they are to service a given dollar volume of accounts so that the organization does not lose a customer. Perhaps they are to do a little of both. But these two kinds of standards—the production of new business and the maintenance of existing business—can require totally different behaviors of the individuals charged with the commitment. Nonetheless, these definitions of productivity are end results of the salesperson's performance and are therefore useful in setting objectives for the sales department.

For purposes of changing behavior, though, these standards are too generalized for application. For example, after questioning a number of sales representatives of a casualty insurance company, all of whom carry out aggressive cold-canvass new-business actions, it was found that when dollar volume is the only standard, no discriminating differences can be found in the way high and low producers do their job. It is nearly impossible to define sales behavior on the basis of dollar volume, yet to establish and maintain a training program of any kind, the trainer must be able to identify key behaviors and the constraints within which they are appropriate and successful. Thus an organization must clarify its expectations of sales performance in terms of all variables that have possible significance. A change in approach is needed in analyzing the insurance sales group: In addition to premium volume, we will have to consider policy mix by profitability, territory makeup, time in territory, account volume, and additional sales volume. These further expectations permit us to group sales personnel with a degree of homogeneity and to identify elements of behaviors as a basis for discriminating between satisfactory and unsatisfactory performance.

DEFINING PERFORMANCE STANDARDS AS A TRAINING PROBLEM

To get a behavioral profile that will give us a set of performance standards usable in training, we must examine the four sets of expectations with which a salesperson deals. First are the expectations of managers, who, according to those expectations, determine whether or not a salesperson is successful. Second are the expectations of the customer, who is most likely to buy from someone who "behaves like a salesperson." Third are the expectations of the organizational subsystems supporting sales, such as the order department, the shipping department, and, in the case of insurance sales, the underwriting department. The subsystems expect certain behaviors of the salesperson in order that they may operate efficiently, and the efficiency of their operation profoundly affects the success (or failure) of the salesperson. And fourth are the expectations of the salespersons themselves, for these expectations determine the performance criteria.

Management expectations Management must define such variables as the differences in: territory, product mix, product value or cost, seasonal effects, and career stages. How do management's expectations of a salesperson change throughout his or her career? Certainly management expects different standards of performance for a salesperson who has been in the organization for one year and one who has been with it for 10, 20, or 30 years. Other variables to be defined are differences in the support subsystem and the workload mix. Does management, for example, expect the salesperson to service the accounts, to take orders as well as to do missionary work and develop new accounts? If management, for example, expects missionary work for which the end results are not measured in sales volume, how are those end results measured?

Each organization probably has a number of other variables applicable to itself, but once these variables can be discriminated, individuals with the title of "salesperson" can be classified in accordance with their common functions and performance requirements. The account service representative in San Diego, California, will not be expected to perform in the same way as the missionary salesperson in Dallas, Texas, or the new-account representative in New York. In most selling organizations this imposes a severe burden on the management group. The idea that each of 12 territory salespersonnel spread throughout the country must meet individual standards, with each standard requiring distinct behaviors and having its own selection criteria, could complicate the job of sales management! But for the trainer, the development of training actions depends on the specification of standards. The trainer does not expect management to have its salary or reward structure totally congruent with the training standards. It would be nice if rewards were based totally on performance against individually defined standards, but this is not likely in any organization, even a commission-sales organization.

Customer expectations This same sort of investigation has to take place at the customer level. Experience shows that an individual successful in selling to manufacturers of women's garments in New York may not be successful in selling to this same market in, say, Atlanta, Georgia; customer expectations seems to differ geographically. This is the least of the differences that may be discovered. Different expectations will probably be determined by the product line, the number of people a salesperson must see before meeting the person who makes the purchase decision, buying volume, business traditions, and so on, depending on the individual market.

Our purpose is to discover how the customer's expectations affect the success, or lack of it, of a qualified sales representative. One of the steps in training a new hire is to bring about behavior appropriate to one or more classes of customer. We can expect that different behaviors will be necessary. Consider the door-to-door salesperson who memorizes a sales presentation. We assume that the sales pitch has been designed to meet the expectations of enough prospects to enable the salesperson to gain some degree of success. However, the fewer the prospects whose expectations are met by this canned pitch, the greater the energy required by the salesperson to meet management's expectations, and the greater the reward per sale the salesperson must receive for success. In any event, most salespeople are taught to interpret customer reactions and to produce behaviors appropriate to these reactions, so that they can respond in ways acceptable to the prospective buyer. The fact that such behavior may meet the expectations of neither the salesperson nor the sales manager is beside the point; the customer prefers to buy from someone who acts in a way *he or she believes appropriate* to a salesperson.

Subsystem expectations   The analyst looks closely at the expectations of the subsystems receiving the salesperson's inputs. For the salesperson to be successful requires some commitment from individuals who carry out the balance of the organization's responsibilities to customers, such as the order department, shipping department, etc. Here is where paperwork training seems to come in, for these support systems expect the inputs they receive from salespersons to meet their own needs; usually the individual salesperson will have a far higher likelihood of success if these expectations are satisfied. Although it is a relatively small part of the overall training action, paperwork training can be critical, since these administrative functions can absorb a large amount of a salesperson's energy and time.

Salespersons' expectations   Finally, the analyst must investigate the expectations of the salespeople. What behaviors do successful salespersons feel are appropriate to their function? And what kinds of behaviors have unsuccessful salespersons expected of themselves? Experience with a large number of salespeople in various training activities shows that unless the individual salesperson's expectations can be met within the organization, likelihood of success is quite low; there is a loss of motivation. Management often accuses such people of having the wrong attitude, but essentially their attitudes are quite right from their own point of view. Here the analyst tries to discover which sales behaviors are rewarded by the organization, whatever the unit of payoff. After all, the only thing that makes a salesperson successful is the fact that he or she is rewarded in some way—with money or recognition or some other unit of value which the organization deems the reward of success. However, the salesperson's expectations may be quite different from those management assumes him or her to have.

Once this information has been collected, the training analyst must collate the data and attempt to find a set of expectations which can be used as performance standards which will discriminate between success and lack of success. It is not suggested that these standards be highly quantitative; it is perhaps practical to consider that just the simple terms *success* or *failure* be used. At any rate, with these standards, we should be able to create a fairly accurate model for each sales representative. Unfortunately, this still will not satisfy the economic requirements of the organization, for it is doubtful that any organization could consider each individual in it as a separate training problem. And so the compromise begins!

BUILDING A PERFORMANCE MODEL

In developing a general model, the trainer will bring together as much data about expectations as possible. Collecting information about the various expectations with which a salesperson deals not only is the easiest approach to the development of the general model, but it also plays an extremely important role in the measurement of sales performance. This point of view is necessary because purely quantitative standards present only a partial picture of sales performance. True enough, many salespersons are evaluated on the basis of a given dollar volume and/or product mix, but many are also expected to meet standards just as important though somewhat less quantifiable. For example, the missionary salesperson working for a distiller or as a medical detailer for an ethical drug company is not expected to take orders or to bring in a volume of sales dollars; he or she may meet a call quota or be measured by inference based on a change of product volume in a territory of a given class of possible customer.

Another class of unquantifiables is frequently used to measure cold-canvass salespeople: the development of prospects for future closings. Often the sales function itself is divided between the cold-canvass prospectors and the closers. Because so many of the variables in the situation are beyond his or her control, the cold-canvasser is usually evaluated on the basis of the number of prospect cards or interest reports turned in to the sales organization or judged on the number of actual sales made through his or her prospects (although this may be inferred, as it was in the case of the missionary salesperson). But as in the other levels of expectation with which a salesperson deals, a number of possible measures exist: sales reports, expense accounts, prospect quality, attendance at sales meetings, conformity to the rules of the organization, etc.

In most cases the various measures applied are directly pertinent to the selling job, for the actions being measured affect sales results in terms of dollars brought in by the orders. Converting expectations into performance standards becomes even more difficult when one considers that most of the expectations have to do with the salesperson's interpersonal skills. At each level, although perhaps less so in the case of the support systems, the behaviors expected of the salesperson are based on the ability to get other people to do things. "Getting other people to do things" is probably the most pragmatic definition of interpersonal skill we can find. In the training of salespersons more than in any other area of training, the kinds of changes to be brought about operate directly in the interpersonal areas. It is perhaps for this reason alone that sales training has remained a mystique rather than a practical business problem.

The trainer has still to develop a set of standards or criteria which can be used to create effective training actions. Once the various expectations are noted, they must be listed, with related behavior requirements grouped into common sets. This is done to simplify training tasks so that the trainee/salesperson can receive reinforcement for a given set of trained behaviors from a number of sources.

SETTING PERFORMANCE PRIORITIES

The trainer's next task is to establish priorities for these expectations. These are split into two headings: the "must haves" and the "pluses." In the first group are those expectations that must be met before the salesperson is considered trained.

This would be the major area of compromise mentioned above, and the purpose of the training actions is to bring performance to this "must" level. This means that the "musts" will be met, but that most of the "pluses" will be treated through task training, as in the industrial situation. The trainer is again looking for the generalized skill areas.

MEASURING THE RESULTS

At this point the trainer must ask, "How do we know when expectations have been met?" The best place to seek the answer is from representatives of the four levels of expectation. Barring this possibility, the trainer will probably have to rely on the sales-system managers for their best judgments. Now the process of setting standards differs little from that for administrative training. The major difference is that more of the standards will be based on subjective judgments than on consistent measurements of outputs. Further, some of the standards set for the salespersons will not have economic value. The values themselves will be subjective, drawn from the various levels of expectations within which the sales force operates. We will have to accept from the beginning that many of the standards will be qualitative and subjective and, further, that they will change as both the situation and our knowledge of the subject change.

With this in mind, the trainer must obtain the agreement of management that the model of a salesperson created from these standards is acceptable. At the same time, this model must be tested against quantitative standards. This is important for future revisions of the training system and to justify effectiveness of training in the sales environment. Essentially, this means that a trained individual who conforms to the general model will meet given quantified objectives appropriate for that particular salesperson and for the sales system itself. Thus at some point all trained salespeople will meet quantified standards, whether in terms of the number of new prospects obtained or of dollars brought in during a given selling period. We must expect that the salesperson's performance after training—achievement of the subjective and objective standards set after investigation of the four levels of expectation—will lead to the accomplishment of quantifiable sales-system objectives!

PROBLEMS IN DEVELOPING EXPECTATIONS

It would be dangerous to underestimate the real difficulty of developing these expectations through analysis. The danger lies in the fact that we are dealing with interpersonal skills. The components of these skills have only recently been explored, and as yet there is no vocabulary to accurately describe or discuss them. Considering how difficult it is for the experts in the behavioral sciences to accurately communicate with one another, it is no wonder that in discussing these kinds of skills, customers, managers, support people, and salespersons themselves have an even smaller basis for meaningful communication! The training analyst will be dealing here with areas of behavior which are very difficult to grasp. Neverthe-less, it is still possible to develop expectations, standards of performance, and dis-criminating criteria.

As a case in point, one expectation of a salesperson's behavior relates to eliciting the trust of others. This expectation has very important implications in a number of industrial sales and cold-canvass selling organizations. Interviews with customers result in such answers as: "I buy from someone I can trust. When I decide to make a purchase, I want to be sure I'll get everything I pay for, and I don't want to have to ride herd to do it! I like to feel I can trust the salesperson at first sight—or at least before I sign on the dotted line."

Questioning a sales manager in this type of organization turns up a very similar set of expectations: "To be successful in my organization, a salesperson has to be a self-starter and follow through all the way. I don't want to have to keep checking every minute of the time to make sure he or she is doing the right things. You might say that a successful salesperson is a person I can rely on!" The same expec-tations are voiced in support organizations: "I don't want to feel that I have to check every part of an order before I fill it. I want to feel that everything is right." "When I ask a salesperson for credit background on a new customer, I want to know I'm getting it straight. I don't want to have to second-guess everything. Be-lieve me, if I feel I can't trust a salesperson to give me accurate credit information, there's going to be trouble!"

A salesperson expresses the same expectation: "I want people to take me at face value. When I say something, I want to be believed. I expect people to trust me! Nothing is more discouraging than to get that fish-eyed stare from a prospect who doesn't believe a word I'm saying—or that questioning look from my manager reviewing my weekly call report."

Summarizing expectations at the four levels: The salesperson will be expected to behave in a way that others perceive as trustworthy. Then how does a sales-person behave—or, for that matter, how does anyone behave—to instill trust in others? The trainer now seems to be operating in an area in which common vocabu-lary is lacking. On closer examination, there are really two different kinds of behav-ioral situations. First, the individual's actions (behavior) must demonstrate not only personal integrity, but also that this integrity is of benefit to the person with whom he or she is interfacing. Second, and perhaps more important, the salesperson must behave in a manner that other people find trustworthy. In considering qualitative standards for this kind of behavior, the trainer can begin with the behavior of people who are considered trustworthy. A group of these trustworthy individuals (colleagues in the organization, customers, etc.) can be assembled and presented with a series of decision situations. The trainer could compile a series of case situa-tions in which choices must be made between two courses of action—one perhaps with greater gain or ease of accomplishment, but demonstrating a lower degree of integrity; the other more complicated or with less potential gain, but demonstrating greater integrity and potential for trust. The group would have to make and evaluate its choices in terms of another person's performing the actions. The group members could then be asked why they feel their choices of action demonstrate integrity and future trustworthiness.

With such a body of decision criteria, the trainee/salesperson could be put through a step-by-step training process structured to reinforce choices of action indicating trustworthiness in a given area. For example, given a situation in which failure to disclose certain facts about a customer will result in credit acceptance, whereas full disclosure of these facts would result in partial refusal of credit, the trainee will select the second alternative. With enough time, it should become possible for the trainer to reinforce this kind of behavior through repetition; in effect, the trainer will be training the salesperson to behave as someone considered worthy of trust.

So far the trainer has solved the first critical problem—discovering what particular salespeople are expected to do and developing with management the means to measure their performance in terms of expectations met. He or she has, in the process, established an evaluation system for future use, employing the quantified standards of the particular sales system.

SELECTING SALES TRAINEES

The trainer now faces the second critical problem: selecting criteria for trainees. With sales training, the individual responsible for the training actions must not only identify entry behaviors of prospective salespeople, but also participate in establishing criteria to select them. In other words, the trainer must take part in the system which establishes guidelines for new sales trainee hires, as well as help select people currently in sales positions who are to be retrained. Thus the trainer must find a means of identifying trainable individuals. This is not to deny the old saw, "Salespeople are born, not made!" In fact, it admits some grains of truth there. In dealing with such complex interpersonal behaviors as those mentioned in connection with trust, the trainer and the sales organization must recognize that, like the motor ability needed in manual-dexterity skills, the abilities involved in the interpersonal skills can be trained only if they are present. There is little agreement, perhaps even little knowledge, about how these skills are learned. Therefore, unless the organization has enough time and money available for trial-and-error learning, the sales-training system will become a hit-or-miss proposition if the potential for success is not increased by the hiring of people with ability to learn the necessary skills. In other words, the selection system increases the success potential of the training action by acquiring partially skilled new hires, then using the training time and effort to develop these skills and transfer them to the sales situation. A trainer's fundamental contribution to the selection process is to provide the acquisition system with performance expectations and standards for use in measuring trainee performance at the end of training. Then the kind of prior behavior or experience which will indicate similar performance on the part of the candidate can be determined. If the selection were based on these criteria, the organization could obtain salespersons who would be more successful in not only training, but also performing their sales functions—which is the real training mission.

The thoroughness of the trainer in developing expectations and performance standards ensures obtaining data which will permit the selection of candidate salespersons with a high degree of ability/skill and therefore consistently greater potential success. The same approach can be applied in dealing with salespeople already in the organization whose performance has not measured up to standards. People who fail to meet quantitative standards should be analyzed to learn which qualitative and subjective standards they do not meet. A decision can then be made as to which individuals should be rehabilitated. In reaching this decision, the trainee/candidate's entry behaviors should be carefully delineated. If the person cannot meet the selection criteria established for new hires, it would probably be wiser for the organization to find him or her a new position, one for which the particular substandard behaviors would not be critical. If, however, the trainers, management, and the individual are all highly confident that the substandard areas can be corrected, the trainer will know where to concentrate efforts.

ENTRY BEHAVIORS OF SALES TRAINEES

The sales trainer meets three kinds of entry behavior: (1) the new hire, such as the sales trainee or junior sales representative; (2) the salesperson performing below standard; and (3) the individual entering sales training from a nonsales position within the organization. In the case of the new hire, selection has been based on the person's performance prior to entering the organization; the person has been measured against selection criteria used in the organization's acquisition process. In the case of the substandard performer, the decision to retain and rehabilitate has been made, and the trainer need attack only those areas in which performance is below standard.

The third case is more complex. An employee who decides to become a salesperson is a special case. When originally hired, he or she had to meet criteria entirely different from those met by a newly hired salesperson. Further, if present job performance merits promotion, he or she will have been successful in a job in which the standards might be contrary to, or at least different from, those required of a sales representative. If the organization is consistent in its approach to sales training, it will apply the same selection criteria to the employee within the organization as it does to the new hire coming in from the outside. The individual selected from within has the advantage of experience with the organization, and there may be strong pressure to waive or suspend some of the selection criteria. This is dangerous, however, for management is, in effect, saying to the sales trainer: "This person does not meet our normal selection criteria and has therefore less than normal potential for success, yet we expect the same kind of results, perhaps even better results, from training because we have a commitment due to his or her previous work in the organization." In such a case the potential for success in training the future salesperson is increased if he or she can be hired into the organization in a position using skills transferable to the sales job. For example, he or she might be selected by the criteria used for salespersons, but put into a position allied to the sales function, such as sales correspondence, product distribution, or credit.

Whether an individual enters directly into sales training or is brought into the sales function from another position, those making the decision to hire must be trained to use the selection process as a method for defining entry behaviors. The implication, of course, is that the sales trainer is in a position to train selection personnel in the use of entry behavior criteria and to obtain the data required to define such behavior.

STRATEGIES FOR SALES TRAINING

Assuming that expectations, standards, and selection criteria have been established, the training system can begin to develop strategies for behavior change. A logical first step in this development is to make a model of the process a salesperson goes through in daily activities. As an example, we might look at one part of a cold-canvass casualty insurance salesperson's job: making a cold call and obtaining the potential customer's insurance coverages or policies so that a comparative analysis may be presented in the form of a sales proposal. For each of the elements in this processing system, the instructional designer will need to define five aspects: (1) the entry behaviors desired, with criteria for qualifying those behaviors; (2) the expected performance of behaviors that will fulfill organizational needs; (3) the training criteria to be used in indicating accomplishment of those expectations; (4) the inputs, tools, or resources needed by the individual; and (5) the physical outputs that can be used for measurement of performance. Now here is the process model of a cold-canvass call.

Element 1: Completion of a daily work plan

Entry behaviors The trainee must show aptitude or capability for developing short-term written plans and indications from prior background that such plans have been developed and carried out. Possible criteria areas are: household budgeting, educational planning, work planning, report writing, care and neatness in personal appearance, etc. Responses to questioning throughout the interview should indicate ability to organize answers and a level of detail demonstrating capability for short-term planning.

Expected performance The trainee should complete a work plan each day prior to beginning calls in conformity with organization requirements. This plan will provide for minimum time spent in travel between calls and be flexible enough so that unplanned calls may be made between planned calls. It is expected that this plan will be followed and will be extensive enough to maximize the number of cold calls made.

Training criteria Given a series of territorial assignments, available expiration cards, prior-call records, a city directory, and a telephone directory for the area, the trainee will prepare a daily work plan for making a minimum of eight planned calls and four unplanned calls on potential prospects.

Inputs These are work-plan forms, city directory, telephone directory, territory map with high-potential areas blocked out, and information from successful salespeople on their methods for preparing the daily work plan.

Output A single output is expected: completion of the work plan to meet criteria in element 3.

Element 2: Precall qualification

Entry behaviors The trainee should indicate ability to use available information to reach logical and consistent conclusions. Testing for mental alertness can give one indication. Another can be discerned from the interview: Each candidate can be given a series of problems and information to make a decision, with decisions measured by the standards of the organization.

Expected performance The trainee will answer the question "What reasons will this prospect have for buying?" on the basis of expiration cards, prior-call cards, and a visual inspection of the facilities. This precall qualification will be made for every potential prospect and will be well enough used in opening to accurately gauge the prospect's needs in at least 50% of the calls.

Training criteria Given typically available data, the trainee will express orally or in writing an evaluation of the prospects' insurance needs and will prepare opening strategies, using these evaluations to sell. In each case the trainee will perform to the satisfaction of the trainer or sales manager.

Inputs In addition to those used in preparation of the daily work plan, inputs include information gained through visual inspection of the prospect's premises. The trainee will also receive information from successful salespersons on their approaches to prospect qualification in the precall situation.

Output One output is expected: a prepared strategy for opening.

Element 3: Precall opening

Entry behaviors The trainee will indicate on first impression confidence in what he or she is doing and will give a reason why this will lead to direct benefit to the recipient. Careful evaluation of first impressions during a series of interviews is probably the best method of identifying such behavior.

Expected performance These expectations demonstrate the complexity of behaviors in interpersonal sales skills. The salesperson is expected to talk to a receptionist or secretary in order to gain, without an appointment, access to the individual who makes the buying decision. In most cases the receptionist/secretary has been directed to screen salespeople to prevent just such an occurrence; at the same time, however, the buyer expects sales representatives to bring potential benefits to his or her attention, notwithstanding the prior directive to the receptionist/secretary.

Training criteria In a series of simulated calls, the trainee/salesperson will respond to such statements as: "Whom do you wish to see?"; "Do you have an appointment?"; "Ms. X sees no one without an appointment. May I have her call you?"; "May I tell her the purpose of your call?"; "We already have insurance. Would you like to call for an appointment?" The trainee's responses will obtain for him or her the name of the person to see and in five out of eight attempts, an interview. Conditions will be established in advance for the required responses to obtain face-to-face meetings, using the experience of successful salespersons in the organization.

Input Statements in the section on training criteria constitute the input.

Output The names of the buyers and appointments or interviews with them make up the output.

SIMULATION AS A SALES-TRAINING PROCESS

The five aspects mentioned above would be described for each element in the cold-canvass process before program development could begin. Since the trainer is dealing with complex interpersonal skills, it would seem that the way to bring about the behavior changes in these areas would be to have the trainee/salesperson actually simulate the real-life process. Many of the interpersonal skills can be generalized through most of the process elements. For example, responding to the questions or statements of the receptionist utilizes some of the same skills required in the opening, in prospect qualification, and in obtaining the survey which is the objective of this particular kind of sales call. In developing sales simulations for this training, there are three important factors. The first is the need for feedback so that the trainee can observe and correct behavior. Next, there must be provision for direct reinforcement when the trainee's behavior meets the training requirements. Finally, the simulation will have to approximate the real world as closely as possible. This means that having a salesperson face the sales manager in a room with other trainees present is not likely to produce the desired behaviors. A way must be found to create credibility in the demonstration in both physical setting and evaluation of performance. Further, a means must be found to recall demonstrated behaviors to the sales trainee in such a way that the training experience can be replayed, beginning at that point which demonstrated successful behavior and continuing until all required behaviors are obtained. To do this we will probably want to use some kind of recording device, either tape or video, or have an observer present who can accurately repeat the trainee's demonstration. The trainee must also be provided with standards against which to compare his or her performance. These standards could be provided by videotapes, or a successful salesperson or sales manager could provide the required feedback and reinforcement.

The development of sales-training materials is not easy. In deciding on simulation as our general strategy, we are left with the problem of how to develop such simulations with enough care and detail to provide the kinds of feedback and reinforcement needed to bring about the desired behavior changes. As always, this must be accomplished without introducing extraneous or even damaging behavior changes. Fortunately, there is available a large body of off-the-shelf material and a great number of consultants, many of them highly effective in the development and presentation of such training. With the expectations, the criteria, and the entry behaviors applying to the various elements of the sales activities known, the qualification of consultants should not be too difficult. The consultants can be presented with this information, and we can examine their approaches to meeting our requirements. If we are not satisfied in questioning them and observing their programs in another organization, we can certainly evaluate their processes against our criteria in a trial run. The major pitfall in dealing with outside sources for sales training, or for that matter any kind of training requiring complex responses, is in the way the responses are structured. The trainer must not accept paper-and-pencil response systems when the organization's criteria require responses in interface situations. He or she must be assured that the trainee/salesperson will meet the training criteria in all cases where a consultant's requirements are met.

The trainer will also have to decide whether the simulation training actions proposed will meet the criteria and expectations of management. Probably, training will have to take place partially in simulations and partially on actual field calls. In other words, the training will move from paper-and-pencil responses to in-house simulations and then to actual sales situations. If this is the course, interim or transition criteria must be developed to determine when the trainee is ready to go into the field. Again, these standards or expectations must be consistent or valid within the organization.

It may even be necessary to place the trainee/salesperson into a situation exactly like the selling one, which means being in the field without a trainer. Presented with this requirement, the trainer will have to develop a series of training objectives with measurable standards of performance which can be recorded by the salesperson in the field. In the simple cold-call system, the establishment of objectives, such as "eight planned calls per day" or "agreement from four prospects per week to a comparative survey of insurance coverages," provides the trainer with feedback points. These objectives can also provide the sales organization with step-by-step interim standards for use before the trainee/salesperson is given a sales quota.

PRODUCT TRAINING

So far we have discussed actions to train individuals to carry out the sales function. For most organizations sales training also covers the area of product training. The introduction of new products or services is a continuing problem in a selling organization, and it requires training actions directed toward all individuals in all sales functions. For the sales trainer, there are two problems to be solved in product training, neither of which has much to do with the product itself; at least, they have very little to do with the technical aspects of the product. The sales trainer's job is not to train the salesperson to describe or defend a product—or even to use it— but rather to cause the salesperson to deal with the product in such a way that someone buys it. So the trainer must first examine the product from the buyer's viewpoint and determine what benefits it has to offer. Second, the trainer must deal with the product by answering the question "Why should I sell it?" Any training actions developed, then, will have to do with the actual situation at the point of sale, and the product must be handled as any other part of the selling job is handled: in a face-to-face situation between a salesperson and a potential customer. Any training action resulting from this analysis is directed at the total selling situation. Such an approach should simplify the job of developing these training actions, since the usual orchestration provided by the production and design people will generally be avoided, and the salespersons' responses will be to activities at the point of sale rather than to interpretations of design or production technicalities. Selling this point of view to a sales organization should not be too difficult. In fact, this analytical approach for developing sales-training actions for new or substandard salespeople should be welcomed in any selling organization.

THE EXPERIENCED SALESPERSON

A frequent occurrence in sales training is the need to retrain sales representatives who have been in the field for some time and whose performance for some reason or other is seen as deficient. Unless, of course, new products are involved, the experienced sales representative probably already knows "how" to do it. If we assume that the original training was effective, the basic skills have already been developed and have been exercised in the field. At some point or another, the sales representatives have met standard; otherwise, they probably wouldn't be there any more. The performance problem, then, may not be one of knowledge acquisition.

Recalling our performance-management model, we know that four factors affect the salesperson's performance in addition to training: expectations, feedback, consequences, and job design. Feedback and consequences are particularly important issues to be dealt with in relation to field sales performance. Often the sales representative receives very little feedback other than from the prospect during a sales process. Rarely does a sales representative receive any positive reinforcement for his or her activities until a sale is closed. Before bringing an experienced sales representative into a training program, one should carefully examine the ways in which feedback and reinforcement are applied.

One successful approach to providing timely and usable feedback is through the medium of a well-designed sales-reporting system. In this kind of system the sales representative is given the means to objectively record data after each prospect contact. The report itself provides guidance to the sales representative in using this information to gauge his or her own progress and to objectively evaluate activities. This kind of feedback allows the sales representative to adjust his or her approaches to the prospect and assists the representative in recalling and sharpening learned skills.

More often, successful feedback and consequence-management processes are involved in sales management training. A significant part of the sales manager's training focuses on performance management so that he or she learns how to effectively provide feedback and positive reinforcements.

SALES MANAGER TRAINING

In training sales managers, the trainer might find a systematic approach difficult to implement. In most selling organizations the route to sales management is paved by successful performance as a salesperson. Traditionally, this is the same as in other systems in which, for example, selection of a supervisor in an industrial situation has been made on the basis of successful performance as an operator; thus the punch-press operator becomes a supervisor of the punch-press department. Recently, however, this trend has changed, at least in the industrial situation. More and more individuals are going into systems as trainee/supervisors, rather than as operators when possibility of assignment to a supervisory position is considered. The movement toward apprentice/supervisor, trainee/supervisor, or assistant/supervisor positions as entry jobs is becoming more and more part of our industrial environment.

Sales organizations by and large remain much more conservative. In nearly all of the organizations investigated, the primary criterion for promotion to sales manager is, as it has been, better than average performance as a salesperson. If a systems approach is taken to training, however, the same kind of criteria would be used for the selection and training of sales managers as are used for the selection and training of the sales staff. If we accept the premise that the basic experience to demonstrate the entry criteria behaviors can best be developed in a sales environment, the selection and training problem properly belongs in the sales-training system. Yet the ultimate objective of such training is a sales manager, not a salesperson, a fact that leads us to place the training of sales managers into the realm of supervisory or manager training rather than into the field of sales training per se.

Perhaps the sales-training system could deal with the selection and transition of a salesperson into a sales manager, leaving the training common to all managers to a management-training system in the organization. Whether separate systems are to be assigned to sales training or to management training isn't really very important. What is important is that the same systematic approach be taken to prepare training actions recommended for the candidate sales manager as was taken to prepare training actions for the new-hire salesperson. The first step, then, is to develop a set of performance standards, or at least expectations, which apply to the sales manager's job. If this approach is used, we will find that the model developed for the sales manager is quite different from the one developed for the salesperson. In fact, we will find that many of the performance standards established for a salesperson will be inappropriate for a sales manager. For example, the salesperson is expected to handle an "opening" alone. The sales manager should not do this part of the sales job, but rather expect to make each salesperson do it.

The actions and results obtained by the sales manager which are rewarded by management may be not only different from those of the salesperson, but also contradictory. For example, in some situations the organization may not expect the individual salesperson to conform to administrative rules and regulations in formal reporting and record keeping. It may, however, have very high expectations that a sales manager will conform in those areas. In this situation the highly successful salesperson tends to have little concern for these administrative matters. Yet suddenly, on promotion to sales manager, he or she will be expected to conform to those procedures and to be highly motivated to maintain them as a priority item. In another example the salesperson is expected to concentrate attention on the soliciting, qualifying, and closing of individual sales and is expected to apply his or her greatest energy to this end. This is, after all, the sales job. Yet on promotion to sales manager, he or she will not be considered effective if a great proportion of time is spent repeating this process with individual customers. It is expected that the sales manager will see that these actions are carried out by sales personnel. But the person who has been rewarded for behavior directed at the individual customer will find it difficult, if not impossible, to comply with the change in organizational expectations. Nevertheless, it is very likely that in most selling organizations performance standards and expectations applicable to salespersons will differ considerably from those applicable to the sales manager, and the selection criteria for sales manager may require behaviors quite different from those of successful salespersons.

The performances expected of a sales manager can be built into criteria for selection of salespersons as candidate sales managers. The trainer must then develop a process that can carry the potential sales manager over the bridge from sales to sales management. Where possible, this process should probably follow very closely that developed for the more complex kinds of administrative training. Where such an apprenticeship process is not possible, it may be necessary to propose to the organization that a separate designation be given to sales manager trainees. A common and successful approach is to assign the trainee/sales manager to a sales trainer's job for a period of time in order to reinforce a number of managerlike behaviors: administrative procedures, sales training, and salesperson selection. The most important action, however, is the careful development of the performance standards or expectation and selection criteria for sales managers, keeping it clearly in mind that the sales manager is quite different from the salesperson.

Although sales training deals with very complex skills and with behaviors less well understood than those involved in the training of industrial operators, it appears that the processes of analysis, development, and operations are more often than not similar to those of such training. The idea that sales training differs from all other kinds of training appears to be more myth than fact. Although the complex entry behaviors required for successful sales training are not always quantifiable, the fact remains that it is not necessarily true that good salespersons are "born, not made!"

CHAPTER 13

New-Hire Orientation

DEFINING THE PROCESS CALLED "ORIENTATION"

Although each aspect of an operating training system is important, each application presents its own particular problems. In industrial skill training, definition of the system approach to developing a training mission and separating skills and tasks presented the "go/no go" problems. In the administrative skill area the major problem was the design of the training action itself. Sales training had as its critical problem the accurate definition of a trained individual by the identification of behaviors.

For a training system designed to orient new hires, the critical problem arises in defining the very object of its action: orientation. Taken literally, the training action should point the new hire in the right direction. But in practice, the meaning of orientation is much more difficult to fix. At some point between being screened for a job and receiving the first salary increase a new hire undergoes a process called "orientation." During this period the new hire becomes part of the organization! Ideally, he or she will have adopted, or at least have been exposed to, the company point of view. The new employee may even be expected to have developed a commitment to the organization—perhaps to learning the formal and informal rules of the social group he or she has joined. Any or all of these changes in a new hire's behavior could be part of a definition of orientation.

It would appear that we are dealing with attitudes rather than definable skills or tasks. Further, we are dealing with them in a rather general way. The particular tendencies toward actions which the proposed orientation training system is to develop will result in a whole set of behaviors, some of which may be job-directed, others of which may not. A productive approach to defining orientation could be the specification of the kinds of behavior an oriented employee demonstrates. Of course, this approach sidesteps the issue of attitude change, but it provides a workable basis for producing an orientation program. Here again, as in some kinds of administrative and sales training, analysis will form the basis for a behavioral model.

This model will be quite different from the others. If the problem of attitude change is to be attacked, a model must describe the ways an individual *feels* about what he or she is doing.

In the best of all possible worlds, the trainer would not be expected to tackle this kind of problem. Ideally, training deals with performance that can be measured against standards. In this case change actions are undertaken not for performance, but for internal tendencies which may lead to performance. In the real world the trainer is expected to orient new hires, with or without standards or measures.

Considering the problem of definition and the difficulty of identifying behaviors that will demonstrate desired attitudes, the need for orientation requires justification. From management's viewpoint, the justification is clear: A new hire's first months with an organization have greater influence on his or her future than does any other period. During this period the new employee has the highest visibility and is searching for a behavioral pattern that will give the desired payoff. Management hypothesizes that if new hires can be led to develop a commitment to the organization at the beginning of their careers, they will maximize their worth and be well on their way to success in the organization.

This view provides an acceptable, if somewhat imperfect, definition of the term "orientation," the process through which a new hire acquires a commitment to the organization. The economic value of this commitment, like the economic value of high morale, could be inferred through productivity, turnover, absenteeism, etc., but this is probably an area in which management's desire for employee commitment is the only unit of value.

It may also be useful to look at the problem from the new hire's point of view. Studies have shown that new hires enter the organization with considerable desire to succeed. They are already committed to the organization as they know it. They want to be successful and are far more likely than not to want to behave in a manner leading to some kind of payoff. If they know the organization as one in which employees must check their brains at the door, they will tend to pretend not to think. If orientation is successful, however, the new hire will not only be committed, but will also know the organization as management knows it.

COMMITMENT AS A BASIS FOR DEFINING TRAINED BEHAVIOR

Substituting "commitment" for "attitude," the trainer is still looking for behavior which management will accept as the model. First, management expects conformity to organizational rules of behavior. The new hire is usually exposed to the formal rules of the organization when processed in; he or she is given the company booklet, or at least is told the hours of work, the clock procedure, relief schedule, etc. Conformity here might be behaving to expectation. Unfortunately, the formal rules only barely demonstrate the commitment expected in this category. The new hire normally receives orientation in the informal rules from peers and from the direct superior. At first the scope is limited to a rather small circle of instructors whose expectations may be quite different from management's and often in conflict with the aims of the organization as management knows it. For example, colleagues may tell a new salesperson that in their experience, the credit department causes trouble with customers; or a boss may tell a new secretary not to spend any time with Jones's secretary because Jones is a little too nosey! These true-life examples demonstrate how conflict in orientation goals can arise, leading to behaviors different from those characteristic of commitment. An instructional design that will satisfy the organization's first requirement—conformity to rules—has to cope with both informal and formal rules of behavior.

Besides conforming to organizational rules of behavior, the new hire will be expected to demonstrate an active desire to meet organization goals. Identification of the behaviors that meet this requirement demands a high level of skill from the training analyst. These behaviors are complex, difficult to define, and often not directly related to job performance. The new hire will find questions directed toward the subject difficult to answer honestly; such a line of questioning can be a threat. Any employee quickly learns the expected safe responses to questions from a member of the staff or management. Asking members of management what constitutes acceptable behavior is just as difficult. Dealing with an internalization such as commitment, we find ourselves working with abstractions; if observable behaviors are arrived at, they usually give only partial or indirect measures.

The manager above will say, "Committed employees have the right attitude."

"Fine. How will we know they have the right attitude?"

"Well, they are motivated."

"What will they do that will tell us they are motivated?"

"They will work hard and be productive. They want to get ahead . . . with us."

This will probably be as far as the trainer will get. Unlike other behavioral problems, this cannot be tied to specifics. The argument is untenable; the "hardworking" employee is committed, but an employee can work hard without being committed! For many, work volume and work tempo are out of their control. For some, high productivity indicates strong ego involvement rather than commitment to the organization. If productivity is the standard, commitment is immaterial, except as a possible contributor to this objective. Logically, the trainer would attack production directly, treating the problem of commitment as one part of it. Orientation would then become task-centered, and the new hire, instead of being oriented, would be trained for the job!

This does not really solve the attitude problem as it was posed, however. Assuming that action can be taken to bring about commitment and that commitment can be defined behaviorally, it should be possible to explore the kinds of behavior expected. How does a person behave who has this state of mind we are calling "commitment"? What set of stimuli and response expectations can be structured to test for its presence? Verbal responses are the easiest. We can describe how committed employees talk about themselves, their jobs, and their organizations. They tend to consider themselves competent at their jobs; they feel that their contributions to the organization are valuable and that they have worth to the organization. They talk about their jobs in terms of value. They usually see their jobs as complex, having special requirements, and their organizations as having importance. To them, their functions and organizations are "the first team." They are in the "big league."

Elements of the committed employee's work performance can also be examined. Outputs are often exemplary and are used as standards for other employees. He or she tends to meet or exceed targets and is independent, drawing planing and control elements to tasks. He or she resists outside influence, which may be unacceptable to others, since change is resisted when he or she does not influence it. Evidence of commitment may also be found in behavior not directly relating to tasks. The committed employee tends to seek the company of fellow employees and to participate in the organization's social functions, with his or her family when possible.

One characteristic of the committed employee's behavior seems to be its predictability. Associates expect certain behaviors as does management; and they get it. This is not a judgment of the value of responses; commitment does not necessarily mean high quality. A poor performer may be deeply committed. As the boss puts it, "At least the poor devil tries!"

It appears from the foregoing that we are dealing not with induction, but with the motivation of the work force in general. To meet the organizational mission of "commitment," the new hire must become committed during the orientation process, and this state of mind must continue beyond what is known as the "orientation program." The changes required to bring about the kinds of behaviors described here will be most effective in the actual job environment. Reinforcers not carried into the job environment will tend to permit behavior to be extinguished by the impact of the multiple stimuli of the job. The individual who behaves as though committed in the company classroom may not be so committed on the job. It is difficult to maintain a behavior so loosely defined when the same level of reinforcement and feedback available in the classroom is not available on the job.

MISSIONS FOR AN ORIENTATION SYSTEM

A valid orientation program becomes a more complex training system than is contemplated in most organizations. The training missions require more than a single action. These missions are to:

1. maintain the motivation of new hires, or their desire to succeed at a level the same as, or higher than, that at which they were inducted into the organization;

2. develop in new hires a feeling of belonging together and a sense of satisfaction in being members of the organization;

3. bring about the commitment of new hires to organization goals;

4. develop in new hires an acceptable conformity to the organization's formal and informal rules of behavior.

The first three missions require trainee behaviors not easily attained in the short run. In time, the individual completing the orientation actions will have been with the organization long enough to demonstrate motivation, satisfaction, and commitment. Such an evaluation should be made after the person has had time to demonstrate by performance that he or she is a committed member of the organization. Barring the 5, 10, or 20 years of loyal service needed for quantitative measure, the trainer and management may have to accept qualitative measures based on verbal responses.

For the fourth of these missions, fairly objective criteria can be developed once the rules of behavior have been identified. Stipulating the response sets, collecting responses that will satisfy criteria, and demonstrating trained behaviors will be less difficult than establishing the conditions under which the responses are to occur. The criterion might be: Given the question "How do you feel about promotional opportunity within our company?" the trainee will respond, "I think the opportunity is very good, and I want to do my best to be promoted." If the person's boss presents the criterion question, one could probably count on very rapid acquisition of the learning that will result in that particular response. The same question presented by an employment agent to a job hunter might bring out a very different response. The problem, then, is to determine the conditions under which the stimulus is presented. The trainer might have to put it this way: "Given a nonstructured situation three months after hire, in the absence of boss/subordinate relationships, the trainee, when presented with a range of occupational goals including advancement with the company, will choose this goal and support the choice with reasons indicating to others in the unstructured situation motivation toward success with the company." If these conditions can be created, reasonable judgments can be made about the success of the training action.

THE ORIENTATION PROCESS AS A BEHAVIOR-CHANGE SYSTEM

Fulfilling any or all of these missions will require the trainer to look at orientation not as a single program or training action, but as a processing system made up of several kinds of actions. A typical model for an orientation process is presented in Fig. 1. Each of the elements of this model includes actions that contribute to the training missions. The trainer will need to determine the manner in which each element can be used as a change agency, the criteria for the training actions, the individuals or systems which will implement these actions, and the feedback media which will be used to control the process.

Application element

The first element, *application*, defines that part of the process during which a candidate is first stirred to apply for a job. The potential employee will answer an advertisement, be processed through an employment agency or service, be solicited by

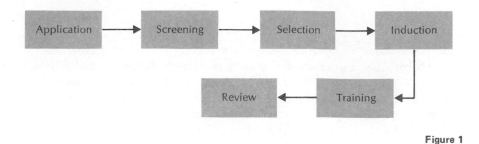

Figure 1

a search organization or company employee, or possibly simply come in off the street. In any case, he or she will have been motivated to take action because of an expected payoff, employment, and will then complete some sort of application in hopes of achieving the expected payoff. Actually, he or she will be preparing to move on to the next step in the process, being hired. Thus, before a candidate ever begins the normal employment process, orientation has begun.

A number of change agencies are possible, among them the advertisements placed to attract candidates, agency presentations to candidates, and the way present employees talk to prospective candidates. Criteria can be set for advertisements which will work toward the orientation missions. For example, an ad could describe important work rules, cite specific rewards for achievement, or give examples of group spirit in the organization. Effectiveness of the ad could be measured in terms of the applicants' responses to questions such as: "What in the ad attracted you to us?" The organization's recruitment function would probably be accountable for this action, and applicant response would provide it with feedback for control. It would probably be helpful if the training system could assist the recruitment function to prepare the advertisement, in which case accountability would be shared.

Employment agencies and similar sources could be treated in the same way. As potential change agencies for orientation, they would be expected to do more than simply provide the organization with candidates. The use of the employment agency situation as a training environment for orientation would present some interesting possibilities. An instructional design and training materials would be needed, and the agency representative would have to be trained to carry out the orientation actions. The objective could be to bring about such a level of commitment that the applicant would choose the organization over another offering similar job specifications but more money. The same possibilities exist when company employees are considered potential change agents; there are also the same requirements: an instructional design, material, and training for the job.

Screening element

The remaining elements in the orientation process can be treated in the same way as the first element. The screening-element change agency would be the screening interview itself, and individuals responsible for conducting these interviews would be accountable for the training actions. The criteria established would stress the benefits of commitment to the organization and the ways commitment is to be demonstrated. The applicants' responses to questions about organizational commitment would be the measuring points. A series of situational questions would be used to ask the applicant to decide which of two points of view was appropriate.

At this stage in the process, the applicant should be quite eager to respond to questions in the way he or she thinks the interviewer wants. The interviewer, therefore, is in an ideal position to reinforce desired responses, since the applicant is highly motivated to give them. A purely behavioral view of the stimulus/response situation is taken here: The more often the applicant responds in a given way, the greater the likelihood of such responses in similar situations in the future. As these responses are reinforced, they become more and more part of a given response repertory; in behavioral terms, an attitude change is taking place.

The interviewer will have to be prepared to use the interview situation as a training vehicle, with a conscious intent to change behavior and will then have to structure the screening questions to bring about the planned stimulus/response sequence. Since the interview itself is the feedback medium, questions selected will be the measuring points, and, if possible, they should be recorded so that if changes in training are needed in the interview, they can be made consistently and on the basis of sufficient data.

Selection element

The selection element of the process provides the same change opportunities as the screening element. Here the process will usually be carried out by a line manager, normally the person to whom the applicant will report if hired. The criteria developed for this element will center on responses involving formal and informal work rules and further reinforcement of commitment responses. The advantages of having the person's future supervisor carry out this part of the training are obvious: Feedback can be provided by having the supervisor use a job aid such as an evaluation sheet to help him or her decide whether or not to hire. This sheet would state the criterion questions and provide space for the supervisor's evaluation of a candidate's answers.

Induction element

The induction element, usually considered the orientation program in most organizations, is the step in the process where the new hires are brought together and told about the glories of the organization: the marvelous benefits program, the basic formal work rules, etc. The two most common change agencies in this element are the lecture/discussion session itself and information distributed during or after the session in the form of employee handbooks, manuals, etc. Accountability for this element should probably be shared by the personnel functions of selection and employee services and members of line supervision whom the new hires will see as representatives of the organization's management. The criteria established for the training actions carried out in this part of the process attack three aspects of the established missions: work rules, potential benefits from commitment, and further reinforcement of the new hire's commitment. The feedback device most useful here is in the form of the questions the new hires ask the conference leader. A refinement might include an unstructured discussion by the new hires of how they feel about the organization and what they expect from it. An additional feedback device could be a formalized attitude survey, similar to those in common use by organizations polling employees' attitudes and morale levels.

Training element

After induction, the new hire will begin work on assigned tasks. This period from entry into the actual work environment to the time of the first review is labeled the "training element" of the process. The job itself is the major change agency, and there are at least two control aspects: first, the supervisor's individual counseling sessions with the new employee; second, informal interactions between the two on the line. The criteria developed here should further reinforce the new employee's conformity to formal and informal work rules as well as level of commitment to the organization. The most useful feedbacks would probably come out of unstructured situations during which new hires were faced with problems and had to make decisions demonstrating such commitment. These data can provide the opportunity to evaluate both employees and training actions and to gauge overall attitude and morale.

Review element

Review is the final element of the orientation process. The appraisal or evaluation session itself is the change agency. From the point of view of orientation training, the criteria involved do not center primarily on the evaluation of performance or attitude. Rather, they are additional instructional media for reinforcing conformity and commitment. The supervisor who carries out this evaluation interview will probably need some kind of job aid as a reminder of the dual purpose of the meeting. Feedback to the training function will come from the evaluation report or the job aid, which should be patterned after the job aid used in the selection interview.

SUMMARY

From this discussion it becomes clear that the orientation process proposed is long and involved. The accountabilities are quite varied; the number of media and agencies used for change is high. It is suggested, however, that if orientation is considered as the entire process from application to first review, the probability of bringing about the desired changes to meet the four stipulated missions for orientation is greater than if the induction program alone is considered the orientation process. Almost all of the requirements for successful training are present, including immediate reinforcement and proximity to the job. The major problem to be faced at this point in the orientation process is the training of personnel in all functions related to the process to make best use of the available change agencies.

It should, of course, be quite obvious that the orientation training system will at several points be operating simultaneously with other training systems, as for example a task-training system. Indeed, the difficulty of training orientation personnel is partially due to the fact they must be so widely dispersed throughout the organization and that the interfaces of the orientation elements with other training and process systems elements must be so carefully structured.

One way to overcome some of these blocks to successful orientation is building in an orientation plan with each new employee. In its simplest form, the plan is a checklist given to the new hire. The checklist details the criteria for successful orientation, the activities to be completed, and resources available to help. Placing orientation in the control of the new employee increases the probability that the activities will be performed. The new hire has the most to gain; his or her own self-interest provides powerful motivation.

The resource people will need to be aware of their roles and will need to have acquired some coaching skills. Where this approach has been implemented, resource people have made themselves available without too much difficulty, often preferring this approach to formal classroom lecturing.

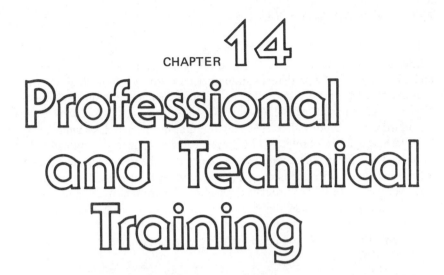

CHAPTER 14

Professional and Technical Training

FORCES FOR PROFESSIONAL TRAINING

The rapid technological changes in today's industrial and business environment bring increasing pressure on the training function to play a more active role in technical and professional training. Although the need is greatest and most obvious in research and development organizations whose products and services are based on advanced states of the arts, product-producing organizations also feel the increasing need to maintain an up-to-date technology. The growth of research and development departments and product development facilities is a case in point.

Technical and professional training is a widespread requirement of business organizations today. Professional training programs in the scientific laboratory or engineering department can be found in almost every function from junior technician to chief engineer. But this requirement is spreading from the laboratory; it extends to production functions as well. Changes in production methods—numerical control, automated production control techniques, and, in fact, the introduction of computer applications to every system of the organization—require new technical arts for the managers and their specialists. With so many job areas and functions affected, and with changes coming so rapidly, nearly every function in the organization may be the subject for training actions in the technical and professional areas.

Many functions long thought to be purely on-the-job learning experiences are becoming professionalized, creating additional reasons why the training function should take a more active part in technical and professional training. Northeastern University's development of a degreed curriculum in purchasing is one good example; another is the growing attention to the development of institutes and seminars by the National Association of Purchasing Agents. Whether a professional engineer would consider purchasing a professional field may be questionable. However, the important point is that a growing body of formal discipline is being developed by this association, and it is a body of formal discipline, after all, which delineates a profession.

Traditionally, the approach to technical training has been to leave the maintenance and advancement of a particular "state of the art" to each individual. On the surface, in our free enterprise system, this would appear adequate, given the expectation that professional and technical people are self-motivated. If this were true, however, statistics would not indicate, as they do, that the electronics engineer, for example, is technologically obsolete within seven years after receiving a degree. In other words, a 1980 EE graduate will be more current in the technological state of the art than the engineer who graduated in 1973 and has had seven years' experience on the job. Nor would we see the product engineering department of an automotive products company going outside the organization for senior technicians and accepting for this position recent graduates of technical schools—and this when they have technicians with years of experience in their own shops!

MISSIONS FOR A PROFESSIONAL AND TECHNICAL TRAINING SYSTEM

Four possible missions can be proposed for a technical training system. The first is the maintenance of the organization's state of the art. This mission would make the training system responsible for the development of actions which would enable a trainee to explore recent changes in a particular discipline and to evaluate the utility of these changes.

The second mission has to do with a change of discipline within the organization; this might be called "technical broadening." Training actions in this category will add to the flexibility of the organization by increasing its abilities to move into new but ralated product areas. In addition, training actions should give it the technical flexibility to shift productivity into entirely new fields. A wide-ranging example of this particular change would be the movement from metal stamping to thermosetting plastics as a means of producing formed products.

A third mission that might be assigned to the training system is the assimilation of the new college graduate into the organization. This mission would require actions to provide a smooth and rapid transition from the educational environment to the work environment. To be productive on the job, the recently graduated design engineer must be trained in the use of cost constraints, manufacturing applications, and value engineering, since these kinds of constraints have seldom entered into design problems in the university atmosphere. Such a mission might help the technology-oriented organization solve the problem of overdesign, which so often contributes to the failure to win profitable contracts. Also important in this training area is the development and implementation of training actions to enable the new engineer to make use of resources available within the organization. Technically, how does an engineer deal with a technician in the development of a breadboard or prototype device? What proprietary tools and systems are available, and how does he or she go about making best use of them?

A fourth mission is upgrading as a means of acquiring competent technical and professional personnel. Actions taken to satisfy this mission parallel other recruitment, selection, and self-improvement actions as another means of furnishing the organization with the personnel it requires. Such a training system develops actions to increase the technical capacities and capabilities of individuals already in the organization. This kind of mission is particularly appropriate to an organization that cannot secure a high enough level of technical or professional competence because of a shortage of qualified personnel. Such a training system would work to bring the technician up to the required level of engineering capability to assume duties usually delegated to a qualified engineer or technical specialist.

SPECIAL PROBLEMS OF TECHNICAL TRAINING

A distinguishing difference between technical and professional training and other training systems is that those to be trained will probably know a great deal more about their needs and the required standards of performance than anyone else involved in the system, except possibly the educational resources who will be used. The trainer's major problem is the happy marriage of the two points of view involved: that of the organization and that of the trainee. This could be a major problem, since the technical specialist or professional looks at the state of the art from an extremely personal point of view and tends to pursue his or her strengths and areas of greatest knowledge. Professional standing is, after all, strengthened most by such an approach. On the other hand, from the organization's point of view, the *utility* of the learning carries the greatest emphasis. Left to his or her own devices, then, the highly motivated individual would pursue fields which are of "interest," while the organization would like this individual to pursue fields which have utility to the organization.

The search for this happy marriage can be extremely difficult if the management responsible for this program is also comprised of professionals, since they would probably give the potential trainee the freedom to pursue the art. Often such state-of-the-art opportunity becomes part of the reward system of the organization: The chief engineer or lab manager allows best people time off to pursue whatever objectives they wish. Such a reward system can be invaluable to the organization; the individual in a profession or in a technical field usually has, as an important motivational want, the desire for professional recognition. The organization, in giving time off and possibly financial support to pursue particular interests, gives such a person that recognition and satisfies that need. However, since the missions of the training system and the reward system differ, the organization will have to establish its own priorities before either system can be successful.

SOURCE SELECTION

In actions taken to bring about the smooth transition of college graduates into the job environment and to upgrade technical personnel into more advanced levels of responsibility, the training system's primary problem is source selection. The nature of technological training makes source selection critical. Instruction is highly specialized within a fairly narrow range of expertise. Qualified instructors, teaching facilities, and instructional materials are limited. The problem of source selection exists whether the need is highly sophisticated, as with metallic oxide semiconductor technology, or more universal, as with Master Standard Data techniques. Most often, outside sources will be used. Educational institutions, through regular undergraduate or postgraduate curricula or through institutes, symposia, and special programs, are the richest resources in technical areas. The second major source consists of programs offered by professional trade associations in the form of conferences, conventions, or seminars. A third source can be found in consulting organizations and proprietary schools which combine some form of technical training with their regular consultative fields.

Depending on the organization's technical needs, one or more of these sources will be used. The choice of a specific source for any action should be made on the same basis as it would be for any other proposed training action: the capability of sources to meet predetermined needs. The usual sequence in choosing sources for technical or professional training makes such an evaluation difficult, if not impossible. Usually the potential seminar attendee makes the choice on the basis of fairly generalized expectations and normally without specific content or behavioral goals, because of the reputation of the sponsoring institution or the announced instructor or seminar leader. Quite often disappointment follows, and the trainer frequently hears such complaints as: "The seminar was too basic"; "The group was so heterogeneous that the instructor had to cover ground I already knew"; "The instructor did not cover the material I expected"; or, most often, "The seminar added nothing to my state of the art."

The training function can effectively help in the evaluation of sources without dictating course attendance. First, an organization policy committee is established to outline rules for company-directed attendance in technical or professional training programs, as separate from educational assistance programs. Next, the organization's technology and state-of-the-art needs are determined by the chief engineer, or other qualified members of management, prior to course selection. Third, the training function works with potential participants to specify their expectations and to correlate them to organization needs so that both individual needs and organizational requirements can be fulfilled. Finally, the training function investigates potential sources to find those which best satisfy these expectations.

One successful approach to source evaluation makes particularly good use of the participant's knowledge of his or her own needs. The trainer asks the trainees for a list of questions they expect to have answered in the seminar. In most cases, little probing is needed to develop a series of very specific questions, since most individuals interested in pursuing state-of-the-arts education have a fairly clear idea of what they would like to learn. Very little time is needed to examine possible sources with the potential participant to narrow them down to those most likely to answer these questions. (Of course, this is possible only if the training function maintains a fairly complete file of source information.) Sources identified, the trainer can make a phone call to the instructors or seminar leaders named in the various announcements to ask which on the list of questions will be covered. If the instructors are not specifically listed, a few questions directed to the department or bureau offering the course usually locate the person who can give the needed answers. If the training function maintains a file of course evaluations including feedback by prior participants, this will also help in choosing a source. Experience with such feedback evaluation shows that if nothing else, the negative aspects of the prior participants' experience will be stated in no uncertain terms!

Seminar evaluation

Preattendance evaluation of outside seminars is not a particularly difficult process. There are really only three questions to be answered:

1. What are the participant's learning objectives? What does he or she want to learn and to be able to do with that learning?

2. Does the seminar have the potential to meet the learning objectives? Do descriptive materials support the objectives? Do the seminar sponsors confirm that the objectives can be met? Do the instructors support the objectives?

3. Has the seminar met similar objectives in the past? Do former participants confirm that the objectives can be met?

IN-HOUSE TRAINING

Although outside training sources will meet most state-of-the-art and technical information needs, in-house training will still be imperative. Most obvious are the in-house requirements for technical upgrading and new-hire training, but even where the state of the art is concerned, in-house actions may be needed. The introduction of a new technology or new technical approach to large numbers in the organization, especially where all must have it simultaneously, is one situation in which the only cost-effective medium will be in-house actions. Similarly, organizational needs may be such that no outside resource is available. The particular technology may be so new that institutional training has simply not been formulated, or it may be that the technical know-how is so proprietary that instruction cannot be obtained from any other source at all. These latter situations occur frequently enough to force consideration of in-house state-of-the-art training.

A discovery that the organization's needs cannot be met outside—that the local university is teaching material one or two years behind—requires the trainer to look for another approach. The possibility exists that there will be a training requirement for which no competence is available either outside or inside the organization. The question then is: "How can a training action be contemplated without any subject-matter expertise?" Assuming capability—that is, assuming that the time and human resources are available—the problem, though difficult, is not insoluble. The answer might be an intensive in-house self-development program. Here is an example of an approach to this kind of training problem. The management of the organization identifies a problem as follows:

> Advanced technological competence is considered to be a primary reason for this organization's ability to obtain new business; technological obsolescence restricts the effectiveness of this organization in gaining new business and can weaken our market position. The recent failure of our proposal to gain the XYZ contract award and the subsequent debriefing are evidence that we have failed to demonstrate technological competence in design accomplishments in advanced areas of solid-state technology.

Here management describes a very clear problem in state of the art: The organization has failed to show that it is able to handle electronics problems using advanced solid-state applications. When an organization sees a problem in these terms, it will probably also find that qualified people are leaving because they need an environment in which they can keep current and qualified in their state of the art. Further, the organization may find itself unable to attract highly qualified personnel who seek the kind of environment in which they can demonstrate state-of-the-art competence. If such a problem is present, the training function's effort will be directed toward the development of a program to provide the competence needed. The objective for such a program might be stated as: the development of technical currency which will enable the organization's future contract proposals to demonstrate sufficient technological competence in solid-state applications to satisfy customer needs in areas of signal and power line filters; miliwatt logical applications; linear circuit applications including range estimators, integrators, differentiators; analog circuits embracing special communication systems, A to D converters, D to A converters, and synchronizing systems; mechanical packaging; thermal studies; wiring connectors; frames; and device packaging.

This technical statement of objective, of course, applies to the requirements of a laboratory dealing with data conversion and computer design. The statement of objective specifies the state-of-the-art requirements. Two kinds of criteria might be proposed for a program that will meet this objective. The first is a set of practitioner criteria describing the behaviors for individuals in the organization immediately concerned with the application of this state of the art to these kinds of problems. A second order of criteria would be given in terms of individuals within the organization who wish to broaden their own state of the art, but who do not have immediate practitioner-level applications in mind.

At the practitioner level, the criterion to be used might be simply to design and "breadboard" circuit designs to solve design problems typified in the situations described in the objective by using three kinds of solid-state technology: metallic oxide semiconductors, thin film circuits, and hybrid circuits. Other solid-state approaches might be added, but these three serve as examples. At the second level, verbal or written response criteria might be selected instead. The expectation is that these individuals are working to gain knowledge or understanding that will have some future use.

IN-HOUSE STATE-OF-THE-ART DEVELOPMENT

With some idea of what the organization expects from this particular state-of-the-art training and accepting the premise that no one within the organization is now competent in the art, the trainer might recommend a three-phase program. In the first phase, two- to five-member teams that will make up the "practitioner" training group are assigned to investigation and research in state-of-the-art literature and hardware. Under the direction of a team leader, each team is assigned one specific area described in the objective. Working with the organization's purchasing department and local university people, if they are available, each team develops a basic theoretical body of literature to provide sources for materials or hardware, etc. These same groups then make proposals for design applications to solve the training-criteria problems assigned to them.

In the second stage of this training approach, the teams, with the assistance of technicians, apply the results of their research to experimental models. They carefully maintain an engineering journal, making entries each step of the way as the bases of data for phase three of the program. In stage two they also continue working with breadboarding until they obtain acceptable results in the specific areas described in the objective. To be acceptable, their results would equal or better current performance in the art within the organization. The training teams are also expected to exploit the advantages of these solid-state technology applications to a degree acceptable to the organization.

In the third phase, the individual members of the teams prepare seminar papers outlining their experimental procedures and the results they obtained, together with state-of-the-art projections for further applications to organization products.

These seminars, then, would be the same kind of state-of-the-art training operation that would be expected from institutional resources. Members of the organization would attend as they would a university special course. Possibly personnel from other firms and the university in the immediate area would also be invited to participate in them.

Development of an immediately applicable technology and the technical education available via the seminar program add to its value as a contributor to meeting both training missions and the organization's technical goals. In this kind of program, the training function's role is minor, or at least less important than that of the participants and line management. This is generally true in all elements of a technical/professional training system. However, the training function's relatively minor role in analysis is notable. In most training areas, analysis is that function's most critical role; here, the organization's technical management will be the most important contributor to the outputs of the analysis element. The definition of current state-of-the-art requirements, as in the program described above, and its projection of future needs must be the responsibility of the organization's technical management. The training function's role is to coordinate these efforts so that state-of-the-art needs are defined and reviewed as training problems and so that the definition and review are carried on as a regular accountability of technical management. Technical management has a further responsibility for needs analysis: the upgrading of technical and professional personnel to fill future openings anticipated in organization planning. Like management development, technical development should meet future organizational needs and should, therefore, evolve from regular organizational planning.

ROLES OF THE TRAINING FUNCTION

Even in the analysis of content requirements, the training function's roles are secondary to those of technical management and to those of individuals who will be subject to the training actions. The participants, after all, are qualified subject-matter experts to the degree that they can present accurate and valid statements about their expectations. The roles of the training function can therefore be considered consultative as far as need analysis is concerned. By calling the technical manager's attention to learning problems and the need to establish criteria, the trainer will be making a major contribution. The analysis element of this training system must be part of the technical system involved, whether it takes the organizational form of an engineering training committee or possibly of assignment of an in-house consultant with expertise in both the behavioral technology and the engineering technology required. The second alternative could call for a job title in the organization such as "Engineering Education Director," probably reporting to a function like that of chief engineer or independent research and development.

The development element of the system presents more direct requirements for a training expert. Program-development activities here will be different from other training areas in that much less time and energy will be directed toward instructional design or the creation of training materials. Development will center more on the design of systems to make effective use of available instructional sources. There will be a far greater reliance on outside resources and on existing materials, such as equipment and facilities within the organization which can be adapted to instructional use. In technical upgrading, the synthesis of existing in-house and outside resources may be the only way to achieve the desired results. A program that can bring technicians up to engineering competence, for example, will have to call on a number of resources. First, a committee or board made up of technical managers and specialists will have to be created to develop the criteria for certification and to implement qualifying examinations. This board will have to persuade the organization's management and technical personnel that an individual it certifies can be considered equivalently competent to an engineering graduate. The training function would be accountable for developing the criteria test sequence to ensure that individuals passing the board will be able to perform on the job to both the board's and the organization's expectations.

Knowing the criteria and testing sequence, the training function would develop a number of learning systems and counseling sources for use by the technicians in preparing to "pass the board." A system is needed for making job assignments to provide the trainees with work experience that will help them pass the testing sequence. Such a system makes job rotation feasible, since there is an acceptable and recognized goal for rotation. It also controls the rotation so that experience gained is cumulative and directed toward meeting board criteria; that is, the rotation is designed and carried out so that it is not merely a series of job assignments, but rather a method for ensuring that each job assignment adds to the technician's repertory.

A system for off-hours formal education will probably also be needed. The development of such a system means a search for available courses. Often, it means working with the local university or technical school to assist it in modifying or expanding its curriculum and schedules to meet the organization's needs. Such efforts, of course, may mean cooperating with other organizations having similar needs to persuade the educational source that such curriculum change or expansion answers a widespread need. It can often mean underwriting the educational institution's expenses for curriculum expansion and perhaps assisting its faculty in obtaining qualified part-time instructors. The organization itself may be called on to furnish some of these instructors.

Finally, identification of potential subjects for upgrading requires development of selection and counseling systems both within and outside the organization. Selection committees may have to be created, selection test batteries assembled and validated, and both career and educational counselors obtained and/or trained within the organization.

NEW-HIRE TRAINING

Transitional training for the new hire imposes the same order of development actions. The analysis of needs will combine the efforts of the training function and the operating system using training. The trainer's role will not be the definition of behavioral needs, but rather the translation of technical needs into terms which can be used for program design. For example, much of the training effort will be directed toward cost decisions. The technical constraints on these decisions will depend on various project requirements. The trainer is unlikely to have the technical competence to generalize these requirements and to create criteria for them. Rather, the trainer's role will be to create typical or model requirements for the training action. Solving the development problem will most likely require the use of such available in-house sources as departmental rotation programs, special project assignments, and out-of-department assignments to other functions. Bringing these possibilities into a consistent system is the training function's primary development task.

The training operations will be the responsibility of the system using them. For those training actions that use the organization's educational assistance program, the operating system and the training function share the responsibility. The evaluation element, as well as the operations element, is most effectively placed in the system using the training. Its evaluation of the results of the training actions is likely to become a very important part of its state-of-the-arts and personnel planning.

The training function's role in both training operations and evaluation is that of a gadfly, perhaps, reminding technical management that the participants in the training action should be able to do something after the training that they could not do before it. The persuasion needed to make this part of the technical management's evaluation system must not be underestimated; the traditional view, again, is that state-of-the-art education builds knowledge, and evaluating knowledge is considerably different from evaluating observable behavior change. But if such an overall technical and professional training system is to be successful, it will have to improve the technical outputs of the organization or, at the very minimum, increase the organization's attractiveness to qualified technical people as a place to work!

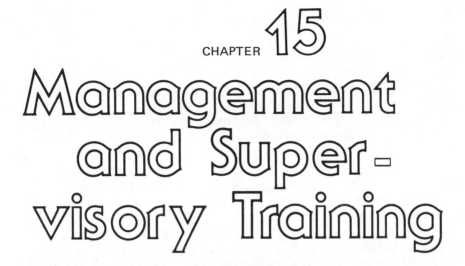

CHAPTER 15

Management and Supervisory Training

IMPORTANCE OF SUPERVISORY TRAINING

Judging from the large number of management and supervisory training programs published and promoted during the 1960s, this area of training became the primary center of attention for organizations selling training services. In the 1970s this growth has continued with further increases in management models and approaches as well as a growing interest in career planning and development. During the 1950s, the greatest apparent growth took place in sales training efforts, but today the consultants have turned to improving the performance of people who "get things done through others." Whether these programs have dealt with "first-line supervisors" or with "managers of managers," interest in them points out the conscious expression of a need on the part of organizations employing them.

The term "supervisory training" implies that some kind of behavior change is the objective of actions taken and that further, the performance change resulting from those actions will be planned and evaluated in terms of some sort of performance standards. Such training may be used as part of a management-development system, but not as a substitute for actions directed at individual long-term growth. Whereas management-development actions are designed and implemented to concentrate on the strengths of individuals who already meet or exceed some sort of a standard, training actions are directed at substandard or nonexistent performance in a significant group of supervisory employees. In the first instance, management says, "Find our best people—those with the greatest potential—and get them ready for new or additional responsibilities"; in the second instance, management is saying, "We are not getting the kind of performance we expect or need from a particular group of employees. Find a way to bring them up to our standards."

DIFFICULTY OF SUPERVISORY TRAINING

From the beginning, supervisory training programs have little chance for success in terms of behavior change. There are formidable problems when we try to define the supervisor's job in terms of performance. Determining what a first-line supervisor or a middle manager does is not a matter of textbook definition; the job varies from organization to organization and within the organization from system to system. Even within a system it will vary from one time to another. To say that a supervisor is one who gets work done through others is an oversimplification and not altogether usable. This tells us not what a supervisor does, but rather that what he or she "does" will be measured through the performance of those supervised. Yet this is not usually a fact. If it were, a supervisor's performance would be measured by the individual outputs of the people reporting to him or her. But supervisors are not usually measured by the individual outputs of their subordinates. At best, this performance is measured in terms of the total outputs of the group supervised and at worst, by ability to avoid "exceptions" which require the intervention of superiors.

It is conceivable that a supervisor of a group of inventory clerks, for example, could obtain all of the results required of the clerical group by doing the work personally. If the group's objectives were set low enough, a few extra hours of work on the part of the supervisor would make any activities on the part of the clerks unnecessary. Certainly in this case the work would not be done through others. There would be no delegation of work at all. Subjectively, we would say that this person is an extremely poor supervisor, yet the requirements of the system are met! Impossible as this appears, it is at least partially true in the cases of many supervisors and managers who do not delegate a significant portion of decision making or work production to their people. In fact, it is considered a common ailment of those promoted through levels of management that they carry upward certain operational work better delegated to people reporting to them.

In one organization, first-line supervisors may have no supervisory duties at all. They may instead be troubleshooters for breakdowns, supertechnicians who advise setup people on the proper installation and adjustment of jigs and dies, or perhaps messengers between the general supervisor and the machine operator to deliver task assignments and other instructions. In some organizations the supervisor's job is so proceduralized that there are no options in behavior allowed. In fact, in the event that a situation arises for which there is no procedure, the general supervisor or superintendent is apprised and makes decisions. On the other hand, some organizations expect quite a bit from a supervisor, giving that person the freedom to make a large number of decisions at his or her own discretion and to carry out necessary actions, reporting to superiors only when particular problems occur. In some instances even greater authority is delegated, and the supervisor makes regular reports to management on the status of assignments.

The job of a middle manager is as varied as that of a supervisor. The traditional view that the job of a manager is to plan, organize, direct, coordinate, and control the work of others permits a unified approach to training, but does not provide an objective definition of managerial tasks. Lack of objectification of the tasks and roles of supervisors and the failure to provide measurable performance standards make it difficult to structure training. If a means could be found to work toward rational and applicable behavior criteria for supervisors, there would be a wide range of potential missions for training. First, supervisory training could be the means for bringing about technical and organizational change in the management of an organization; that is, training could be the agency to bring about system modifications such as the introduction of computer technology or automation. Second, it could also be the means for bringing about changes in the management structure itself, perhaps permitting delegation of greater decision-making authority at lower levels, potentially eliminating layers of middle management. Third, it could be the agency for selecting and preparing individuals for promotion to supervision. Thus training could become a powerful tool for the acquisition and maintenance of supervisory personnel. Fourth, it could serve as a change agency to bring the individual behavior of supervisory personnel up to the established standards of performance. Fifth, it could be an agency for coordinating the efforts of a number of supervisors, taking the form of "team training" to develop a higher degree of cooperative spirit within an organization and greater goal centering of various interfacing subsystems. Finally, it could serve as an agency for attitude change, to bring about the desirable condition of having even the lowest levels of supervision, traditionally caught between the work force and upper levels of management by their role demands, adopt an attitude which would place them fully within the "management camp." This last mission has the potential for developing more satisfying human relations between peers and with subordinates.

TRAINING MIDDLE MANAGERS

The middle manager presents a most difficult problem in the determination of training needs. This results from the wide discrepancies between system require ments and management expectations and between each of these and the expectations of the supervisors themselves. Throughout this book the basic premise has been that when performance is unacceptable, it is due to behavior different from that which is necessary to obtain the results the system requires. For most training actions, the system requirements alone can determine behavioral-change needs. The organization's management sees individual performance as directly related to a set of observable results in terms of system requirements. Behavior is proximate to the results. Thus the salesperson's performance produces orders; the secretary's, letters; the press operator's, processed stock. In all of these situations, performance can be defined in terms of system requirements. As for manager or supervisor performance, we can say that the system requirements are imposed, because in order to produce the expected results, any operating system must have certain functions performed and certain actions taken, and some of these functions or actions are assigned to individuals in supervisory capacities.

But the behavior of individuals assigned to management or supervisory functions often affects the system design itself, due to the wide variance between system requirements and management's view of the supervisor's roles. From the chief executive down, the supervisor's superiors all expect certain kinds of performance. A production system may require a supervisor to assign operators to tasks so that production is maximized within quality, scrap, and rework constraints. Management may expect the same supervisor to make operator assignments in a "fair" manner, so as to avoid grievances or work slowups. To the supervisor, the job is one of "keeping everyone busy." Here is the dilemma: In order to meet system requirements, the supervisor must be "unfair," because of the need to show favoritism to the most skilled, most efficient, and most motivated workers, placing them in key tasks. Every attempt to meet the needs of the system can result in charges of favoritism, and as far as management expectations are concerned, performance will be substandard; that is, the supervisor will be demonstrating poor "human relations." Most often, system requirements are ignored by the supervisor and the overall performance of the production system is affected. It should not be surprising that where there is a difference, the supervisor is more likely to meet management's expectations than the system's requirements. After all, in most production systems there is maximum feedback from the supervisor's superiors, usually quite direct and quite immediate, whereas seldom is the supervisor wholly part of the feedback loop of the system design itself.

The discrepancies are further increased because of the management group's emotional involvement in defining supervisory performance. Upper-level managers look at those below as though they themselves were still in these positions, and all too frequently they define these roles and performances in terms of their idealization of them. One organization uses the supervisor as a firing-line decision maker, participating in shaping the destinies of the organization; another sees the supervisor as a necessary evil who rides herd on a lazy and incompetent work force.

DEFINING SUPERVISORY TRAINING NEEDS

The trainer is faced with the monumental task of translating these often irrational idealizations of supervisory performance into training criteria which can be met and accepted as measures of performance. The key to developing training actions for supervisory performance is the analysis process. Analysis will bring together system requirements and the various expectations to a point where performance can be identified. It will also develop standards acceptable to management, and ideally it will meet system requirements. At the very least, analysis will bring to the attention of management discrepancies between system requirements and management expectations. If there is no possibility of bringing them together or changing one to conform to the other, the trainer, in consultation with management, will be able to defend the supervisor from performance measures which require unobtainable behavior. The analysis, then, will provide a set of required behaviors together with their related actual behaviors. It will result in a set of requirements to be met by changes in the system, in performance expectations, or in individual behaviors. Any changes brought about should be acceptable to management and at the same time contribute to meeting organizational goals, missions, and objectives.

Following such an analysis from beginning to end is probably the best way to examine the kinds of problems which will be encountered. We might first consider a project involving first-line supervision in a manufacturing system. In this case the project under discussion was requested by the organization's chief executive and an operating committee consisting of key staff and the general managers of the manufacturing divisions involved. This first step, gaining an operational commitment from general management, may be thought of as the first gating factor for any project involving supervision. Therefore, before any further action can be planned, the objectives of the project will have to be established, and the trainer will have to receive not only the approval, but also the acceptance, of top management.

The objectives of this project were to provide the company with an analysis of the foreman's job in the "A" manufacturing division so that the company could: (1) specify the job of the foreman; (2) relate the job of foreman functionally to the goals of the division; (3) redesign the position of foreman to make it a more effective component of the division in terms of system requirements; (4) set performance standards and measures for a foreman; (5) establish criteria for foreman selection; and (6) conduct training relevant to the foreman's job as it exists or as it might be redesigned. In endorsing objectives like these, general management accepts the possible consequences of the analysis, namely, that change actions may be expressed not only as training needs but also as changes in the expectations of the systems or of management. Management will anticipate recommendations for job redesign or redefinition and, ideally, by endorsing these objectives will be open to such recommendations.

Considering real-world problems, the implications of these objectives could be a considerable threat for the management of the system which will be investigated. It is relatively easy for a member of management to accept a first- or second-line supervisor's performance as resulting from lack of ability or poor attitude. But it is often difficult to accept the possibility that substandard performance is due to the organization's structure which he or she has personally designed or to conflicts created by permitting wide discrepancies between system requirements and personal expectations of the supervisor's performance. Yet if effective training is to take place in this kind of situation, the trainer must avoid being trapped into limiting analysis to the upper levels of management; in other words, the trainer must not take the easy route of looking to the plant manager for descriptions of what supervisors do on the job, but actually work with the supervisors. At the same time, the trainer will have to work very closely with members of management in the system to gain their commitment as the analysis proceeds. The trainer must not be guilty of cutting management people out of the feedback loop.

ANALYSIS OF SUPERVISORY TRAINING NEEDS

In the project under discussion, the first step in maintaining a close interface/ communications/feedback relationship with the managers involved meant developing a well-defined project design which detailed a series of required feedbacks to management. The system model for the project looked like that shown in Fig. 1. The model follows the entire project from the first step of scheduling through the completion of all proposed training actions. It breaks down into three main sub-systems: the analysis itself, the development of a foreman selection action, and the development and implementation of foreman training actions.

With this overall project model, management was given a task schedule carefully outlining the approval points. These approval points are decision junctions at which the system's management was called on to approve the project's outputs (Table 1).

There are two reasons for presenting this kind of schedule to both the general manager and the subject division manager. First, it lets them know what to expect and assures them that they will participate in every important decision. Second, it gives them a means for measuring the training function's performance, for they can use this schedule as a statement of target dates for each of the outputs expected during the course of the project.

Elements one through five of the model (Fig. 1) comprise the analysis portion of the project system. The output for element one is, of course, the schedule itself, which will describe the kinds of outputs management may expect and give the target dates for them. Element two, the sytem analysis, results in a report to management identifying change needs of the division under investigation. When this analysis is completed and the needs both specified and summarized, the report is presented to

TABLE 1. FEEDBACK AND APPROVAL SCHEDULE: FOREMAN PROJECT

	Task	Target [Plus ( ) Calendar Days]
1.	Project schedule approved by president and division general manager	(7)
2.	Report of change needs and recommendations presented to president and division general manager	(36)
3.	Selection and training proposal approved by division general manager	(36)
4.	Performance standards approved by division general manager	(48)
5.	Selection criteria approved by division general manager	(63)
6.	Foreman assessments reported to division general manager	(77)
7.	Training objectives approved by division general manager and reviewed by president	(84)
8.	Training plan approved by division general manager	(90)
9.	Selection-team training-program evaluation reported to division general manager	(156)
10.	Foreman training-program evaluation reported to division general manager	(300)
11.	Foreman candidates list approved by division general manager	(224)

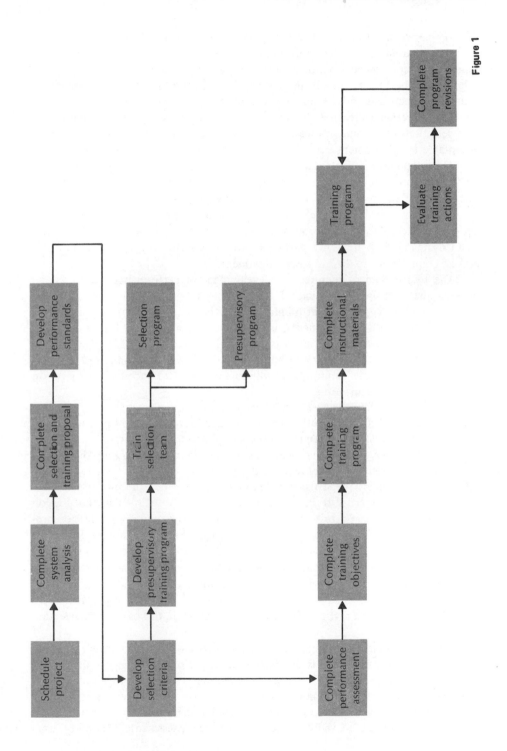

Figure 1

the company's chief executive and the manager of the subject division for their confirmation and approval. The confirmation comes from a mutual discussion of the report's contents and an attempt to obtain management's agreement that the report validly describes the manufacturing system. Agreement means that management accepts these facts and understands the relationship to the performance of the foremen. The agreement precedes the next element of the training system—completion of a selection and training proposal. The output of this element is a general strategy acceptable to management for bringing about the changes required by the system.

The proposal is important for a number of reasons. The general procedure to be followed must be approved and accepted by management, since further investment in time and money will be required. The proposal itself is the basis for all future planning for the balance of the project and determines the kinds of change actions selected. This kind of proposal makes it necessary for the two levels of management involved to not only participate in the selection of strategies, but also make a commitment to the proposed investment.

The fourth element requires the development of performance standards and criteria, the basis for evaluation of the training actions and for evaluation and assessment of the supervisors in training and on the job. A set of performance standards, together with measurements, is presented to management for its approval.

The fifth element of the analysis portion produces criteria for selecting new foremen, and again the approval of both levels of management is required (element six), since considerable commitment will be made toward the shaping of future supervision in the organization.

As a result of the processes carried out in the seventh element of the system, a selection team is brought together and trained to use the planned presupervisory training program as a foreman-selection medium. The actual selection of team members is made by the division manager, drawing individuals from among the general foremen, production superintendents, and members of the division staff. Thus the direct participation of the division manager in carrying out the processes of this element is quite explicit. It becomes important, therefore, to plan the division manager's attendance in a test run of the presupervisory training and selection procedures in order to develop confidence in the proposed selection system. From this point forward, as the selection program is implemented, the selection team itself can provide the necessary feedbacks to the division manager on progress in the candidate-evaluation reports. In effect, the staff trainers involved in the project will be turning over actual operation of the selection program and the presupervisory training program to the division manager for delegation, in this case to the selection team.

The tenth element produces a performance assessment of each foreman within the division. This assessment is an evaluation of performance against the performance standards in element four and the selection criteria developed in element five. Participation of the division manager in at least the first few assessments is important in obtaining further commitment, so that there will be confidence in the ability of this process to validly make performance assessments. Obviously, each assessment report will go to the division manager, and the plan includes a detailed discussion of as many of these assessments as necessary. A summary report on over-all performance of foremen in the division is made jointly by the staff trainer and the division manager to the company's chief executive to ensure key feedback on overall performance at the top.

Element eleven will produce a detailed set of training objectives and criteria statements to be given to both the chief executive and the division manager of the subject division. Their approval is necessary at this point, and these statements will provide the staff trainers with an opportunity to describe the limitations of the behaviors to be produced in the formal training action and permit them to recom-mend a reinforcement system to be carried out on the job. With the recommenda-tion accepted, instructional design can begin; the next feedback should be a dry run of the training actions, with the division manager and possibly the company chief executive participating as a means to gain their future commitment to the processes.

From this point forward, the evaluation reports implied in element fifteen will be communicated to the chief executive and the division manager and discussed in detail with them to give them confidence that the planned changes are coming about. These planned feedbacks to the decision-making levels of management are intended to force participation in the training action by line management. This in-volvement is more critical in supervisory training than in any other training effort. There must be commitment to not only the specific actions to be taken, but also the philosophy or style of the underlying management approaches. The system model points out that if all of these processes are going to take place, new perfor-mance standards, behavioral criteria, and assessment processes will have to be de-veloped, which will have far-reaching implications for supervisory performance in the organization. The training actions, then, cannot be separated from the normal operation of this particular division. The project plan has as part of its intention the integration of selection and training with other management processes.

SETTING UP A TASK MODEL

The task model used for carrying out the analysis of change needs for this project consists of ten task elements. The model shown in Table 2 could be used as a gen-eral approach to analysis for any subject of training, with the possible exception of the tasks involving organizational relationships. The latter are less appropriate to industrial skill and administrative skill training, which do not normally impose such demands. These tasks become important in undertaking analysis for supervisory training, because the supervisor is involved in far more formal and informal organi-zational relationships which have far more effect on performance than do the limited interfaces of an individual machine operator or administrative employee.

The first task is the development of a formal organizational model with the ob-jective of determining management's view of the foremen who are the subject show-ing the reporting authority and accountability relationships one level below and one level above the foreman in the organizational line and those functional relationships

TABLE 2. FOREMAN PROJECT: TASKS FOR SYSTEM ANALYSIS

Task	Output	Method	Sources	Objective
1. Develop model of formal organization	Organization chart showing reporting authority and accountability relationships	Conduct interviews; create model	General manager, function managers	Determine management's view of reporting relationships
2. Develop model of operational organization	Organization chart showing interfaces, feedback points, and control points	Conduct interviews; create model	Function managers, supervisors	Determine relationships required to get job done
3. Develop model of material flow	Flow chart showing movement of material from receiving through shipping	Follow material flow—record movement, process changes, and storage points	Production scheduling and control functions, supervisors	Identify points at which supervisory action is required to get job done
4. Develop model of information flow	Flow charts showing major information models: material, people, accounts, facilities	Conduct interviews and file search	Representatives of functions using or processing information, supervisors	Identify supervisor's information points, media, and sources
5. Make functional analysis	Descriptions of all systems relating to first-line supervisors: missions, outputs, input requirements and sources, interfaces, feedback points, performance measures	Follow outputs in (1–4) by interview	Function managers, supervisors	Determine management expectations and system requirements
6. Make analysis of supervisor performance	Descriptions of existing supervisory performance: responsibilities, accountabilities, authorities, decision points, feedback, standards, measures	Interviews: superior on subordinate, subordinate on superior, subordinate on subordinate, subordinate on self	Supervisors	Determine current performance and standards; identify "will do" and "can do" behavioral items

7. Develop performance standards	Set of measurable performance standards	Compare actual performance from (6) to expectations and requirements in (5): identify critical standards and sensible measures; obtain general manager's approval	Project coordinator, general manager	Establish practical standards
8. Develop performance criteria	Set of criteria for use in evaluating performance	Identify on-the-job activities and outputs which measure performance against standards set in (7)	Project coordinator	Establish means to measure performance
9. Validate criteria and standards	Management approval of standards and criteria	Use criteria from (8) to evaluate performance of range of best and worst supervisors	General manager, supervisors	Establish management confidence in criteria
10. Identify training problems	List of training needs with specifications	Use criteria from (8) to evaluate performance of supervisors. Substandard performance is specified: standard, substandard behavior; change required in skills, knowledge, or attitude	Supervisors	Identify training needs

which management recognizes as including the subject foremen. If a formal organizational chart exists, its contents must be confirmed through interviews with the division manager and staff members who have the authority to recommend changes or make revisions in the formal relationships. If an organizational chart does not exist, the training analyst must work with these same sources to create one.

The second task develops an "operating" organizational model to determine the relationships really required to get the job done. This results in an organizational chart showing the actual interfaces, feedback points, and control points with which the foreman is involved. Thus this task identifies the differences between management's formal view of the organization and the actual operating organization. The task would include interviews with managers of functional units designated in the formal organizational chart, members of their departments, and interviews with foremen and general foremen to identify the organizational relationships they see and use.

In creating this model, the analyst will attempt to describe not only the recognized organizational relationships, but also relationships imposed by the various informal demands of the organization. In the example used here, one such description highlights the fact that the informal organizational relationships built up over a period of time forced a significant number of assembly department foremen into the position of having no direct authority over lift-truck operators, thought by higher levels of management to be reporting directly to these foremen—at least, that is what the organizational chart showed! Actually, however, an informal coordinating function had grown up in production control as a cost-reduction effort to decrease the number of truck operators. This had taken place at some previous time when production demands were lower, but there were no changes as the assembly demands had increased. The foremen were now faced with using their powers of persuasion to compete with fellow foremen for the services of the operators. Since some of the foremen involved were relatively new to the organization, they thought that this was part of the formal structure—"the way we do things here."

The third task develops the flow of materials through the system in order to identify the points at which supervisory action is required to move or process material. The output of this task is a flow model showing the movement of material from the point of receipt through shipping, from beginning to end. This task is carried out on the floor following the processes in their physical reality. Then it is checked against the model of production flow of the processing engineering department or industrial engineering department, which in the example was available to the analyst. Interviews are carried out with production scheduling and production control functions and with individual foremen, with questions such as: "Where do you get your processed stock? Where do you start? How do you know you're going to get it at the right time and in the right quantities? If it's not where it's supposed to be, where do you go to find it?" etc.

The fourth task develops an information-flow model similar to the material-flow model, but has the objective of identifying the supervisor's information points.

Incorporating information formats and sources, the output is a flow chart showing the major information models: models of information about material, people, controls, and facilities. The task is carried out through a series of interviews with members of the functions involved and with the line supervisors, using questions such as: "If you are supposed to set priorities for the operation of your department, how do you know how to set those priorities? What schedules do you use? What other information do you receive? May I see copies of them?" etc. The analyst follows each formal communications medium, tracking each copy of it and making notes about changes in content, ending up with flow models of such things as production cards, time cards, production schedules, schedule explosions, scrap reports, maintenance job histories, downtime reports, and the like.

Task five is to make a functional analysis of the supervisory jobs. Using the data developed in the first four tasks, the analyst determines management expectations and system requirements for each function involved. The outputs are descriptions of all systems relating to first-line supervisors that describe the missions, outputs, input requirements, sources for those inputs, interface points, feedback points, feedback media, and methods presently used to measure the performance of the function or methods which might be proposed for such measurements. These outputs become a basic tool in developing recommendations for changes not involving training. Improvement in feedback, for example, so that foremen will have more timely and accurate information about their performance, is probably the most frequent kind of system change recommendation that will be made, and it grows from the data developed in this task.

The sixth task is to make supervisory performance analyses in order to determine current performance and current performance standards. A further objective is the identification of performance items in the behavioral terms "can do" and "will do." For example, part of the task will be to identify substandard or nonexistent performance which is either expected or required in the present system and to find out whether individuals involved have the necessary skills or knowledge to carry out the tasks required, or whether their substandard performance is due to other causes such as improper or invalid information, unacceptable attitude, or conflicting demands. The outputs of this task are descriptions of existing supervisory performance in terms of responsibilities, accountabilities, authorities, decision points, feedback points, performance standards, and performance measures. The task is carried out through a series of interviews, with selected foremen talking to their superiors about their subordinates, to their subordinates about their superiors, to subordinates about other subordinates, and to the subordinates about themselves. If enough supervisors are subject to the training project, then a random selection could probably be made to cover about 20% of the foreman group. If the total number of foremen involved is too small to allow confidence in random selection, a useful tactic could be to talk to the most experienced and least experienced, two of the best and two of the worst, youngest and oldest, making sure every function is covered so that variances in job requirements can be identified and considered in making the analysis.

Task seven develops performance standards to be used in identifying performance areas that require some kind of change action. The analyst's objective here is to establish workable performance standards. The standards developed in the analysis task will be validated in terms of the organization as it is. A set of measurable performance standards forms the output of this task: Outputs from tasks five and six are compared, giving a picture of actual performance as it relates to total system requirements and management expectations. The analyst will be attempting to identify critical performance standards and to develop some reasonable means to measure the performance. A very close working relationship is needed here between the training analyst and the division manager and probably each level of supervision down to the foreman. These standards will, after all, form the most critical basis for decisions about foreman performance, and the organization's management must be committed to them if any training actions are to be successful.

From these standards, the analyst will go on to task eight and develop performance criteria. Here the output will be a set of criteria to be used in evaluating performance in the organization as it exists. These criteria will be used to measure existing performance in terms of the standards developed in task seven.

Task nine validates these criteria in order to establish management's confidence that the criteria do adequately and validly measure performance in the organization. Again, a sampling of incumbent foremen is used, on either a random basis or by selection of a worst-to-best performers range. Identification of best and worst can be made subjectively by general supervision and/or production management personnel. In essence, the analyst is asking, "Who is your best person? Who is your worst? Who is your next best? Your next worst?" Subjective evaluation or ranking is, after all, the means the organization presently uses to measure performance. The analyst is attempting to validate the objective criteria developed by means of the subjective measures in use in the organization. If, after performance evaluation, there is a wide discrepancy between objective criteria and the subjective value judgments of the managers, it will be necessary for the analyst to go more deeply into system requirements and to test performance against those requirements. If the criteria prove valid in terms of real-system requirements, the analyst then has the opportunity to persuade members of management to adopt the objective criteria as more accurate, and therefore more useful, management tools.

When the analyst finally has workable criteria which are accepted by management, the task of identifying training problems can begin. The objective is the identification of those areas of behavior that cause the substandard performance. The complexity of dealing with supervisory training problems then becomes very clear as performance problems are finally identified. The analyst finds, for example, that the system requires production foremen to maintain a specified production level as material is processed through their departments. In the course of this analysis, the analyst discovers that a significant number of the foremen are failing to meet this requirement: Their performances are substandard. After following the material and information flows through their departments, the analyst finds that indeed, the foremen's performances are substandard, but the degree below standard is unknown because there is no accurate standard for production levels. (Consider, for example, the job-shop operation making a wide variety of related products.) The foremen involved do not know what their standards are; they have no information regarding performance in terms of production requirements. In fact, from their point of view, the major portion of their job is devoted to the prevention of machine shutdowns through breakdown or setups. Foremen face a wide range of problems: They must rely on other departments to supply them with parts; they must rely on their own judgments in matters of scrapping and reworking processed goods; they must face a final line inspection which has the authority to close down their lines; they must obtain setup services which they may not control; they even have to spend a great deal of time trying to find the lift-truck operator who can bring the stock to their areas. In this kind of situation, what, indeed, are the training needs? The analyst may propose a number of system changes to provide the foremen with feedback which can give them the kind of information they need to identify the problems in their own performance and in their departments. Further system changes might be recommended to give the foremen more control over the people and materials they need to get their job done. If some of these system changes can be effected, the analyst will be able to identify some very specific training needs: The foremen need to be able to use the feedback, and this is a training matter. They may need to be brought to a skill level at which they can identify substandard work in process, so their decisions on scrap and rework will be valid. But in this particular case, it is a foreman's lack of information that is the primary cause of substandard performance, and the analyst can make a predictable improvement if feedback can be provided.

In another situation, the analyst discovers that machine operators' performance varies, depending on departmental assignment. In other words, there is a difference in productivity level from department to department. The analyst seeks out differences in the performances of the foremen in these departments and discovers that when operator performances are below expected standard, the foremen involved seldom interact directly with their people. By itself, this is not necessarily a behavioral problem, but if the analyst discovers that there is a relationship between productivity and supervisory interaction, a "human relations" problem is likely. Yet what is that specific problem? In the course of analysis, the trainer finds that a particular foreman involved feels unable to personally influence the behavior of operators. This foreman has discovered through experience that attempts to use disciplinary procedures against them result in his "eating the warning slip." Further, although the foreman considers the operators incompetent, the analyst discovers that this foreman has never taken an action to train the operators or communicated. work standards to them. The foreman never felt that this was necessary, since most of them are on incentive, anyway!

EXAMINING ALTERNATIVES FOR BEHAVIOR CHANGE

In examining the system's requirements and asking questions about management's requirements, the analyst has also found that the foreman is both expected and required to develop and maintain a specified level of operator performance. However, the system does not provide staff assistance or step-by-step procedures for carrying out this role.

It is at this point, perhaps, that supervisory training presents the kind of problem that makes it so unique. There are two ranges of alternatives available: the analyst can recommend a change of procedure which would eliminate the expectation from the foreman's job or else can take action to train the foreman to "motivate" employees. The direction taken must depend entirely on the underlying management philosophy or style of the organization. Oversimplifying, the choice is between "Theory X" and "Theory Y," or possibly some shade of definition in between. Now management's commitment to the entire project becomes critical. The analyst has to exact from the chief executive of the organization a decision, possibly tentative, on the direction to be taken. Thus the approach to the supervisor's performance is profoundly affected by the organization's concepts of what that performance should be.

If the choice is to eliminate this function from the foreman's requirements, then, of course, training is not the answer. The answer must be sought in a system redesign that will somehow remove the need for personal interaction between operators and foremen. Although this approach might not be called "soul-satisfying" to the social scientist, it has been used and found to be quite acceptable and successful. The training analyst and his or her colleagues responsible for instructional design and development can certainly assist line management in preparing a set of procedures for the interaction functions. They might, for example, use the industrial relations function to "counsel" with employees, either directly or through the bargaining unit. Or, they could use the foreman as a liaison between the operators and a special staff function responsible for maintaining "fair practices."

If, however, management decides that the foreman is to have the function of using personal influences to improve or maintain performance, the analyst will begin working on the identification criteria for use in developing training toward this end.

ENTRY BEHAVIORS

A further problem, often more critical in supervisory training than in any other area, involves entry behaviors—the problem of the controller promoted because she was an excellent accountant or the foreman promoted because he was a very good, hardworking setup man. An accurate description of the functions performed by a supervisor is needed if a valid definition of minimum entry behaviors is to be reached. In the foreman-training project used here as an example, pressroom foremen had been selected primarily on the basis of their ability to set up dies and adjust jigs. The functional description showed that technically the press room foreman needed only to be able to identify a correct setup and to describe corrective action to an employee designated as setup person. In fact, 75% of the grievances filed in the departments involved resulted from the foreman's actually doing work on setups in violation of the union contract. The technical skill so important in selection thus contributed to substandard performance, and the application of the skill affected the system. The foreman performed setups because the setup people lacked the skills to satisfy the foreman's expectations, and foremen carrying out the tasks prevented the setup people from developing the required skills. The result was a closed circle.

The analyst can recommend three alternatives: (1) that a skill requiring identification and evaluation of setup-person performance be used to "extinguish" setup skills; (2) that the foreman be punished for making a setup; or (3) that responsibility for setup be eliminated from the foreman's function. Some form of the first recommendation would have to be considered the most likely choice. Punishing a foreman for doing what he knows he can do better than anyone else leads to a number of potentially dangerous situations. He would probably suffer the effects of incompetence and malingering on the part of the hourly people, and management would no longer be on his side. Management expects the foreman to meet performance standards, but slaps him down when he takes action to meet them. The third alternative, of course, means that the foreman would no longer control one of his basic resources; he would have to negotiate with another department for needed services. Adequate staffing and procedures would be needed and would probably add to the overhead cost of the operation.

The strategy recommended is to first assign accountability for the training of setup men to the foreman and make setup operator performance part of the measure of foreman performance. In other words, substandard performance by setup men would affect the organization's evaluation of foreman performance. Next, the foreman should be trained as a setup training expert with stress on the identification of performance problems and the use of a training process to correct them. Finally, the foreman's superior, in this case the fabrication department superintendent, should make periodic audits of setup activities and take direct actions to recognize satisfactory performance as trainers on the part of foremen. The superintendent in this case would undergo further training in coaching and counseling activities as an effective "rewarder" through direct influence.

CHANGE AND THE ROLES OF THE SUPERVISOR

This small part of the entire analysis shows the implications of any supervisory training actions; like the ripples from a stone thrown into a calm pool, they grow and grow! The complexity of system change, expectation change, and behavior change, because of their mutual dependency, must be carefully thought out and painstakingly structured. In the setup situation described above, the end result is a training program foremen can use to train setup people, a change in foreman function and responsibility, a training action for the foremen's superiors, and a change in management's view of the foreman and the foreman's roles in the organization.

What has been applied here in the case of a foreman-training project becomes even more complex when we move into the middle levels of management. The interactive elements of the jobs involved are more complex, and the role demands on those in management positions are increasingly complex and less clearly defined. The role that analysis plays in defining and revising the existing organization systems can be seen as a potentially powerful management tool. The involvement of top management in the analysis process must be secured and their commitment made part of the trainer's course of action.

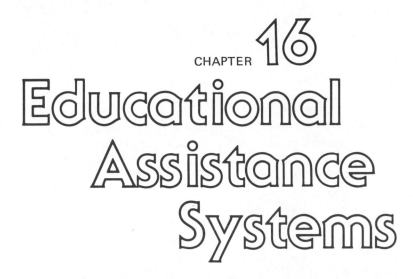

CHAPTER 16

Educational Assistance Systems

FINANCIAL SUPPORT FOR SELF-IMPROVEMENT

Educational assistance programs have been part of the business scene for several generations. Today the medium- or large-size firm employs such a program almost as a matter of course. The purpose of these programs is to encourage individual employees to participate in educational activities toward self-improvement. Normally, the program provides financial support; sometimes time off from work is included. Some programs restrict support to courses leading to degrees in accredited institutions; others broadly permit registration in technical schools or even correspondence schools. Specialized fields are often included in the assistance program, as in the case of computer programming or methods and motion studies. Technically oriented organizations use such a program to support attendance at institutes, symposiums, and seminars sponsored by appropriate professional and trade groups, such as IEEE or NAPA.

MISSIONS FOR AN EDUCATIONAL ASSISTANCE PROGRAM

Programs of this kind can serve the organization in a number of ways. Three uses are most commonly seen, however. Educational assistance can be considered as: (1) a fringe benefit needed to attract and/or retain employees; (2) a system for upgrading personnel which can be incorporated into the technical or management development system; and (3) an integral part of the organization's training system.

Setting missions and establishing administrative policies and procedures for the program becomes of more than passing interest. If the program is considered a fringe benefit, it must be designed to satisfy the wants of the people it is supposed to attract and retain. This means the maximum possible freedom of choice in courses and programs and extremely broad definitions of the acceptable sources. If the program is to attract people to the organization, it will have to be structured to meet important competition. In other words, if several organizations are competing for the same people and if educational assistance is offered as a special fringe benefit, the program will have to be at least on a par with those of other organizations. It may have to include time-off provisions or cooperative education opportunities. If, however, retention of employees is critical, the program may need to incorporate provisions for stretching reimbursement over a period of time or possibly a structure for counseling or directing course attendance toward a narrower company-oriented range of subjects and institutions so that the participant becomes more closely tied to the organization and to the community.

As a method for contributing to technical or management development, the educational assistance program requires a well-structured career-counseling system to make sure that courses taken do indeed contribute to the participant's organizational growth. This could mean working with a local institution to create an "honors" program, allowing part-time class attendance where such enrollment is not normally permitted. The program might also include sabbaticals when local institutions lack either the needed curricula or provisions for part-time enrollment.

Most difficult is the use of educational assistance as an integral part of training. In this case course participation becomes a matter of a make-or-buy decision. Is a course available which will bring about planned, trained behaviors? If so, how does it compare in cost and time to possible in-house actions? Thus participation is at the organization's discretion rather than the employee's. This approach may be required if the organization intends to carry out training actions, but doesn't have the competence or capability to do the job internally.

SETTING CONDITIONS FOR FINANCIAL SUPPORT

Ideally, educational assistance programs should be flexible enough to fulfill missions for each of these uses, but such a multipurpose program necessitates careful evaluation of alternatives before procedures are implemented. A decision on the conditions for support will have a profound effect on the applications of the program. If payment is limited to courses taken "at the direction of the company," it is doubtful that the program could be considered a benefit to employment with the organization, yet this point of view would control course attendance to an extent that outside institutions could be used as an integral part of the training. At the opposite extreme, the organization's support of all formal courses or programs would put the assistance system on a par with the organization's other employee recreation programs and would negate most of the training or development impact.

Within these boundaries, the decision will be based on answers to the question of job-relatedness. Payment could be made only for courses or programs "directly related to the applicant's current job assignment." This approach certainly lends itself to applications involving development and ties any program participation to the individual's contribution to the organization. Definition of the term is the difficulty; if "job-relatedness" is limited to the individual's current assignments, for example, how could the program be used as a development agent for future assignments? Relating course content to individual growth would be likely to require participation outside the scope of an employee's current job content. Finding a definition for relation to the job is complicated further by the assignment of approval levels. If payment approval comes only from the function administering the program, support could be given for "any course or program that is expected to increase the participant's contribution to the organization." This breadth of definition is feasible when a knowledgeable central authority is used and the central decision-making authority has available enough information to make valid and consistent decisions. But centralized approval is more difficult for the employee, increasing the amount of time spent obtaining approvals. Unfortunately, when the system is centralized in this way, there is a tendency to build a formal application process requiring course descriptions and justifications for the applicant. Giving approval authority to lower levels of staff or to line managers simplifies the process, but requires more careful definitions to ensure consistent and valid decisions. The situation can arise in which a department manager may approve a personality-improvement course for a subordinate to improve his or her public speaking, for example, while another manager turns down a production engineer's request for a course in budgeting because budgeting, after all, isn't really part of the production person's job! Yet from a broader view, the personality program would make less of a contribution to the organization than the budgeting program.

When course content is considered in terms of its relationship to a job, we are probably saying, first, that taking the course should result in some new behavior which has real value to the organization; that is, it should have a measurable effect on the person's work. If this is an acceptable premise, then course content is job-related when it is clearly within the scope of the work assignment as outlined in a position description or through planned work objectives. Second, the course must add something new to the individual's skill or knowledge inventory. Third, there should be some expectation that a behavior change will occur as a result of participating in the course. Finally, should the course content become part of the behavioral repertory of the individual, there must be an opportunity for him or her to make use of what has been learned in order to avoid extinguishing the learning experience. Considering these aspects of the definition, we might say that a course is job-related, and will therefore be supported, if the course content is within the scope of the applicant's position description or part of planned objectives and will contribute directly to competence in meeting present job requirements. This still allows the applicant considerable freedom of choice, although it might be necessary to expand such a definition to include support for courses considered prerequisite to a job-related course.

If educational assistance is to be used as a means for bringing about behavior change that will contribute to organizational needs, creating a definition that totally eliminates management judgment is nearly impossible. But any definition that limits these judgments enough to ensure consistent and valid applications will have to consider the elements described above. This still does not solve the problem of defining conditions of course support in terms of the participant's development, since the definition so far restricts support to courses contributing to present job assignments and job content. To allow for future development will require further enlargement of the definition to include courses or programs with course content which will significantly contribute to the applicant's potential for planned promotions or job changes. Now the choice of basis for course approval can be tied to planned growth, but the planning will have to become a necessary part of the process. This makes the judgment process more complex, because, again, justification may be needed before enrollment is permitted. In other words, both the participant and the manager will have to have some idea of potential applications of course content.

The mechanics for an educational-assistance procedure can be used with some compromise for all three missions. A reasonable definition of "job-related" will still allow the program to be used as a fringe benefit. An expansion of this definition to include future assignments will make it possible to use the program as part of the development system, and since courses taken at company direction can always be made part of a training program, it will lend itself to potential use as a training resource.

REIMBURSEMENT VERSUS DIRECT PAYMENT

The next decision has to do with the way the support is provided. There are really two alternatives. Direct payment can be made to either the participant or the institution at the time a course is begun, or some form of postcourse reimbursement can be used. From the employee's point of view, direct payment of the course is the most desirable. For the organization, however, reimbursement has distinct advantages. It can be used as a quality control, since reimbursement will be made only on completion of a course. Further, reimbursement can be tied to a grade level so that not only must the course be completed, but a passing grade must be obtained. Of course, the direct-payment system can also be used in this way when no courses can be taken unless all prior enrollments have been completed and passed. An interesting question is raised, however, when an individual who failed one course is not permitted to take any courses afterwards. Even if failure was within that individual's control, there is no natural law that says one cannot be successful after once failing. It would seem that control of course completion and passing would be more equitably controlled through a reimbursement program.

A second advantage of a reimbursement approach lies in the fact that an individual who has to make an investment in the undertaking tends to be more motivated toward its completion, particularly when successful completion will mean not only course credit but also reimbursement of the investment. A third advantage comes from the flexibility of a reimbursement program. Reimbursement can be stretched out for a period of time so that, perhaps, partial reimbursement is provided on completion of each individual course, with full reimbursement on completion of a degree or some other objective goal. Or, reimbursement could be split over a period of years, perhaps 20% per year for five years, and could act as a means for retaining employees.

FULL VERSUS PARTIAL SUPPORT

The next decision settles the problem of full or partial support. The organization may reimburse the total cost of participation for all courses taken, paying for not only tuition and fees, but also books and materials. It could restrict itself to tuition only, or could provide only partial support. From the employee's point of view, an ideal system would pay or reimburse 100% for all courses. This is also desirable from the viewpoint of the person making the approval decision, since it eliminates one judgment; with full reimbursement rather than a sliding scale, one need not bother with decisions about the amount of reimbursement. But proportional support has some advantages; for example, it can be used to encourage participation in job-related curricula by paying 100% for course content within the scope of present assignments, and it could make a partial payment, perhaps 50%, for other courses. An alternative system would be to provide 100% reimbursement for courses directly job-related, perhaps 50% for courses related to career development, and 25% for courses without existing organizational applications.

In this way, a degree of support can be provided for every employee want within reasonable limits. The organization can exclude certain kinds of courses if it wishes, but in any event, restricting the amount of payment or reimbursement can serve to control course participation without taking away the employee's sense of benefit. By giving greater support or reward for taking courses of value to the organization, the program makes it possible to exert a great deal of influence on employees to undertake job-related programs.

LONG-RANGE OBJECTIVES

Another important decision involves the long-range objectives of such a program. While educational assistance can be directed at specific course content, it can also place emphasis on completion of a degree or certification program. If the objectives of educational assistance include the concept of educational upgrading or growth through education, the problem of job-related courses reappears. How shall the program support six semester credits of English literature required for a bachelor's degree? The course content is certainly not job-related. A program based on course content is often ineffective in stimulating or supporting completion of degree programs. This kind of problem exists not only at the undergraduate level, but also with graduate programs. For example, a manufacturing employee enrolled in an

MBA program could be refused reimbursement for a required course in personnel management; a personnel staff member could be turned down for a course in production management. Both of these courses could be required for a degree. A number of rationalizations will have to be made in this kind of situation to justify a variety of courses as related to the jobs of those to be enrolled.

DEGREE PROGRAMS

Degree programs are an important asset in attracting and retaining people, since the participants have the opportunity to achieve the special recognition reserved for degree holders in the current business environment, and they are often tied to such a program for an extended period of time. Part-time enrollment in a master's curriculum normally takes from four to six years, and once begun, the individual enrolled has more and more difficulty in picking up and leaving the community. Not only is the present educational situation familiar, but often courses are not totally transferable. Enrollment in graduate technical curricula usually poses less of a problem of credit transfer but more of a problem of personal transfer, considering the advantages of familiarity and rapport with a faculty group. Interviews with part-time graduate students indicate that the more course credit they build up in an institution, the easier course participation becomes. Participants become more familiar with the standards of the faculty and the requirements of the institution in which they are enrolled.

One way out of this dilemma appears to be the approval of an entire degree program. Once the individual is accepted as a candidate, the amount of support that will be provided for each course can be settled in advance. For example, the decision could be made to reimburse 100% for courses within the individual's approved major, 50% for courses required by the department or college in which the person is enrolled, and possibly 25% for all courses applicable to the degree. On the graduate level the decision could be made to reimburse 100% for all courses. The matter of job-relatedness, however, is still present. The manager approving such a long-range program may find it difficult to decide six years in advance how job-related the degree will be. We can easily imagine a young trainee foreman who begins work on a degree and during the six to ten years it takes to get a bachelor's degree ends up in marketing and sales. This person's curriculum will have contained numerous courses in production control, inventory control, etc., and possibly not very many at all in the field of marketing. For most organizations that feel that a degree is primary, this possibility of nonrelated degree programs should be a negligible deterrent to preapproval, at least at the undergraduate level.

Enrollment in a degree program is complicated further in some communities and in some colleges and departments by the fact that at more advanced levels, courses may not be offered during nonwork hours. Consideration must then be given to the possibility of offering time off with pay during course attendance. Whether this can be a broad policy decision offering, say, eight hours per week, or whether judgments will have to be made on an individual case-by-case basis is another matter for policy decision. If the organization were to embark on an honors program, and if one could be developed with a local university, the time-off requirement would be almost absolute. For example, the Stanford University Honors Program for an MBA degree requires approximately six hours per week away from the job. (It should be noted that this particular honors program has been a long time in the building and requires the participating organizations to pay a premium in terms of tuition and fees.) The success of this program in retaining and developing management personnel is notable. Then, too, cooperative programs in which work time and course time are alternated on a quarter or semester basis are possible, particularly with junior-level employees. But how much should the organization support the participant attending school full time? Should there be a kind of fellowship grant, or should there be a salary allowance? Present-day co-op programs by and large do not provide for payment during full-time school attendance. Rather, cooperative attendance in courses is made a condition of employment.

Another possibility is the use of sabbaticals with full or partial salary payment during school attendance. The advanced degrees sought can be obtained in one year or possibly a year and a half—one year full time and one-half year part time. If degree programs are to be part of the management-development system, it would appear that sabbaticals could be treated in the same way as attendance in the special management courses offered by universities. Whether an individual attends the 13-week Advanced Management Program at Harvard or embarks on a year program working toward a master's degree at a nearby university is more a matter of management policy toward educational assistance than of time off with pay.

EDUCATIONAL RESOURCES

Once policy approaches have been determined, other considerations remain in making educational-assistance programs effective. One area that must be seriously planned is liaison with educational resources. The educational resources can be of considerable help in structuring the curricula to fit the needs of an organization if the organization takes the trouble to work with the institution's faculty and staff involved in course counseling and curriculum approval. It is often possible to obtain credit by examination if it can be shown that the individual making application for such course waiver has had practical job experience equivalent to or beyond the level of that course. When such permission is granted, the institution's faculty can often provide special tutoring to ensure that the examination will be passed. Good relations with the local university can also bring about time changes in course offerings so that more of the institution's curriculum is offered after hours. It may even be possible to get the university to bring its facilities closer to the organization, cutting down travel time and thereby making still more courses available. A group of electronics manufacturers and research and development organizations outside Boston persuaded and supported Northeastern University in bringing a facility out of the city and into their midst. Such a coordination of efforts can be quite successful, but the organization must be prepared to spend a good deal of time in the endeavor, possibly even designating an individual in the organization as a college-relations coordinator, not for recruitment but for educational purposes. The organization may also have to furnish faculty members and guarantee enrollments. All of these actions are possible and can improve the effectiveness of local educational resources in fulfilling organizational needs.

While consideration is being given to effective liaison with the educational resources, provisions must be made for counseling within the organization. Whether this counseling function is set up as part of a management-development system or whether it is purely an educational-counseling function, the objective is to provide help and direction to employees so that there is the widest possible participation in the educational-assistance program. The availability of this kind of counseling within the organization, especially if it is competent in educational planning and heedful of both educational resources and organizational needs, will make an educational-assistance program effective as both a development tool and a fringe benefit.

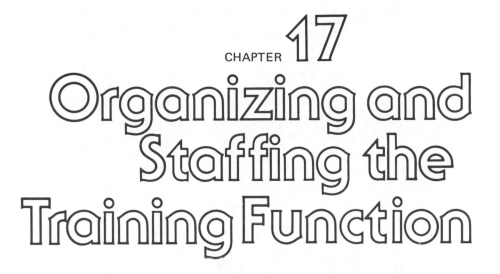

CHAPTER 17

Organizing and Staffing the Training Function

ORGANIZING FOR TRAINING

This book has been devoted to the problem of creating and managing training systems that will be more effective agencies of behavior change. Two aspects of the problem have been discussed in some detail: efficiency as a system and effectiveness as a producer of predetermined behavior. This chapter discusses a third aspect: the administration of the training system as an organizational unit.

There are two major administrative considerations: first, the problem of designing and installing a formal organizational unit as a training system; and second, the problem of acquiring and maintaining an effective staff, the "people" part of that system. In some respects these considerations are independent of each other, and in others they are completely intertwined. The organizational shape of a training unit is dependent on the type of staffing it can obtain; similarly, once the unit has been established, its form is a strong limiting factor on the acquisition of new staff. But the integration of an effective training system as an organizational unit will depend to a great extent on finding a formalized shape that can realistically be expected to work in the larger organization. This brings us back to the problem of "real-world" thinking. The system designer must say, "We are searching for optimal, not maximal, solutions." There is a wide variety of possible forms the organizational training unit can take and with them an infinite number of potential reporting relationships to other units in the organization. Still, there is only one way the problem can be validly approached. Effective design of the organizational training unit is dependent on its functions and its missions.

FUNCTIONS AND MISSIONS

A training department to carry out all functions included in all elements of the administrative-skills training system will be designed very differently from that for a department for research, development, delivery, and evaluation elements of an industrial-skills training system, where the analysis and operations elements are decentralized throughout a dozen plant locations. Design considerations include training areas, missions for each area, elements to be assigned, and the nature of the training department, whether operational, consultative, or directive for each element. This last consideration determines whether the organizational unit will actually carry out the training actions (delivery unit), whether it will provide subject-matter expertise and advice to the systems carrying them out (consultative unit), or, finally, whether it will initiate the implementation of training actions relying on other systems for subject-matter expertise (directive unit).

In addition, the organization's existing structure will impose such design considerations as reporting level, degree of centralization, training competence and capability, and organizational expectations. An organization that expects to employ a human resources development function in the same way that a financial control function is used would probably make training part of the organizational planning and development function, reporting to the organization's chief executive. If training is separated from organization development, a training function might report to the personnel department, while the management development unit would account to the chief executive or to the organizational planning and development function. The organization that provides centralized consulting services to decentralized profit centers in other functional areas is unlikely to create a centralized training function as an operational unit even if the profit centers lacked training competence and capability. Instead, the central training staff would be temporarily assigned an operational role, with the added mission of creating operational units in the profit centers. The probability of success in this situation would not tempt a sensible gambler! Resistance of the profit centers to the direct expense of a training function, added to the availability of operational services from the centralized staff, tends to stretch "temporary" to "permanent." In this situation the central staff tends to keep and expand its operational roles, as a matter of both effectiveness and organizational status.

PRINCIPLES OF ORGANIZATION DESIGN

No single design will satisfy the needs of every organization, nor is it likely that any one design will be able to meet the requirements of a single organization for a long period of time. Whatever the formula, these basic assumptions can be used to improve the odds that the design will be workable:

> The design must account for each of the five training-system elements.

> Each element must be assigned on the basis of the areas of training required by the organization.

> Each element must be assigned on the basis of capability, competence, and cost.

> The design must conform to the organization's traditions wherever possible.

> The design must be acceptable to the systems that will use the training services.

Whether the final organizational design results in total centralization or in a consultative service, these assumptions apply. With this in mind, we can look at some examples of organizational training units, beginning with a totally centralized operation.

THE CENTRALIZED ORGANIZATION

A completely centralized and fully specialized training unit is a system in which all training areas are covered, with missions assigned to handle every action for each area. It contains all elements of the training model and is operational for each. As a specializing *training* system, it is separate from organization development and management development functions and probably reports to the chief personnel executive or the organization's chief executive. Such a training system would contain the total training competence and capability of the organization, and other systems would not be expected to furnish it subject-matter expertise. Further, when inputs beyond its competence were required, it would be expected to go outside the organization to find them. Expectations for such a unit would be all-inclusive; it would be expected to furnish the behavior change required by the organization's objectives and to initiate, implement, and maintain training actions and procedures and processes to carry out those actions.

For many training executives, this is the "ultimate" training department. Such an organizational unit would contain seven sections reporting to a training manager: research, industrial skills, administrative skills, sales training, supervisory training, professional and technical training, and training operations. (See Fig. 1.)

The *research section* would be responsible for inquiry into and investigation of new systems, technologies, and training methods from a purely behavioral point of view and would in effect be the training department's state-of-the-art repository.

The *industrial skills section* would be comprised of two groups—one accountable for development and the other for operations. The development group would carry out needs analysis, instructional design, and development and production of aids and materials and would probably be assigned copy-writing, including the design and production of programed instruction. The delivery group would have classroom instruction, on-the-job training, vestibule training, and hourly employee orientation.

The *administrative-skills section* would be made up of three groups—training development and training operations, with many of the same functions as the industrial skills section, and college graduate training programs, with responsibility for both individual counseling and classroom instruction.

The *sales-training section* could most effectively be broken into two groups—"home office" training and "field" sales training. The first group would carry out analysis, instructional design, aids and materials production, programed instruction, classroom instruction, and sales orientation. In other words, it would combine the functions of analysis, development, and operations, covering all aspects of home office training.

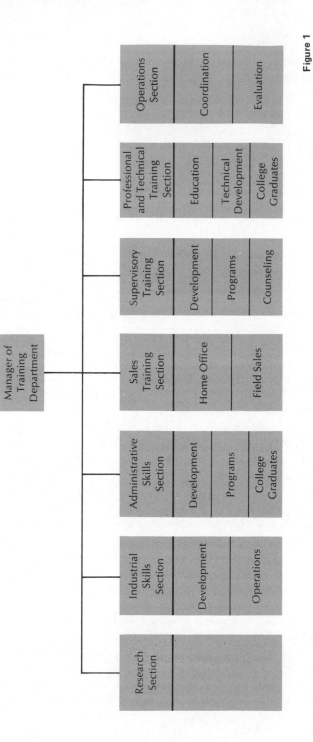

Figure 1

The *supervisory-training section* would also have development and training programs groups, with functions similar to those in the administrative-skills section. In addition, it would have a counseling group to handle supervisory selection programs, counseling, and the training of managers as counselors.

A *professional and technical training section* would have three groups. The first, technical education, would administer educational-assistance programs, provide educational counseling, and act as a program coordination unit with outside institutes and seminars. A technical-development group would be responsible for in-house training and individual career counseling. It would carry out training analysis, instructional design, and production of training materials and would provide for classroom instruction. The third group would handle college graduate programs for new technical hires, with responsibility for orientation, classroom instruction, and career counseling.

The seventh section, *training operations,* would be made up of two groups—program coordination and program evaluation. The coordination group would acquire and maintain audiovisual aids, text materials, a central library if one were necessary, and training facilities. It would also keep the training records and provide clerical support to the other sections, particularly for the production of training materials. The program-evaluation group would develop and implement devices to measure both the quality of the programs and the performance change of the participants.

THE TRANSITION ORGANIZATION

Changing the design from a totally centralized functional training system radically changes the model, even where a high degree of centralization is required. The organizational unit that has missions in all training areas, but that is eventually to be responsible for decentralized training operations, would have to be structured quite differently from the "ultimate" training department just described. In this example the unit is responsible for management development as well as training. This "start-up" training and development department is directed by a training and development manager, who in turn reports to the chief personnel executive or the organization's chief executive, and it is structured on the basis of functional elements rather than training areas. It has four sections: research, programs, management development, and the last section, rather unusually designated "training" (see Fig. 2).

The *research section* has two groups—research and program evaluation and performance assessment.

The *programs section* carries out analysis and development of all training programs for all training areas within the organization.

The *management-development section* is made up of three groups—one to carry out all supervisory-training program operations, using the program section as a resource; an individual-development group to handle management appraisal, counseling, and coaching; and an education group to administer the organization's

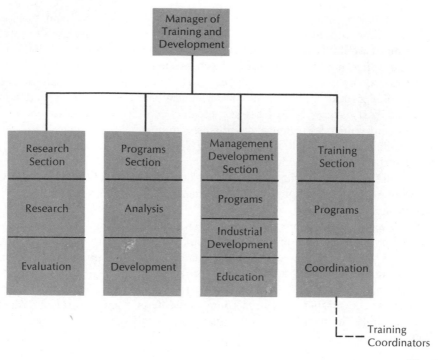

Figure 2

educational-assistance programs and coordinate special outside seminars, institutes, etc. This last group might be eliminated in the future, by assigning educational assistance to another system.

The *training section* has two groups—one to carry out the training-operations element of the training system for training programs used in other organizational systems and another temporary one, called "training coordination," to handle training of trainers and, on a consultative basis, to assist other systems in developing their own training functions. The entire training section would eventually be split off from the central unit and assigned to the operating systems. Thus the organizational unit would be designed in advance to facilitate the decentralization of training actions when the organization has developed the competence and capability in its subsystems to carry out the necessary training actions.

THE CONSULTATIVE ORGANIZATION—TRAINING AND DEVELOPMENT

Where the organization has training competence and capability in its divisions or cost centers, organizational expectations may change to the point where a centralized training department would fulfill a consultative role in training. In this situation, of course, the operations element would not be included in the organizational unit structure. Such a central consultative unit would probably report to a chief personnel executive. Since this kind of training unit seldom initiates or directs actions, it is unlikely that there would be a situation in which it would need to report to the chief executive of the organization.

In the example of a central staff unit, management development and organization development are not within the scope of the training system, but it has been assigned operating responsibility for the organization's educational assistance programs. Four sections are under a manager of training and education: research, management education, training, and educational assistance (see Fig. 3).

The *research section* contains two groups—one accountable for state-of-the-art research and the other for research and development of evaluation devices. The evaluation group also assists the operating training head in making evaluations of both training-program effectiveness and performance of participants in training actions. A training specialist assigned to this group would probably be called on to make evaluations of the training actions carried out in the systems, but in this role would report to the individuals in the decentralized unit accountable for the training actions rather than directly to the manager of training and education. This really is the way an internal consulting operation should function, since its services are provided to specific subsystems and not to the organization as a whole.

The *management-education section* is separate because frequently the administration of supervisory- or management-training actions or self-development actions cuts across systems and requires a central administrative function for cost-effectiveness. A training specialist in this section would be assigned as a conference leader for supervisory-training conferences and also as an administrator of special programs where outside sources are used. For example, a training specialist in this section might act as a liaison and coordinator between the organization and a local university offering an extended management-training program.

The *training section* is comprised of two groups—production and development. The production group produces aids, materials, and specialized training devices such

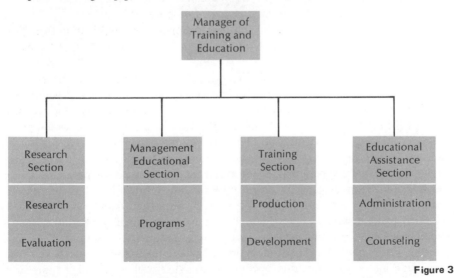

Figure 3

as programed instruction as a centralized service to training units in other systems. Copy-writing, editorial skills, art makeup, etc., are the repertory of training specialists in this area. The development group provides consultants in training analysis and instructional design to the decentralized units. Although it does not directly interface with potential trainees, it provides local training units with background data and analysis and design techniques. It might also run trainer-training programs to assist those units in building their own competence and capability.

The fourth section, *educational assistance,* also has two groups—one for program administration and a second to provide direct career counseling when geography makes such a centralized service possible.

THE SPECIALIST ORGANIZATION AND DECENTRALIZED TRAINING

Organizing a centralized staff training unit into this kind of alignment permits a high degree of flexibility in its roles, permitting both potential for innovation through the research section and the rapid response capability of an efficient consulting group. Since the operations element has been carefully left out of the organizational structure, it is unlikely that such an organizational unit could infringe on the prerogatives of the individual cost centers. Such a structure implies that training competence and capability exist in the systems being served, however, and that the managers of those systems are highly motivated toward bringing about behavior change through training actions in the systems under their direction (see Fig. 4).

In organizations in which individual systems or locations do not have or cannot afford to develop their own competence and capability in all training areas or in all elements of a training system, the organizational unit can usually be structured so that the operations element at least can be decentralized. With the help of a consultative central training staff, the analysis and instructional design can also be carried out by local systems. In structuring such a compromise staff the main orientation of the organization must be considered. For example, a manufacturing firm with decentralized plant locations might find it effective to develop a central training staff consisting of three sections.

First, a *program section* would operate in a consultative role for research, analysis, and program development. Second, a *section for personnel development* would carry out operational functions for the group of employees closest to the central office of the organization. The third section, also consultative, would be an *industrial training section* and would handle both coordination and subject-matter expertise in behavior change for operator training, on-the-job training, trainer training, apprentice-training programs, and hourly employee orientation programs. Using the program section as its main technical source, it would work with the decentralized plant units for the development and implementation of training actions.

Each plant location would then have an operating training coordinator who would serve three functions: (1) a classroom instructor; (2) a supervisor of full-time or part-time training specialists in classroom instruction, hourly new-hire orientation and instruction, and vestibule training, as well as including apprentice

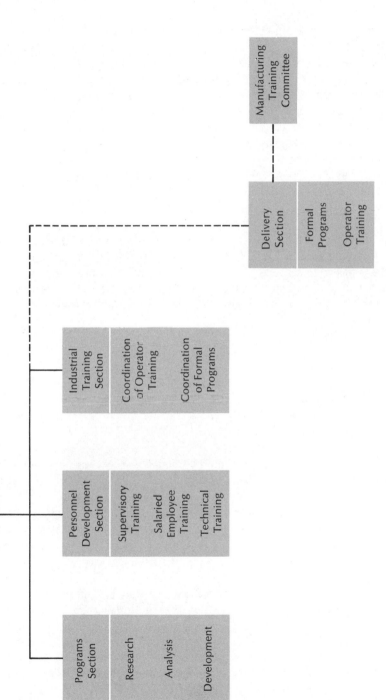

Figure 4

training and on-the-job training; (3) a head of a training committee accountable for training needs, analysis, and evaluation. Such a committee would most likely consist of the manufacturing manager, the production superintendent, the industrial engineering manager, some general foremen, and possibly some line foremen. The operation training coordinator would be accountable to the operations manager either directly or through the employee relations manager.

In a manufacturing firm this kind of training structure could be the best of all possible solutions. Separated from the central staff, using it only as a resource, each operational unit would be able to direct its own efforts, patterning its training directly to its own unique requirements. It would still have available to it expertise in behavior change and would have the final say on whether to accept or ignore the consultative advice of the central staff unit.

The degree of freedom and authority such a structure would give to the local unit would make it imperative that expenditures for training actions be taken from the location's own overhead budget. Without the motivation necessary to allocate budget money to training, a loss of effectiveness could be expected. Therefore, it would not seem logical to organize in this manner unless the operations manager involved is persuaded that such investment in behavior change will contribute to the unit's profit position.

THE TECHNICAL TRAINING ORGANIZATION

A similar approach might be suggested for a technically oriented organization, where special attention will be paid to technical and professional development. In this case the local unit accountable for training would report to someone like the chief engineer and would probably be assigned to someone at the level of section head, thus making a training manager in this case a section head for technical education. Two groups would report to the training manager—one for professional education and the other for training coordination. The professional-education group would administer the educational system's program for engineering personnel and would coordinate special seminar attendance, association memberships, and sabbatical programs if they were part of the organization's education program. The training-coordination group would coordinate and administer in-house training programs and handle instruction and instructional design for new college hire orientation actions.

The section head in charge of technical education would have two other very important functions: first, as head of an engineering training committee which would serve many of the same functions as the training committee in the manufacturing situation; second, as chief member of the engineering board which would develop and administer a certifying and upgrading program.

The committee approach to training-needs analysis gives rise to the possibility of utilizing a program-management approach to training. In this approach once a training need has been identified, a task group can be put together to carry out the development and operations of the training action required to meet this need.

Calling on a central staff group for competence in behavioral technology, the local task group could be organized using subject-matter experts within the engineering organization to develop the level of technical programming needed. The task group would be a temporary assignment and could be put together with members from various places in the organization, depending on the area of training under investigation. The training coordinator's job in this case would be to act as a "program manager" for the task group. This kind of organization would be drawn up as shown in Fig. 5.

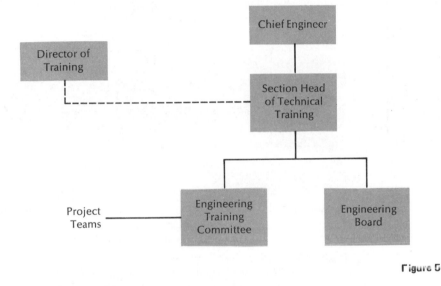

Figure 5

THE TASK-TEAM ORGANIZATION

The task-team approach can be extended to account for all training actions if the organization has enough flexibility. Traditional concepts of organization structure with static reporting relationships and rigid lines of authority prevent such an approach, since it lacks the formalized structure such concepts demand. If it can be used, however, the task-team approach offers a number of advantages. It places both responsibility and process in the system using the training action; it makes maximum use of existing competence, involving the organization in individual training actions without committing it to training as an institution; and it permits a training function to invest its time, money, and personnel at points of greatest need.

In this environment the training department has two functions. First, it operates like a program-management office to coordinate the activities of task teams. Second, it provides technical experts to the teams. When an operating system expresses a need for training or when a performance problem is thought to exist, a task team is organized to tackle the specific problem or need. Members of the team

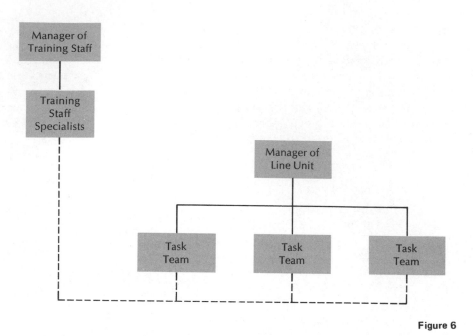

Figure 6

are drawn from the system itself. The team obtains technical help from the training department, as needed, in the form of analysis methodology, instructional design help, production assistance, etc. The training department also furnishes a coordinator to assist the team in solving any interface problems.

When the training task has been completed and its objectives met, the task team is dissolved. If the training actions involved are continuous or long-range, part of the team can continue to function as needed. The size of the team will vary as specific subtasks are begun and finished. At any one time a number of such teams might be functioning (see Fig. 6).

The instructional designs, aids, materials, and evaluations produced by the teams would be retained by the program-management office as a resource for future task teams.

STAFFING THE TRAINING ORGANIZATION

Once missions have been established and the organizational training unit designed, staffing it can be undertaken. Both the missions established and the organizational design contribute to setting the selection criteria for searching, screening, and selecting this staff. The organization's ability to successfully compete in the labor market and to attract individuals with the competence to meet the selection criteria will determine whether it will meet its design requirements. In other words, the organization may be forced to modify both mission and unit design to meet its ability to pay for or locate individuals who meet the selection criteria. Without a search of the market and its own organization, however, it is unrealistic to modify the training unit. An attempt to obtain staffing to meet organizational needs rather than modify organization requirements for available personnel is, from a systems point of view, a more realistic approach. True, modification may be necessary, but any modifications should be made grudgingly as a last resort rather than lower the potential contribution of the training function to the organization at the outset.

SELECTION CRITERIA

Selection criteria must be based on the answers to three questions. First, what do the training-system requirements demand that individuals under consideration do? Second, how will their efforts be measured? Third, what have they done in the past that gives reasonable assurance of their ability to do what is required? Ideally, these are the same three questions asked in acquiring anyone for the organization, but since the training organizational unit is using a systems approach, they must be part of its acquisition process.

In a specific case, a training unit in a central staff function is looking for an instructional designer to service plant locations in the development of training actions for operators.

What is the individual required to do?

This designer is expected to produce instructional materials for hourly employee orientation, safety and housekeeping training, and vestibule training, as well as materials for training the supervisors who will carry out OJT actions and the job aids they will use. In this particular situation, both analysis and operations are carried out by the decentralized plant. These expectations can be further narrowed in this instance by noting the major processes in the plants. For example, plant operations are primarily sheet-metal processes, although a variety of such processes are carried out.

How will trainer output be measured?

We can begin by saying that instructional strategies and designs will be evaluated on their ability to bring about behavior change to meet training criteria established in the analysis and that the evaluation element is assigned to individuals in the training system in the plant. Since the instruction developed will be carried out by the local training units, they will evaluate the instructional design in terms of their ability to use it. This leads to the need for another measurement: acceptability to the systems using services. The designer will be measured on his or her ability to function smoothly with the units serviced, without the intervention of directive authority from either the central staff or the plant management. A final area of measurement is the time/cost aspect of instruction, and for this, budgetary standards will be specified on a per capita basis, on a training-hour basis, or on estimated return per dollar invested in the training action.

In establishing measurements to evaluate individual performance, it is necessary to specify conditions for performance, just as it was necessary to specify conditions in establishing training criteria. For staff-selection purposes, these conditions become extremely important, for if we say that this instructional designer will operate independently with total accountability for all aspects of the job, a higher degree of proficiency and experience is required than if we provide the support of direct supervision and technical assistance in editing, audiovisual aid production, etc.

What has the designer done in the past to demonstrate competence?

Assuming for the moment that the instructional designer under consideration is to operate with maximum independence, with the only requirement being to report on a regular basis the status of projects, answers to this third question can be considered.

First, it is important that the individual under consideration have actually produced instructional designs which brought about behavior change and that in the development of these designs, he or she did the writing and at least a portion of the artwork, if this was necessary. He or she should have supervised the development of audiovisual aids and instruction. Although not required, it would probably also be helpful if the person has carried out analysis, evaluation, and instruction of not only his or her own instructional designs, but also those produced by others, in order to demonstrate ability to carry out training actions in coordination with other individuals or other systems. Work samples with evaluations of both training and participant performance will be important judgment criteria. Since analysis, operations, and evaluation will be carried out by the manufacturing organization, there may be no critical need for an individual to have demonstrated competence in the area of sheet-metal work. It would not be very important if the analysis element carried this competence; on the other hand, if the unit being served does not have a high degree of subject-matter competence, it will be necessary that an individual under consideration have created and carried out instructional designs in the particular technical area. For an instructional designer, this matter of subject-matter expertise is relatively unimportant, since the skills with the greatest payoff are in behavioral areas, not in subject-matter areas.

Earlier chapters of this book have detailed at some length the kinds of performance that should be expected from individuals who perform the functions required by the various training elements. Considerable attention has also been paid to particular needs in the various training areas. Working with these data, we can develop a set of selection criteria to meet any organizational structure with almost any existing level of competence and capability. In general, in staffing a research element, we can expect the selection criteria to include competence in the behavioral sciences, with a demonstration that the applicant is able to operate within the state of the art. This means either a relevant educational background or demonstrated competence in dealing with recognized subject-matter experts in the state of the art. Particular skills in the communication arts might also be required, as well as competence in the utilization of communication aids in behavior-change actions. In staffing a research element in some organizations there might also be a requirement for expertise in other disciplines, such as systems engineering, computer programming, government aids, grants and subsidies, etc.

Individuals who will staff an analysis element should, of course, be able to demonstrate that they can design and carry out system investigation and produce objectives and training criteria. Here a knowledge of the organization itself may be a requirement. Since such knowledge may facilitate training-needs analysis, it may be particularly important in a new training system that is in the process of being assimilated into the organization.

The development element will require a staff with instructional-design experience and some expertise in training methods and media suitable to the organization. For example, in the case of the manufacturing system discussed above, specialized experience in trainer training and on-the-job training techniques may be a very critical requirement; in another case—an electronics manufacturing organization, for example—specialized knowledge of vestibule training may be required, particularly where certification of operators is required. Thus a prerequisite for an instructional designer in such an organization may be certification as an instructor by a government entity.

An individual considered for a position as a staff member with accountability for the delivery element should be able to demonstrate experience in the instructional media the organization can expect to use, as well as administrative experience in facilities management and even, perhaps, in design and acquisition of facilities and their equipment. Also needed is audiovisual proficiency in the types of equipment the organization now uses or intends to use in the future. Since such staff may be responsible for administrative functions, the candidate should be able to demonstrate experience and skill in scheduling training, estimating costs, and budgeting.

Finally, in staffing the evaluation element we can expect the potential candidate to have experience in test design and the design and implementation of experimental and interviewing techniques for performance evaluation. Prior experience should prove the ability to develop and maintain evaluation records meaningful to the other elements of the system.

The establishment of clear functional descriptions and selection criteria for the staffing of training functions must be considered a mixed blessing. Together with the advantages of having a clear definition of requirements goes an increasing degree of difficulty in obtaining individuals who can meet these requirements. The most likely source *today,* from a practical point of view, is existing training functions in other organizations. Since there are no formal educational disciplines in our university system for the complete technical preparation of training specialists, the practical answer is to draw experienced talent from existing functions. Not too many years ago the training function was either a stopping place on the way to other responsibilities in the personnel field or an ending-up place for individuals whose contribution to the organization as a whole was considered less than outstanding.

In recent years, however, there has been a change of direction toward profession-alism in staffing an organization's behavioral-change function. Unfortunately, human resources here are somewhat limited, and, at least in the late 1970s, there is a growing shortage of competent, experienced practitioners. Although univer-sities and technical schools do not have well-considered curricula for the prepa-ration of training people, they do provide a growing resource for candidates. Educational institutions with established staff and faculty groups chartered to provide continuing education services to industry are in many cases training com-petent instructional designers and conference leaders. This is particularly true in institutions having very strong business schools, where such efforts have been tied to the business college rather than to the education college.

The organization itself, if the time and resources are available to develop train-ing people, could be the larger on-tap source for talent. By designing an organiza-tional unit to make use of people in other systems through task teams, training committees, and subject-matter experts, the training function has the opportunity to screen and qualify candidates within the organization. With maturity and the stability that come with successful performance, the organizational training unit can embark on its own training program.

In the same way that college graduates are recruited for other functions in the organization, graduates with majors in psychology, sociology, social relations, an-thropology, and the technical areas of education can provide a major pool of po-tential candidates, one from which it is relatively easy to draw, since the "soft sciences" are not yet a seller's market. The greatest possible potential is, of course, in the liberal arts areas, particularly in the areas of literature, language, and speech, in which a high degree of communications skill is developed together with an ac-ceptable degree of discipline, problem solving, and human relations.

Bibliography

Learning theory

Cantor, Nathaniel F., *The Teaching-Learning Process,* New York: Holt, Rinehart and Winston, 1953.

Fletcher, John M., *Psychology and Education,* Garden City, N.Y.: Doubleday, Doran & Company, Inc., 1934.

Guthrie, Edwin R., *The Psychology of Learning,* Magnolia, Mass.: Smith, Peter, 1952.

Hayakawa, S. I., *Language in Thought and Action,* 2d ed., New York: Harcourt, Brace & World, 1964.

Hilgard, E. R., *Theories of Learning,* Chicago: University of Chicago Press, 1956.

Morris, J., *Psychology and Teaching: A Humanistic View,* New York: Random House, 1978.

Mowrer, Orval H., *Learning Theory and Behavior,* New York: Wiley, 1952.

Skinner, B. F., *Science and Human Behavior,* New York: Macmillan, 1953.

Systems concepts

Ashby, W. Ross, *An Introduction to Cybernetics,* New York: Barnes and Noble, 1956.

Brewer, Stanley H., *Rhochrematics: A Scientific Approach to Material Flows,* Seattle: University of Washington, Bureau of Business Research, 1960.

Bross, Irwin D. J., *Design for Decision,* New York: Free Press, 1965.

Eckman, Donald P. (ed.), *Systems: Research and Design,* New York: Wiley, 1961.

Forrester, Jay W., *Industrial Dynamics,* Cambridge, Mass.: M.I.T. Press, 1961.

Gagné, Robert M. (ed.), *Psychological Principles in Systems Development,* New York: Holt, Rinehart and Winston, 1962.

Gross, P., and R. D. Smith, *Systems Analysis and Design for Management,* New York: Crowell, 1976.

Johnson, Richard A., Fremont A. Kast, and James E. Rosenzweig, *The Theory and Management of Systems,* 2d ed., New York: McGraw-Hill, 1966.

Litterer, Joseph A., *The Analysis of Organizations,* New York: Wiley, 1965.

Putnam, Arnold O., E. Robert Barlow, and Gabriel N. Stilian, *Unified Operations Management,* New York: McGraw-Hill, 1963.

Withington, Frederick G., *The Use of Computers in Business Organizations,* Reading, Mass: Addison-Wesley, 1966.

Organizational performance analysis

Argyris, Chris, *Integrating the Individual and the Organization,* New York: Wiley, 1964.

Argyris, Chris, *Personality and Organization,* New York: Harper & Row, 1957.

Beckhard, R., and R. T. Harris, *Strategies for Large System Change,* Reading, Mass.: Addison-Wesley, 1977.

Bennis, Warren G., *Changing Organizations,* New York: McGraw-Hill, 1966.

Bennis, Warren G., K. D. Benne, and R. Chin, *The Planning of Change,* New York: Holt, Rinehart and Winston, 1961.

Bergen, G. L., and W. V. Haney, *Organizational Relations and Management Action,* New York: McGraw-Hill, 1966.

Hicks, Herbert G., *The Management of Organizations,* New York: McGraw-Hill, 1967.

Homans, G. D., *The Human Group,* New York: Harcourt, Brace & World, 1950.

Katz, Daniel, and Robert L. Kahn, *The Social Psychology of Organizations,* New York: Wiley, 1966.

Likert, Rensis, *New Patterns of Management,* New York: McGraw-Hill, 1961.

Roethlisberger, F. V., and W. J. Dickson, *Management and the Worker,* Cambridge, Mass.: Harvard University Press, 1939.

Sherif, M. (ed.), *Intergroup Relations and Leadership,* New York: Wiley, 1962.

Motivation

Beck, R. C., *Motivation Theories and Principles,* Englewood Cliffs, N. J.: Prentice-Hall, 1978.

Hall, John Fry, *Psychology of Motivation,* Chicago: Lippincott, 1961.

Herzberg, Frederick, *Work and the Nature of Man,* New York: World, 1966.

Maslow, A. Herbert, *Motivation and Personality,* New York: Harper & Row, 1954.

Managerial psychology

Gellerman, S. W., *Motivation and Productivity,* New York: American Management Association, 1978.

Haire, Mason, *Psychology in Management,* 2d ed., New York: McGraw-Hill, 1964.

Leavitt, H. J., *Managerial Psychology,* Chicago: University of Chicago Press, 1964.

Maier, N. R. F., *Psychology in Industry,* 3rd ed., Boston: Houghton Mifflin, 1965.

Sayles, Leonard, and George Strauss, *Human Behavior in Organizations*, Englewood Cliffs, N. J.: Prentice-Hall, 1966.

Management principles

Amrine, H. T., J. A. Ritchey, and O. S. Hulley, *Manufacturing Organization and Management*, 2d ed., Englewood Cliffs, N. J.: 1959.

Brown, F. R. (ed.), *Management: Concepts and Practice*, Chicago: Lommond, 1971.

Chapple, E. D., and L. R. Sayles, *The Measure of Management*, New York: Macmillan, 1961.

Drucker, Peter F., *The Effective Executive*, New York: Harper & Row, 1967.

Kepner, Charles, and Benjamin B. Tregoe, *The Rational Manager*, New York: McGraw-Hill, 1965.

McGregor, Douglas, *The Human Side of Enterprise*, New York: McGraw-Hill, 1960.

——, *Leadership and Motivation*, Cambridge, Mass.: M.I.T. Press, 1966.

Odiorne, George S., *Management by Objectives*, New York: Pitman, 1965.

Scanlan, Burt K., *Results Management in Action*, Cambridge, Mass.: Management Center of Cambridge, 1967.

Schleh, Edward C., *Management by Results*, New York: McGraw-Hill, 1961.

Taylor, Frederick, *Scientific Management*, New York: Harper & Row, 1947.

Whyte, William H., Jr., *The Organization Man*, New York: Simon and Schuster, 1956.

Training technology

Blake, Robert R., and Jane S. Mouton, *The Managerial Grid*, Houston: Gulf, 1964.

Broadwell, Martin, *The Supervisor as an Instructor*, Reading, Mass.: Addison-Wesley, 1967.

Craig, R. L., and L. R. Bittel (eds.), *Training and Development Handbook*, New York: McGraw-Hill, 1967.

dePhillips, Frank A., William Berliner, and James J. Cribbin, *Management Training Programs*, Chicago: Richard D. Irwin, 1960.

Dolmatch, Theodore B., et al. (eds.), *Revolution in Training*, New York: American Management Association, 1962.

Jaffee, Cabot L., *Problems in Supervision*, Reading, Mass.: Addison-Wesley, 1968.

Kibbee, Joel M., Clifford J. Craft, and Burt Nanus, *Management Games*, New York: Reinhold, 1961.

Laird, Dugan, *Approaches to Training and Development*, Reading, Mass.: Addison-Wesley, 1978.

McGehee, W., and P. W. Thayer, *Training in Business and Industry*, New York: Wiley, 1961.

Mager, Robert, *Preparing Behavioral Objectives*, Palo Alto, Calif.: Fearon, 1964.

Mager, Robert, and Kenneth M. Beach, Jr., *Developing Vocational Instruction*, Palo Alto, Calif.: Fearon, 1967.

Maier, Norman R. F., Allen R. Solem, and Ayesha A. Maier, *Supervisory and Executive Development*, New York: Science Editions, 1964.

Morgan, John S., *Practical Guide to Conference Leadership,* New York: McGraw-Hill, 1966.

Proctor, John H., and William Thornton, *Training: A Handbook for Line Managers,* New York: American Management Association, 1961.

Schein, Edgar H., and Warren G. Bennis, *Personal and Organizational Change Through Group Methods,* New York: Wiley, 1965.

Zoll, Allen A., *Dynamic Management Education,* Seattle: Management Education Associates, 1966.

Index